The Cambridge Introduction to
German Poetry

German poetry has long held a special place within the Western literary tradition. Its major achievements include Luther's hymns, Goethe's unequalled poetic versatility, the Romantics' lyric songs, and the challenging poetry of Hölderlin, Rilke, and Celan. Combining readings of traditional poems with fresh examples, Judith Ryan conveys the rich rewards that come with reading German poetry. Organized thematically, the book demonstrates the significance of the poems in their time while also showing their resonance in later periods. The nuanced readings in this book serve as ideal examples for close engagement with the primary texts. Quotations are given in the original German and translated into English prose. Special sections give guidance on how to approach an unfamiliar text and how to compose a close reading; an appendix on German metrics and a glossary of technical terms are also provided, along with further reading for those ready to explore more widely.

Judith Ryan is Robert K. and Dale J. Weary Professor of German and Comparative Literature at Harvard University.

The Cambridge Introduction to
German Poetry

JUDITH RYAN

CAMBRIDGE
UNIVERSITY PRESS

CAMBRIDGE UNIVERSITY PRESS
Cambridge, New York, Melbourne, Madrid, Cape Town,
Singapore, São Paulo, Delhi, Mexico City

Cambridge University Press
The Edinburgh Building, Cambridge CB2 8RU, UK

Published in the United States of America by Cambridge University Press, New York

www.cambridge.org
Information on this title: www.cambridge.org/9780521687201

© Judith Ryan 2012

First published 2012

Printed and bound in the United Kingdom by the MPG Books Group

A catalogue record for this publication is available from the British Library

Library of Congress Cataloguing in Publication data
Ryan, Judith, 1943–
The Cambridge introduction to German poetry / Judith Ryan.
   p.   cm.
Includes index.
ISBN 978-0-521-86766-5 (hardcopy) – ISBN 978-0-521-68720-1 (pbk.)
1. German poetry – History and criticism. I. Title.
PT571.R93   2012
831.009 – dc23   2012016544

ISBN 978-0-521-86766-5 Hardback
ISBN 978-0-521-68720-1 Paperback

Contents

Preface

German poetry has a special appeal, one attested to by the many musical settings of poems in the German language. At one point, I had imagined writing a chapter on that phenomenon, but it soon became apparent that a book of this size could not possibly do justice to it. Instead, this *Introduction to German Poetry* restricts itself to poetry in its own right, presenting some of its high points and central concerns. Rather than devoting separate chapters to forms and genres, I have arranged the contents according to issues and problems. Because of the emphasis German studies places on the history of literature, the chapters follow a sequence that accords broadly with literary periods, yet without being inflexibly tied to them. Larger issues often come to a crux at a specific time, and are thus most effectively treated by starting with that time period. While the focus is primarily on the poems themselves, these texts are often best illuminated by reference to the period or movement in which they originated. The more we know about German Romanticism, for example, the more easily we can recognize its characteristic features in specific poems and decide what elements of a given poem need extensive commentary or can be explained more briefly.

Some types of poetry – long poems that are not found in most anthologies of German poetry – are not treated here. In most cases, the poems treated are short enough to be cited in full, or else not so long that the reader cannot easily find lines or stanzas quoted in a broader discussion. In the main, the chapters focus on well-known poems, texts that have been frequently anthologized and that can be readily located in libraries or online. Nonetheless, I have also injected a small number of less familiar poems into the discussion, in the hope of expanding the canon and attracting readers to texts they might not otherwise have discovered.

Although the book treats many poems in depth, none of the readings is intended to be complete or self-sufficient. Each poem is discussed from the angle of vision suggested by the overall topic of the chapter in which it is placed. To have done otherwise would have resulted in detours that would have led too far from the main arguments of the chapters. Much reading in the critical literature informs my readings of the poems, and I owe a great debt to scholars who have paved the way. The suggestions for further reading that follow the last chapter indicate major items from which I have profited and from which others will also learn a great deal. In each case, I have tried to include articles or book chapters in English as well as selected items in German. While trying to keep the individual poetry readings up to date, I have refrained from scholarly notes or a complete bibliography. My aim is, rather, to keep the discussions fresh and appealing.

The opening chapter is intended as a guide to reading German poetry. By examining four short poems of increasing levels of difficulty, it demonstrates different ways of entering a poetic text and how to build up an analysis of the text as a whole from the chosen starting point. The opening poem, a ballad from the Romantic period, illustrates how even a text in simple language can reveal unexpected complexities. The final poem, an evocative text by Nietzsche, is considerably more challenging, but I show how we can make sense of it by beginning with its most problematic elements.

The main chapters pinpoint issues in German poetry that are crucial to the German tradition. It makes "cuts," as it were, into the spectrum of German poetry in order to expose moments when its characteristic features and special contributions appear in sharp relief. Each chapter is organized around an intellectual problem central to the study of poetry in general and German poetry in particular. The issue of "originality," for example, is approached through texts by Goethe and his contemporaries that illustrate the tension between tradition and innovation. The problem of poetic unity is approached through the German Romantic lyric, a reference point for subsequent poetry in the language. Other topics treated include the medieval song-lyric, devotional poetry, political poetry, and the complex question of "poetry after Auschwitz," among others.

The concluding pages of each chapter look forward at poems written later than the period from which the bulk of examples in that chapter are drawn. In this way, the reader will see that no issue ever fully disappears from the German tradition; rather, it takes different forms at different times. This is most strikingly the case with medieval German poetry, which frequently appears in anthologies but is often not covered, or covered only cursorily, in German poetry courses. I believe that we should not allow the de facto divide between medieval and post-medieval literature to stand unchallenged.

This overall scheme allows the book to range widely, without any need to discuss every major German poet or create a continuous narrative about the German lyric tradition. Not every poem is treated in equal detail: some receive close analysis, others more glancing attention. By including prose translations of the texts cited, the volume aims to make German poetry more accessible to students at different levels; but I do not shrink from more complex poetic material. The opening chapter is more overtly pedagogical in approach, but the principles articulated there also underlie the subsequent chapters. My hope is that the book can be used for systematic study, but also for browsing and the sheer pleasure of making discoveries. Even readers familiar with German poetry may happen upon a new text or two. I pay tribute to serendipity by making the first poem I discuss in this book a text I found long ago at the back of a high-school German reader (to my disappointment, our class was reading only the prose material at the front). Naturally, I see that poem differently today, but it is the one that sparked in me a long fascination with the German poetic tradition.

Acknowledgments

The main debt I would like to acknowledge is to the many students who have taken courses from me on German poetry over the years. I have learned a great deal from them, and wish I could name each of them here to say thank you. Longer-running conversations over the years with former students who are now colleagues at other universities have also enriched my understanding of individual poems and the German poetic tradition: I wish particularly to mention Joseph Metz and William Waters. While I was giving this book its final shape, I received valuable help on smaller points from several colleagues in my department. When I finally decided on the poem that would conclude the book's last chapter, I made copies for friends and sent it to others by email. It was fun to see the excitement generated by this small, twenty-first-century poem. That, of course, is how poetry is supposed to work.

In February 2009, I had the great good fortune of spending four weeks at the Liguria Study Center in Bogliasco, Italy. It was an extraordinary opportunity to engage with a group of scholars while also enjoying the unusual hospitality of the foundation. In a spacious studio with a view of pine trees and the brilliant blue sea, I wrote Chapter 5 of this book. Anna Schuleit, a fellow during that session, was instrumental in organizing brief talks, performances, and art shows by the residents, and I am indebted to her initiative for the chance to present a short version of my thoughts on Mignon's song.

I am deeply grateful to my friends in medieval studies who advised me on Chapter 2, "Poetic roles in early song-lyrics." In particular, I wish to thank my colleague Eckehard Simon for his initial encouragement and the care with which he read and commented on a draft of the chapter. Christopher Young, of Cambridge University, organized an informal colloquium on medieval German poetry during a visit of mine to Cambridge in June 2010; I am indebted to him, his colleague Mark Chinca, and their students, Sarah Bowden, Ken Fockele, and Esther Laufer, for a stimulating discussion of key poems. Christopher Young also gave unstinting advice as I developed the chapter. In addition, Markus Stock of Toronto University and Hans Ulrich Gumbrecht offered invaluable thoughts on my chapter draft. Hans Vaget made suggestions and gave encouragement about a version of Chapter 5, "Classical antiquity and modern experience," and Ray Ockenden contributed perceptive and nuanced comments on Chapter 7, "The self and the senses." An anonymous reader wrote a very thoughtful critique of an early version of Chapter 6, "Romantic poetry and the problem of lyric unity."

Charlotte Szilagyi read the manuscript carefully, eliminating inconsistencies, checking details, and thinking along with me about my approach to the poems. Doris Sperber chased down numerous articles in the library and from interlibrary loan, often at short notice; she was also an attentive reader of page proofs during the final phase. Vanessa Ryan read and commented on Chapter 1, and Lawrence Joseph followed the progress of the entire manuscript over its long period of gestation.

I am grateful to Linda Bree for her patience and encouragement, to Maartje Scheltens for her help with the cover image, to David Watson for his astute editing and to Jodie Hodgson for her care during production.

For kind permission to cite copyrighted poems and excerpts from poems, I wish to acknowledge the following publishers:

Arche Verlag: Gottfried Benn, "Ein Wort," *Statische Gedichte* © Arche Verlag Zurich 1948

Berlin Verlag: Gerhard Falkner, "Droben Wohnen," *Hölderlin Reparatur: Gedichte* © Bloomsbury Verlag GmbH Berlin 2008

Frankfurter Verlags-Anstalt: Marion Poschmann, "Kleines Rasenstück," *Grund zu Schafen: Gedichte* © Frankfurter Verlags-Anstalt Frankfurt a.M. 2004

Fischer Verlag: Paul Celan, "Sprachgitter," reprinted by the permission of Regal Literary, Inc. as agent for S. Fischer Verlag. From: Paul Celan, *Sprachgitter. Die Niemandsrose. Gedichte.* © S. Fischer Verlag GmbH, Frankfurt am Main 1959

Klett-Cotta Verlag: Gottfried Benn, "Der Sänger," with kind permission of the Klett-Cotta Verlag Stuttgart. From: Gottfried Benn, Gedichte in der *Fassung der Erstdrucke*, ed. Bruno Hillebrand. S. Fischer Verlag GmbH Frankfurt a. M. 2006

Piper Verlag: Ingeborg Bachmann, "Lieder auf der Flucht" (excerpt), *Werke*, Bd. 1: *Gedichte* © Piper Verlag GmbH Munich 1978

Rotbuch-Verlag GmbH: Helga Novak, "Das Lied vom alten Tee," *Ballade vom kurzen Prozeß* © Rotbuch Verlag Berlin 1975

Rowohlt Verlag: Rolf Dieter Brinkmann, "Einen jener klassischen," *Westwärts 1 & 2. Gedichte.* Erweiterte Neuausgabe © Rowohlt Verlag GmbH Reinbek bei Hamburg 2005

Suhrkamp Verlag: Bertolt Brecht, "Schlechte Zeit für Lyrik," *Die Gedichte* © Suhrkamp Verlag 1981; Paul Celan, "Tenebrae," *Gesammelte Gedichte*, Bd. 1 © Suhrkamp Verlag Frankfurt a. M. 1983; "Fadensonnen" and "Zürich, Zum Storchen," *Gesammelte Gedichte* II © Suhrkamp Verlag Frankfurt a.M 1983; Durs Grünbein, "Gedicht über Dresden" and "Sieben Telegramme" (excerpt), *Schädelbasislektion* © Suhrkamp Verlag Frankfurt a.M 1991; Hans Magnus Enzensberger, "Küchenzettel," *Gedichte 1950–2010* © Suhrkamp Verlag Berlin 2010; Nelly Sachs "In der Flucht welch großer Empfang" and "Du in der Nacht," *Werke*, Bd. II © Suhrkamp Verlag, Frankfurt a.M. 2010

Verlag Klaus Wagenbach: Erich Fried, "Zweifel an der Sprache" (excerpt), *Gegengift* © Verlag Klaus Wagenbach Berlin 1974

Verlagsgruppe Random House GmbH: Ulla Hahn, "Nach Jahr und Tag," *Spielende: Gedichte* © Deutsche Verlags-Anstalt Munich 1983; and Sarah Kirsch, "Ende Mai," *Sämtliche Gedichte* © Deutsche Verlags-Anstalt Munich 2005

Every effort has been made to contact copyright holders. The publishers are willing to correct any omissions in future editions.

Chapter 1

Exploring the poem

We know from poetry in our native tongue that it speaks in a language at once familiar and strange. We also know that poets whose work rises up from the mass of verse written in any given period have developed a language very much their own. How, then, can we be expected to cope with the challenge of poetry written in a foreign language?

Let us begin with a relatively accessible example, Ludwig Uhland's ballad "Das Schloß am Meere" (The Castle by the Sea; 1805):

> Hast du das Schloß gesehen,
> Das hohe Schloß am Meer?
> Goldig und rosig wehen
> Die Rosen drüber her.
>
> Es möchte sich drüber neigen
> In die spiegelklare Flut;
> Es möchte streben und steigen
> In der Abendwolken Glut.
>
> "Wohl hab' ich es gesehen,
> Das hohe Schloß am Meer,
> Und den Mond darüber stehen
> Und Nebel weit umher."
>
> Der Wind und des Meeres Wallen,
> Gaben sie frischen Klang?
> Vernahmst du aus den Hallen
> Saiten und Festgesang?
>
> "Die Winde, die Wogen alle
> Lagen in tiefer Ruh,
> Einem Klagelied aus der Halle
> Hört' ich mit Tränen zu."
>
> Sahest du oben gehen
> Den König und sein Gemahl?

Der roten Mäntel Wehen?
Der goldnen Kronen Strahl?

Führten sie nicht mit Wonne
Eine schöne Jungfrau dar,
Herrlich wie eine Sonne
Strahlend im goldnen Haar?

"Wohl sah ich die Eltern beide,
Ohne der Kronen Licht,
Im schwarzen Trauerkleide;
Die Jungfrau sah ich nicht."

(Have you seen the castle, the high castle by the sea? The clouds drift,
golden and rosy, above it.// It longs to stoop downward into the
mirror-clear tide, it longs to strive upward and climb into the glow of
the evening clouds.// "Indeed, I have seen that castle, the high castle by
the sea, and the moon standing above it, and fog spreading far around
it."// The wind and waves of the sea, did they resound briskly? Did you
hear, from the high halls, the harp and festive song?// "The winds and
the waves together lay in the deepest stillness; With tears, I heard a
mournful song coming from the hall."// Did you see the king and his
consort walking on high? The rippling of their red cloaks? The shine of
their golden crowns?// Did they not lead with delight a beautiful
maiden, splendid as a sun, radiant with golden hair?// "Indeed, I saw the
two parents, without their gleaming crowns, in black mourning dress – I
did not see the maiden.")

One of the first things we notice is that the ballad is structured as a conversation. One person asks questions and another answers (these answers are
in quotation marks). This two-speaker format is not uncommon in ballads.
Nonetheless, we should never take anything for granted about a literary text:
we need to ask whether and how the author has made use of conventional
features. One starting point for thinking about the poem, then, might be why
Uhland opted for this structure.

Another possible entry to the poem might focus on the final stanza. The
second speaker tells us that he has seen the royal couple walking on the ram-
parts, but has not seen the young girl, presumably their daughter. We hear that
the king and queen were dressed in mourning garments, and we assume that
the daughter is no longer alive; but we are not told anything at all about what
precipitated her fate. Why does Uhland refrain from providing the full story
in what, after all, is a variety of narrative poem?

Yet another approach to the poem might be to concentrate on the relationship between the natural setting and the human figures. Stanza 5 is structured around a correspondence between the two, with the winds and waves resting silently while a song of mourning resounds from inside the castle. This kind of analogy, where nature seems to be mirroring the feelings of human beings, is known as the "pathetic fallacy." Working backward from stanza 5, we can see this effect at work throughout the poem. When the questioner recalls the castle in its happier days, nature is presented as suffused with radiant beauty; when his respondent speaks of his experience of the castle in mourning, nature follows suit as it is first cloaked in fog and then steeped in silence. Stanza 2 goes beyond the pathetic fallacy in personifying the castle, attributing to it a desire to look downward to the water and reach upward to the clouds. What is the function of this personification? What would have been lost if it had not been included in the poem?

Another entry point might be to consider the poem in terms of its imagery. Working through the epithets used to describe both human beings and natural phenomena, we notice patterns that connect the one with the other. I find it useful to mark up the text in ways that render these patterns more vividly. The golden clouds link up with the golden crowns of the king and queen and the golden hair of their lovely daughter. The rosy color of the clouds is picked up by the red of the royal cloaks. Radiance is everywhere: in the glow of the evening clouds, the ray of light that is refracted from the royal crowns, and the shine of the young woman's hair. Yet there are also gradations: the beautiful maiden is compared with the splendor of the sun, but in the opening stanza the sun is setting (hence the rosy glow of the clouds), and in the first response to the questioner, the moon, not the sun, is present in the sky.

I have sketched four possible avenues for exploring the poem. One thing I have pointedly not done is to comment on its rhymes: "each stanza employs an abab rhyme scheme." In this instance, the rhyme scheme is not so complex that it requires more than this brief observation. There are no missing rhymes, half-rhymes, or eye-rhymes. All we need to do to include this observation is to tuck it into whatever statement we decide to make about the ballad form of the poem. With some other poems, it is easy to get bogged down in laborious accounts of rhyme schemes. In such cases, it is usually best to focus on the places where there is a break in the regular scheme. Your reader's interest will be held more effectively if you state that "line x diverges from the otherwise regular alternating rhyme scheme" and then go on to suggest an explanation for the divergence. Here, however, that strategy is not necessary.

I have also not commented on the diction of Uhland's "Das Schloß am Meere." Part of its charm resides in its relatively simple word choice, no doubt the result of Uhland's desire to connect with folk traditions and to suggest a much earlier period in poetic history. Simple diction is an integral part of the ballad tradition. Yet he does not observe simplicity throughout: the word "spiegelklar" is a neologism, and the phrase "der Abendwolken Glut" is a genitive construction ("der Abendwolken" is the genitive plural; the phrase means "the glow of the evening clouds") common to more sophisticated German poetry. We find another of these genitive phrases in "der roten Mäntel Wehen" (the rippling of their red cloaks) and "der goldenen Kronen Strahl" (the shine of the golden crowns).

It should be clear from my comments on "Das Schloß am Meere" that there is no single, right way to work with a poem. I have suggested different ways to approach the text and sketched the outline of observations that would need to be reorganized and perhaps expanded in a finished essay. I have posed numerous questions, but not answered all of them. Further, my suggestions and observations assume that the aim is to give a close reading of the poem, but not necessarily to contextualize it. My allusions to the ballad tradition are brief, for example, and I have not said anything at all about the relationship of the poem to its period, Romanticism, nor about Uhland's views on the nature and function of poetry. The larger context is likely to provide more satisfactory solutions to the question why Uhland refrains from spelling out the entire story of the princess's death. This withheld information is undoubtedly a large part of the charm this ballad exerts on its readers: I call it the "puzzle" of the poem.

Indeed, one good way to approach any poem is to consider it as a puzzle. What features of the poem make us stop and think? Before declaring our puzzlement, however, we need to make sure we have as much information as can be gleaned from the text itself. Good knowledge of the language – and a dictionary of at least medium size – is an essential prerequisite. Words that seem familiar may turn out to have additional meanings we might not have suspected. We can learn a good deal about the potentialities of the language, moreover, by studying the ways in which poets stretch its capabilities. This is strikingly the case with Eduard Mörike's short but compelling poem, "Denk es, o Seele!" (O Soul, Remember This; 1852):

> Ein Tännlein grünet wo,
> Wer weiß! im Walde,
> Ein Rosenstrauch, wer sagt,
> In welchem Garten?
> Sie sind erlesen schon,
> Denk' es, o Seele,

Auf deinem Grab zu wurzeln
Und zu wachsen.

Zwei schwarze Rößlein weiden
Auf der Wiese,
Sie kehren heim zur Stadt
In muntern Sprüngen.
Sie werden schrittweis gehn
Mit deiner Leiche;
Vielleicht, vielleicht noch eh'
An ihren Hufen
Das Eisen los wird,
Das ich blitzen sehe.

(A little pine tree is growing somewhere, who knows where, in the
forest; a rose bush, who can say in what garden? They are already
chosen – O soul, remember this – to take root and grow on your grave.//
Two small black horses are grazing in the meadow; they return home to
town in lively bounds. They will go at foot pace with your corpse;
perhaps, perhaps even before the horseshoes that I can see flashing
loosen on their hooves.)

The diction of this poem is relatively straightforward (although some items,
such as the iron horseshoes and the – implied – horse-drawn hearse are no
longer familiar sights for us). The verbs, in particular, are mostly simple ones:
"wissen," "sagen," "denken," "gehen," and "sehen" form the backbone of the
poem. With the exception of "gehn," which refers to the horses, these other
verbs are all connected with human consciousness in one form or another.
The reader will notice the two diminutives, "Tännlein" and "Rößlein": these
are not merely sentimental, but support the concept of growth that is a central
issue in the poem. The pine tree, the rose bush, and the horses – all of them
growing things – illustrate a fundamental contrast between present and future.

The most striking feature of the poem is its use of the verb "denken" as a
transitive verb: it is not coupled with its usual preposition, "an." This is the
first element of what I have called the puzzle constituted by this text. The slight
stress that falls on "es" as a result of this unusual usage disrupts, ever so subtly,
the basic iambic meter of the poem.

Having established this puzzling feature, we need to explore the way it fits
with the poem as a whole. As in the case of "Das Schloß am Meere," we can
do so by taking several routes. One would be to look more closely at the way
stress works in this text. Are there any other metrical divergences in the poem,
and if so, do they support our general impression of the poem's overall theme?

Another route might be to ask about the addressee of the poem, the "Seele"; this leads, however, to a more basic question: who is the speaker of the poem? Unlike Uhland's ballad, there is only one speaker in Mörike's poem, but we need to take care not to assume that this speaker (often termed "das lyrische Ich" in German) is identical with the poet. Yet another way into the poem might be to think about about the word "wo" in the first line, where it is used not as a question word, but as a substitute for the adverb "irgendwo." Does this usage have any connection with the actual questions that follow: "wer weiß" and "wer sagt?" This cluster of issues contains the main pieces that need to be fitted together to solve the puzzle of Mörike's text.

Let us begin with the word "Seele." Is the unnamed speaker addressing his own soul? Or does the word refer to the soul of anyone who may be reading the poem? In the context of the grave mentioned in line 7, either could be possible; and we doubtless do best to keep both possibilities open. In the second stanza, both pronouns, "du" and "ich," put in an appearance: "mit deiner Leiche" is contrasted with "das ich blitzen sehe." Yet this distinction does not unequivocally prove that speaker and soul are two separate entities. The moment in the present, when the speaker perceives the flash of the horseshoes, is seen as a continuum with a future moment when the "du," whether himself or someone else, will no longer be alive. The opening lines of the first stanza set up a related contrast, not simply between life and death, but between the brevity of human life and the relative longevity of natural phenomena. The pine tree and rose bush that are planted on a grave serve as living memorials for many years after the death of the individual. Yet the soul, too, if we consider it in religious terms, lives on after bodily death: indeed, its survival presumably outlasts the long-lived pine tree on the grave. In less religious terms, the "Seele" might represent the human psyche, of course. From that perspective, the human lack of knowledge expressed in the questions "wer weiß" and "wer sagt" is set against a deeper knowledge, precisely because we are mortals, we often prefer to forget: the knowledge that death is inevitable. The poem presents itself as a reminder of this fact, a *memento mori*, in other words. Nonetheless, the force that pre-ordains death is not made explicit. The elevated word "erlesen" bespeaks an irrefutable certainty, but the use of the passive voice lacks religious specificity: we do not know whether a deity or a more abstract fate is at work here. That, too, contributes to the tension between certainty and ambiguity.

Although the poem has a certain folk-like simplicity (and is introduced at the end of Mörike's novella *Mozart auf der Reise nach Prag* (Mozart's Journey to Prague; 1855) as a "Bohemian folk song"), we might also think of it as a meditation. This effect is heightened by a hidden "iambic pentameter" that emerges if we take each set of two lines as if they composed a single line. In

German, Shakespearean iambic pentameter is called *Blankvers* (note that the term does not refer to unrhymed verse as such). If we take "Denk' es, o Seele" as a poem in "Blankvers," then we could readily see it as a kind of soliloquy or monologue. Mörike's other monologue-poems are, however, in free verse (in other words, unrhymed lines of varying length). The most we can say about the "hidden" iambic pentameter is that if it is indeed present here, its presence is in counterpoint with the song-like aspects of the poem.

Especially in the second stanza, questions arise about how best to scan (graphically represent the meter of) certain lines. Does the first line begin with an unstressed and a stressed syllable, "zwei schwárze," or should we give a little more weight to the word "zwei"? Further down, the word "schrittweis" might be read in two ways, either as a stressed syllable followed by an unstressed syllable ("schríttweis") or as a stressed syllable followed by a secondary stress ("schríttweìs"). Similarly, in the penultimate line of the poem, we might wish to give a little more stress to the word "wird" following the strong syllable "los" ("lós wìrd"). This effect is due in part to the reader's expectation that a three-beat line will follow the two-beat line "An íhren Húfen." Finally, although the final line may be scanned with three stresses – in accord with the basic scheme in this poem – it would sound more natural to read it as beginning with two unstressed syllables. In their subtle tension with the poem's iambic underpinnings, these metrical uncertainties echo the central thematic tension between the pre-ordained and the unpredictable.

The striking use of alliteration in "Denk es, o Seele" makes up, in a sense, for its lack of rhymes. Indeed, it harks back to the very earliest forms of Germanic verse where alliteration pulled lines together in much the same way as rhyme later unified couplets or stanzas. The repeating sounds "w" and "sch" (the former mainly but not exclusively in the first stanza, the latter anticipated in the first stanza by "schon" but then predominating in the second stanza as "Schwarz," "Stadt," "Sprüngen," "schrittweis") bring unity to the disparate images over which the mind seems to skip as it picks its way between thoughts of living things and the finality of the grave.

The ambiguous currents that traverse this poem in terms of both meter and imagery underpin its central theme: the knowledge of death that we mostly prefer to keep buried in the deeper realms of consciousness. The speaker is thus not some wiser person, but our own more profoundly attuned inner self. This self, however, hesitates to yield entirely to the knowledge of death, though it accepts with some reluctance that the end of life can arrive more rapidly than we think. The repetition of "vielleicht" articulates this reluctant admission. The final words of the poem allude, on one level, to the present moment, represented by the flash of light struck by the horses' hooves. On another level, though, this flash can be understood as a correlative of the sudden insight that present and future are connected. As sight and insight come together in the final line, the fleeting spark from the horseshoes gives rise to recognition of the eternal. In a final irony, superstition has long regarded the horse shoe as a sign of good luck and a talisman that could fend off evil spirits and natural catastrophes. Yet nothing, of course, can ultimately fend off death. From this vantage-point, we can now understand better the puzzling use of "denken" as a transitive verb in the key phrase "Denk' es, o Seele." What happens in this poem is no ordinary type of thinking, but something more penetrating, a mental process that cuts to the heart of a complex matter, the relation of life and death. This is not idle thinking, but an intense kind of thinking that also is a type of knowing. It is an unusually active form of thinking that brings to the surface thoughts that we sometimes fear. To solve the puzzle of "denken" with the accusative is also to penetrate the mystery of life and death.

At this point, let us reflect on the process of exploration that has yielded this analysis. Some of the work has been done backstage, as it were. This includes work with the dictionary and the grammar book. Since poetry often uses words in unusual ways, it is always wise to check the possible meanings of a given term. There we can find, for example, that "Eisen" means both "iron" and "horseshoe." A grammar book can tell us more about "denken" and "denken an." In the case of a short poem like this one, we can do a complete scansion, which will not only help to establish the basic metrical scheme but also alert us to important divergences. In writing up an analysis, it is always more productive to highlight the moments where the poem departs from its general meter, since these are often moments of heightened significance. Marking up the text in various ways – underlining the alliterating consonants, circling related sets of imagery – provides a view of the poem as a network rather than as a purely linear construct. Identifying the speaker of the poem is essential, because, like other literary texts, poems are crucially structured in terms of perspective (point of view).

Preliminary work on the text avoids some common mistakes. Instead of trudging stolidly through one line after another, commenting on elements of the poem as we encounter them, we now have a view of the poem as a whole. In this case, I began with the diction, which enabled me first to establish what I termed the backbone of the poem, formed by simple words of knowing, thinking, and saying. That also allowed me to move swiftly to the use of "denken" as a transitive verb, a feature I regard as the central "puzzle" of the poem, intricately connected with its meditation on life and death. Preliminary work also permitted me to work more efficiently with such formal aspects of the poem as meter. Eliminating cumbersome sentences describing the metrical scheme, I was able to identify from the outset some important exceptions to the basic pattern. Such exceptions are almost always more meaningful than the underlying scheme, and because they raise questions about their function in the poem, they are certainly more arresting for the reader of the analysis. Finally, having given some thought to the question "who is the speaker?" allowed me to summarize my thoughts about the poem's "ich" and "du" in a single paragraph without sprinkling my observations throughout my reading of the poem. That eliminated back-tracking and kept the focus more strongly on the relation of speaker and addressee that is so complex an issue in this text. Collecting thoughts according to issues makes your reading move better and prevents the analysis from becoming bogged down in description.

I would like to move now to a more conventional lyric, Theodor Storm's "Hyazinthen" (Hyacinths; 1851). Here is the text:

> Fern hallt Musik; doch hier ist stille Nacht,
> Mit Schlummerduft anhauchen mich die Pflanzen.
> Ich habe immer, immer dein gedacht;
> Ich möchte schlafen, aber du mußt tanzen.
>
> Es hört nicht auf, es rast ohn Unterlaß;
> Die Kerzen brennen und die Geigen schreien
> Es teilen und es schließen sich die Reihen,
> Und alle glühen; aber du bist blaß.
>
> Und du mußt tanzen; fremde Arme schmiegen
> Sich an dein Herz; o leide nicht Gewalt!
> Ich seh dein weißes Kleid vorüber fliegen
> Und deine leichte, zärtliche Gestalt. –
>
> Und süßer strömend quillt der Duft der Nacht
> Und träumerischer aus dem Kelch der Pflanzen.
> Ich habe immer, immer dein gedacht;
> Ich möchte schlafen, aber du mußt tanzen.

(Music resounds far off; but here night is still and silent. The plants breathe on me with slumberous scent: I have always, always thought of you, I wish to sleep, but you must dance.// It never stops, it rages without cease; The candles burn and the fiddles shriek, the rows of dancers part and come together, and all are glowing, but you are pale.// And you must dance; a stranger's arms press close upon your heart; oh, do not suffer harm! I see your white dress fly past and your light and delicate form. –// And more sweetly streaming the night's perfume wells up, and more dreamily from the calices of the plants. I have always, always thought of you; I wish to sleep, but you must dance.)

Let us imagine that you have done the preparatory work needed before delving more deeply into this poem. You have looked up the vocabulary in a good dictionary, noticed the contrast between the speaker and the addressee of the poem, and identified its meter and rhyme scheme. You have doubtless also noticed the frequent use of "und" at the beginnings of lines. Now it is time to make note of the elements that leap out of the regular patterns you have observed, and ultimately, to decide on the best way to approach the poem as you write up your findings. Don't forget to look for something puzzling that may open up the text in unexpected ways.

In fact, this poem poses several puzzles. Some lie on the level of syntax: why does the speaker say "anhauchen mich die Pflanzen" instead of using the more normal word order "hauchen mich die Pflanzen an"? Arguments from meter and rhyme do not suffice to solve this puzzle: we should expect an accomplished poet to handle this sort of problem without resorting to bizarre grammar. It is always wise to assume that when a poet strays from normal usage, there may be a good reason for it. In this case, the phrase with the strangely unseparated prefix is also unusual on the thematic level: usually, we think of perfume emanating from flowering plants, but not of plants breathing on us. The poet's decision not to separate the separable verb captures the overpowering nature of the hyacinth scent, which, however sensuous, also represents a kind of threat. The speaker longs to sleep, but does he want to lose consciousness altogether?

Other puzzles are located at the thematic level. Why should the beloved, the person addressed as "du," actually suffer harm if she dances with a stranger? The speaker's cry, "o leide nicht Gewalt!" seems on the face of it a rather extreme reaction. Surely the young woman has the right to dance with an unknown partner at what seems to be a ball attended by other people and accompanied by a group of musicians? Yet why is the speaker himself not dancing? Why is he confined to an unlit space, and why does he long to sleep rather than to dance? Why doesn't he pull himself together and step out onto the dance floor?

At this point in our exploration, we may wonder whether there is a connection between the syntactical and the thematic puzzles. Let us begin with the phrase "o leide nicht Gewalt!" What elements in the poem underscore the speaker's fear that his beloved might come to harm? For one thing, a dance where participants are arranged in rows that open and close, separating couples and bringing them together again, seems to have lost its measured formality and to have turned into a wild celebration. The dance never stops, it "rast ohn Unterlaß," and the violin music "schreit" as if to join in the furious abandon of the dancers, who "glühen," as if to heighten the gleam of the burning candles. Similarly, but with a quite different force, the plants' perfume advances almost aggressively on the speaker: "anhauchen." Scanning this line, we need to give a secondary stress to the prefix "an" as a result of its unusual positioning:

Mit Schlúmmerdùft ànháuchen mích die Pflánzen.

The speaker is overcome by the scent of the plants, which functions like a drug and drains him of energy. The plants, as the title tells us, are hyacinths, a flowering bulb known for its strong perfume. The text does not say exactly where the speaker is situated, and this, too, may be an indication of his increasing drowsiness under the influence of the intoxicating hyacinths. He is certainly not in the candlelit ballroom; but despite his reference to night, he is probably not lurking in the bushes outside the house. Most likely he is in a greenhouse or winter garden attached to the house. In such an enclosed space, the powerful aroma of the hyacinths, a typical hothouse plant of the period, can become overwhelming. The poem's final stanza introduces another syntactic anomaly: "Und süßer strömend quillt der Duft der Nacht/ Und träumerischer aus dem Kelch der Pflanzen." Restoring these two lines to normal word order, we would have: "Und süßer und träumerischer quillt der Duft der Nacht aus dem Kelch der Pflanzen." The displacement of the second adverb, "träumerisch," suggests something of the speaker's disorientation as a result of the penetrating scent. In effect, he is suffering harm as well, although because the poem is presented from his point of view, this occurs less dramatically than the transformation of the ballroom dance into what he perceives as a violent orgy.

This brings us to the pallor of the beloved woman. Her white dress and light, delicate form underscore her pale skin, which does not color even as the other dancers are glowing with energy and excitement. Why does the speaker use the verb "müssen" in connection with her dancing? Does he simply mean that she insists on dancing, or is she subject to external force? Much is suggested in this poem, and the solution to this question is necessarily speculative. Nonetheless, the poem makes more sense if we consider the scene to be a dance of death. In the "Totentanz" tradition, death is figured as a skeleton, but the victim is not. In this respect, a dance of death would fit. Indeed, it would make sense to think of the entire poem as a metaphorical meditation on the impending death of a beloved woman. At the level of his deepest fears, the speaker knows that his loved one is in the grip of a fatal illness; but on another level, he would rather ignore that knowledge – hence his preference for sleep and forgetting.

Within the context of the mid-nineteenth century, "Hyazinthen" is not only a poem about death, but also a poem about problematic aspects of the aesthetic. It is not accidental that the poem mentions music and dance, two of the arts most closely related to poetry itself. Storm's poem poses the question whether attention to these aesthetic forms brings with it a willful neglect of the darker side of human existence. Are the lyric arts a way of numbing ourselves to more serious concerns? Is poetry a hothouse flower that only apparently counteracts confrontations with threatening forces, such as illness and death? Enlarging the focus by moving outward from the poem itself to Storm's novellas, which, as he himself noted, emerged from his early lyric poetry, would create a fruitful context in which to study the central paradox of this poem. Bourgeois realism, with its attention to the problematic relationship between history and fantasy, reason and superstition, smooth surfaces and troubled depths, is at the base of "Hyazinthen"; but it would take a more extensive explication to demonstrate this than is possible in this chapter.

In part because of the poem's relation to bourgeois realism, it was to become a touchstone for the protagonist of Thomas Mann's novella *Tonio Kröger* (1903), who cites its refrain as an emblem of his relationship to his unattainable youthful love, Ingeborg Holm. While a group of young people are practicing the quadrille at their dance lesson, Tonio suddenly recalls "ein wunderschönes Gedicht von Storm"; the first line seems to him to put into words his response to what he perceives as the ludicrous situation of having to practice ballroom dancing while in love with a beautiful girl: "Ich möchte schlafen, aber du mußt tanzen." Tonio's memory of the poem is inflected by his own emotional response to the dancing lesson: the hyacinth perfume becomes the scent from Ingeborg's hair or the delicate white fabric of her dress. He appropriates the poem for his own purposes. Not surprisingly, the dance lesson becomes a comic scene that differs radically from the ballroom scene presented in Storm's poem.

I would like to conclude this chapter by exploring a poem that engages pointedly with the central problem of the modern lyric, the issue of subjectivity. This untitled poem was written by Nietzsche in 1888:

> An der Brücke stand
> jüngst ich in brauner Nacht.
> Fernher kam Gesang:
> goldener Tropfen quoll's
> über die zitternde Fläche weg.
> Gondeln, Lichter, Musik—
> trunken schwamm's in die Dämmerung hinaus . . .
>
> Meine Seele, ein Saitenspiel,
> sang sich, unsichtbar berührt,
> heimlich ein Gondellied dazu,
> zitternd vor bunter Seligkeit.
> – Hörte Jemand ihr zu?

(I stood on a bridge recently in brown night. Song came from afar: it welled with golden drops across the trembling surface. Gondolas, lights, music – drunken, it floated into the dusk . . . // My soul, a stringed instrument, invisibly touched, sang secretly to itself another gondola song, trembling from colorful bliss. – Did Anyone listen?)

Nietzsche's poem is cast as the expression of an "Ich" who speaks in the first person from the outset. The notion of lyric poetry as a personal experience had been established by Goethe's poetry of the 1770s and had become an accepted convention during the Romantic period. Nietzsche's poem invokes this tradition. Time and place are indicated in the first sentence by the words "jüngst" and the reference to a bridge at night. In the second section of the poem, however, the more personal formulation "meine Seele" takes the place of the first-person pronoun at the beginning of the poem. In this context, the word "Seele" does not have religious overtones; rather, it refers to the emotional or responsive side of the speaker's self. Alongside the speaking subject and his "soul," a more mysterious force manifests itself. The English translation cannot do justice to the use of the indefinite pronoun "es," which here does not refer to the song that comes from afar ("Gesang" is masculine). As the song traverses the distance between its faraway source and the experiencing self on the bridge, an unspecified and indeterminate agency emerges as if independent of human perception or understanding: the verbs associated with it are "quellen" (to swell or well) and "schwimmen" (to swim or float). To the customary subject–object relationship of poetic expression, Nietzsche brings a mysterious new subject, an "es" that seems almost independent of ordinary interactions. This "es" consists of emotion and movement, as we can tell from the words "quoll," "schwamm" and "trunken." "Goldener Tropfen" is genitive, an intriguing way of articulating the relationship between the welling up and the drops that seem to form as result. In the final line of the poem, another third instance is posited, but we do not know who or what that "Jemand" might be. Alluding no doubt to Bishop Berkeley's famous thoughts about whether things need to be perceived in order to exist, this last line questions the existence of a deity whose all-seeing eye validates reality. By introducing not only the indeterminate "es" but also the skeptically invoked "Jemand," Nietzsche's poem complicates the traditional concept of lyric poetry as fundamentally an expression of subjectivity.

At the same time, however, the poem also engages with another aspect of the lyric, its musical essence which, according to ancient mythology, originated in songs accompanied by the lyre. In the first section of the poem, music takes the form of song that comes from afar, carrying across a spatial distance that can also be construed as an implicit reference to a temporal distance, as if this music harkened back to the earliest manifestations of human song. But the song is also that of boatmen in contemporary Venice (the gondolas suggest as much) wafting in the nighttime air. In the second section, the speaker's soul itself becomes a stringed instrument played by unseen hands (the word is "berührt," physically touched, not "gerührt," emotionally touched). Seemingly independently of the speaker, his soul sings secretly to itself; the lack of visible agency makes this song appear to emanate from somewhere other than the speaker's consciousness. In this respect, the song joins the effects of the indeterminate "es" that are apparent in the first section. Yet the secret song is also a "Gondellied," echoing the other gondola songs that fill the space experienced by the speaker. Nietzsche deftly transforms the topos of Venice as a city of mirrors, formed by the reflections in its canals, into a city of echoes that connect the inner self to the perceived impressions of the place. Night is a propitious moment for this transformation, since it is a time when the visual is reduced – in this case to lights on the water – and sound can make itself more effectively heard. Song is a primary mediator between inner and outer world, and in the form of vibration it also links the surface of the water with the interior movement of the speaker's feelings. The same word, "zitternd," is used in both cases. Yet while the outer song drifts into the darkness, the inner song vibrates with "bunter Seligkeit." Color, which has largely disappeared from the nighttime scene, takes on a metaphorical cast in the inner world of the speaker.

A broader approach to this poem would situate it not only in the tradition of poetry about Venice, but also in Nietzsche's conception of the "Dionysian" aspect of art (the word "trunken" points to the Dionysian or ecstatic, which Nietzsche contrasts with what he terms the Appollonian or ordering impulse) and his understanding of the centrality of music (in Nietzsche's manuscript, the poem is preceded by a prose text about music). What I have tried to do here is not to give a complete reading of the poem, but rather to show how close attention to issues of subjectivity can illuminate the implications of even a very brief poetic text. One conclusion that needs to be drawn from this analysis is that this is a poem about what lyric is and the conditions under which it emerges. While it brilliantly expresses the ecstatic character of lyric experience, however, it also calls it into question, notably in its disillusioned final line. By countering the conventional question "who is speaking?" with the question "who, if anyone, is listening?" Nietzsche reveals his problematic relationship to the primacy of lyric experience. The poem is a highly sophisticated reflection on poetry and subjectivity.

Nietzsche's Venice poem brings to a head an important debate about the nature of lyric poetry. Critics have often become so caught up in this debate that they end up with very narrow definitions. Rather than attempting to identify essences, this *Introduction to German Poetry* keeps the concept of poetry relatively flexible. One conception of lyric poetry as embodying a sudden flash of insight on the part of an individual speaker is certainly exemplified by a poem like Mörike's "Denk' es, o Seele," but it is subjected to a critical gaze in Nietzsche's Venice poem. No one would deny, however, that Storm's "Hyazinthen" is a lyric poem, even though it does not focus on an epiphanic moment. Uhland's "Das Schloß am Meere" belongs to a different subgenre, the ballad, and as a result it includes some narrative elements; but it still fulfills a crucial task of poetry, the attempt to capture the mystery of what eludes our direct knowledge.

While this opening chapter has consciously focused on texts in their own right, the following chapters also attend to contextual issues that can often bring greater depth to our understanding of individual poems. Here, I have merely suggested some of the larger questions that might be brought to bear on the four sample poems we have looked at. The principal lesson to carry away from this chapter is that there is no single "right" way to approach a poem. The success of the venture depends, however, on careful preparatory work, the identification of crucial issues (what I have called "puzzles" in the poems), and thoughtful organization of more detailed observations into a coherent and well-structured account of your thoughts and findings. The appendices to this book can help you work with greater accuracy on these aspects of poetic texts.

Chapter 2

Poetic roles in early song-lyrics

Medieval German poetry has great power to fascinate, and anyone interested in the German tradition should be familiar with some key examples. Many anthologies include a selection of texts in their original language, Middle High German, often with glosses or modern translations. This chapter is designed to provide a first entry into this very rich material and its afterlife in later periods. I hope that readers will be sufficiently seduced to explore more broadly on their own.

As the chapter title indicates, these texts are song-lyrics, and in that respect they connect with the very origins of poetry: the etymological root of the word "lyric" is the lyre, the instrument to which songs were performed in ancient Greece. In contrast, German medieval poetry was performed by a single singer; we do not know if the melodies were accompanied by an instrument. Certainly, there was no part-singing. The texts were often set to familiar melodies, but the more gifted singers invented their own. Although several song-books from the Provençal troubadours survive, only a relatively small number of melodies from German medieval song-poetry have come down to us. In post-medieval times, of course, lyric poetry also includes poems that are not sung, but whose language still bears distinct melodic traces in the words alone. In modern poetry, we have come, in addition, to associate the lyric with subjective expression. From the late eighteenth century on, the lyric has been the medium of individual perception and feeling: it has been seen as speech uttered by an exquisitely sensitive self, the "I" of the poem. In medieval poetry, the speaker was not in quite the same sense individual: these poems are *Rollengedichte* ("role poems") in which the speaker adopts a fictional persona. This is not to say, however, that the speaker is a one-dimensional figure. Even within the genre conventions, there was sufficient room for poets to shape the poetic persona with considerable flexibility and thus to convey a sense of subjectivity. Some recent scholars have argued that we need to acknowledge this nascent selfhood in poems where it seems to emerge. Essentially, however, this poetry is an art of variation, and the audience was finely attuned to the poets' skill in developing new roles and new situations. The poet's virtuosity is part of what gives it interest and life. The most obvious "role poems" are those where the words are those of a woman, but male speakers should also be understood as roles and not as an expression of the poet's biographical person. In performance, all of these lyrics were sung by male poets, regardless of whether the persona in the song is male or female.

I would like to begin with a captivating Middle High German lyric from around 1160. Its central motif is falconry, a sport restricted to the nobility during the Middle Ages. In nature, the falcon is known for its free-ranging flight; yet when tamed and trained by a falconer, it becomes an emblem of loyalty. This poem, by a poet known only as "Der von Kürenberg" (also called "the Kürenberger"), gives poignant expression to the contradictory characteristics of the falcon: its willingness to submit to its trainer and its desire to fly freely and unrestrained.

> Ich zôch mir einen valken   mêre danne ein jâr.
> dô ich in gezamete,   als ich in wolte hân,
> und ich im sîn gevidere   mit golde wol bewant,
> er huop sich ûf vil hôhe   und flouc in anderiu lant.
>
> Sît sach ich den valken   schône fliegen:
> er fuorte an sînem fuoze   sîdîne riemen,
> und was im sîn gevidere   alrôt guldîn.
> got sende si zesamene,   die geliep wellen gerne sîn!

(I trained a falcon for more than a year. Once I had tamed him as I wished him to be, and braided his feathers well with gold ribbons, he soared up very high in the sky and flew into foreign lands.// Later, I saw the falcon flying gloriously: on his feet he bore silk tassels, and his feathers were golden red all over. May God bring those together who wish to love one another.)

The speaker of the poem is not a falconer, but most probably a noble lady. She does know some technical terms of falconry, however: the notion of flying "into foreign lands" was the phrase falconers used to describe a bird who has escaped. In a sign of pride in her ownership of the bird she has trained, the lady decks it out with gold ribbons. In flying away, the bird resists her ownership. The next time she sees it, evidently after a lapse of time, its feathers are golden red and its feet bear silken tassels. Are these the trappings of another owner, or the same trappings with which she ornamented him and bound him to her gloved hand? Through the most delicate of verbal sketches, the poem suggests the fundamental paradox of courtly love, which is constantly torn between possession and loss. The falcon seems to stand for the lady's lost lover. The poignant wish in the final line, formulated in general rather than specific terms, gives voice to the experience of someone who has loved and lost.

In terms of form, the "Falcon Song" uses the same long line as the *Nibelungenlied*, a German epic poem from around 1200. Each line is divided into two parts indicated by a gap or caesura; the second part of the line has three stresses. Given that the Kürenberger uses the *Nibelungen*-stanza in all of his thirteen poems, his employment of it here may not carry any special meaning. Nonetheless, the falcon motif may possibly allude to a scene in the *Nibelungenlied* where Kriemhild dreams that she has raised a falcon that is then torn apart by two eagles. She interprets her dream as a prophecy of Siegfried's death. The Kürenberger's text, while maintaining the equivalence between the falcon and the beloved man, is more complex, largely because it leaves so much unsaid. The charm of the "Falcon Song" lies in the way it leaves the listener to imagine the contours of the story that lies behind it.

One of the most famous medieval German song-poems in a female voice is "Under der linden" (Beneath the Linden Tree), by Walther von der Vogelweide.

> Under der linden
> an der heide,
> dâ unser zweier bette was,
> dâ mugent ir vinden
> schône beide
> gebrochen bluomen unde gras.
> vor dem walde in einem tal,
> tandaradei,
> schône sanc die nahtegal.
>
> Ich kam gegangen
> zuo der ouwe,
> dô was mîn friedel komen ê.
> dâ wart ich enpfangen,
> hêre frowe,
> daz ich bin saelic iemer mê.
> er kuste mich wol tûsent stunt,
> tandaradei,
> seht wie rot mir ist der munt.
>
> Dô hat er gemachet
> alsô rîche
> von bluomen eine bettestat.
> des wirt noch gelachet
> inneclîche,
> kumt iemen an daz selbe pfat.

bî den rosen er wol mac,
   tandaradei,
merken wâ mirz houbet lac.

Daz er bî mir laege,
wessez iemen –
nu enwelle got! –, so schamt ich mich,
wes er mit mir pflaege,
niemer niemen
bevinde daz, wan er und ich
und ein kleinez vogellîn.
   tandaradei,
daz mac wol getriuwe sîn.

(Beneath the linden tree on the meadow, where we two had our bed, you can find neatly plucked flowers and grass. At the edge of a wood in a valley, tandaradei, the nightingale sang sweetly.// I came to the meadow: my lover had already arrived there. Then I was received, "noble lady" – so that I shall forever be happy. He kissed me about a thousand times, tandaradei, look how red my mouth is.// There he had made a splendid bed out of flowers. If anyone comes along the same path, he will laugh inwardly. From the roses he can see, tandaradei, where my head lay.// If anyone were to know (God forbid!) that he lay with me, I would be ashamed. What he did with me, may no one ever find out except for he and I and a little bird, tandaradei, but it will doubtless remain silent.)

The natural setting includes two elements of the pleasant trysting place or *locus amoenus*: trees and grass. Yet other common ingredients of the pleasant place, water and a gentle breeze, are missing. For good measure, however, there is not only one tree – the linden beneath which the man and woman make love, but also the little wood at whose edge it is situated. The meadow appears to consist of open country with grass and bushes. The woman's lover has prepared a bed made of flowers and grass plucked from the area. Later, the flowers are designated as roses. The bed is thus both natural and artificial, and while it is located in nature, it is on the edge of the wood, not hidden in a clearing within it. As the fourth stanza indicates, the bed can be seen from the path that the two took to reach this spot. The place is thus a liminal space between the human world and the world of nature. To some degree, the place is private, but even when no other people are present apart from the lovers, a nightingale announces its presence by singing the cadence imitated in the refrain, "tandaradei." In the first stanza, the nightingale seems to function as a typical part of the backdrop, but its insistent song acquires a different meaning as the poem proceeds. The way in which "tandaradei" is interpolated into the poem, interrupting the flow of sentences, is itself striking, perhaps even humorous. Why does the speaker insert it in this way? As we shall see, the refrain is more than just "filler."

Although this lyric, like all Minnesang, was sung in performance by a man, the words are those of a woman, and we quickly realize that she is remembering something that has happened recently. The act of remembering turns what at first seems like a conventional nature description into a landscape of the mind. The double character of the scene – its existence as a natural location for the lovers' tryst and as mental scenery for the speaker's act of remembering – adds an extra dimension to the poem. This is not a naïve text. The reference to traces left in the flowers and grass suggests not only that the lovers' meeting took place there, but also that the experience continues to persist in the speaker's memory. The inclusion of the nightingale is not merely an expected requisite of the scene, but also a first hint that the poem also reflects on its own character as a song.

This self-reflexive dimension is highlighted in the second stanza by the interpolation "hêre frouwe." The function and meaning of this exclamation is disputed: does the lover call the woman by a title she most likely does not bear in reality, "noble lady"? Does she invoke the Virgin Mary, in which case it would mean something like "By our Lady." Or – yet another possibility – is the speaker telling her story to a noble lady? Even without scholarly agreement on what the phrase means, we can tell something of its significance by the striking way in which it interrupts the logical syntax of the sentence. In this respect, it echoes the song of the nightingale, "tandaradei," which also interrupts the syntax and logic of the poem. The lover's reception of the woman and the feeling of bliss that she still connects with that moment are separated by a moment that can only be rendered as an exclamation: "hêre frouwe." The poem skips over the actual consummation of the lovers' desire, referring in this stanza to the lover's "thousand kisses" and in the final stanza to "what he did with me." The interpolated cry registers a moment of surprise and joy that cannot be fully expressed in language.

The nightingale is a crucial key to the poem's reflection on speech and memory. To grasp this point, we need to bear in mind that Walther was a well-educated poet who was familiar with works from classical antiquity. Ovid, whose works had been rediscovered in the twelfth century, was widely read by medieval writers of that time. Ovid's retelling of the tale of Procne and Philomela was well known. According to the myth, the two sisters were daughters of an Athenian king; Procne was married to Tereus, king of Thrace. After raping Philomela, Tereus cut out her tongue to prevent her from telling what had happened, but she wove the story in crimson letters into a large cloth.

When Procne received the cloth and read her sister's story, she took vicious revenge on Tereus. The gods intervened, however, and turned all three of them into birds. One of these was the nightingale, whose song continues to repeat the tale of Tereus' rape of Philomela. In contrast to Walther's poem with its refrain "tandaradei," one of the songs in the *Carmina burana* uses a somewhat similar refrain, "lodircundeie" (it's not clear quite what this word means) in connection with a rape that also takes place at a "wunneclîche stat" (wondrous place) where grass and flowers grow. If the nightingale and its song in Walther's poem alludes to Philomela, then it also alludes to song and story (the tale on the cloth and the song of the bird).

The situation of Walther's song is, of course, the inverse of the Philomela story. Its allusion to the story is ingenious and even witty. At the conclusion of the poem, the speaker avers her trust in the bird's ability to keep her secret. Yet the woman speaker has herself been telling the story in her own song. Why does she do so, when she also says that she would be ashamed if anyone knew what had happened beneath the linden tree? One answer would be that, although the poet is singing her story in her "voice," this voice is not meant to be understood as actually speaking aloud. Rather, the woman is presumably remembering the story in thought. Medieval narrative does not have a form that correlates with modern "interior monologue": in courtly epic, characters' thoughts are uttered as an aside, a sort of dramatic soliloquy in a lowered voice. "Under der linden" could be understood as a memory soliloquy of this kind. In any event, it reflects on the relation of speech, memory, and poetry or song in a highly sophisticated manner that is at odds with the poem's seemingly transparent surface.

The theme of consummated love illustrated in this poem and others differs from another important strain in Minnesang, which concentrates on love from afar. The kind of relationship celebrated in Walther's "Under der linden" contrasts with the courtly love model, which plays an important role in medieval German poetry. In a characteristic poem by Reinmar, "Swaz ich nu niuwer maere sage," we can observe many of the knightly attitudes and emotions that give form to a particular type of poetry that co-exists with what we have just seen in Walther. In fact, medieval German poetry exists in many different variations and cannot easily be reduced to one or two predominant types. The genre represented by Reinmar emphasizes some features that have come to be associated with song-poems about unconsummated love. The speaker of Reinmar's poem announces at the outset that he is unhappy: "ich enbin niht frô." Even his friends, he says, have had enough of his constant complaints. The cause of his distress is the refusal of a beloved lady to respond to his wooing. Unhappiness that springs from unrequited love is part of the very structure of this type of poetry, however. In the third stanza, the speaker expresses the paradoxical nature of his situation:

> Sô wol dir, wîp, wie reine dîn name,
> wie senfte du ze nennen und zerkennen bist!
> ez wart nie niht sô rehte lobesame,
> dâ duz an rehte güete kêrest, sô du bist.
> dîn lop mit rede nieman wol volenden kan.
> swes du mir triuwen pfligest, wol im, der ist ein saelic man
> und mac vil gerne leben.
> du gîst al der werlte hôhen muot,
> maht du mir ein wênic fröide geben?

> (Praised be you, woman, what a pure word. How pleasant to pronounce and to hear! There never was anything as praiseworthy as when you link yourself with true kindness, as is your nature. No one can fully articulate your praise in words. He whom you accept in faithfulness, good fortune to him, he is a happy man who can live with great enjoyment. You give the whole world higher spirits – Can you not also give me a little pleasure?)

Courtly love is a kind of ritual or game intrinsic to a particular type of poetry. In spite of much controversy about how the concept may have related to actual practice, we know very little outside of actual texts. Whether or not the loved woman was present at the performance of the song is simply not known. In this now canonical stanza from Reinmar, the address "sô wol dir, wîp" seems to be directed more toward woman in general then toward a specific woman. Woman as person quickly becomes woman as word. It is the term "wîp" that bears the purity that the speaker of this poem attributes to it. Indeed, the purity of the term and the woman who embodies it is so exceptional that it cannot fully be expressed in language. It is a quality that also confers obligations of service and loyalty in the knight who professes his love. The final lines of the stanza give voice to a central paradox of this kind of relationship, which – by means of the song-poem – elevates the mood of the audience even while the lover is deprived of physical satisfaction. The lover himself experiences both emotions at one and the same time. The last two stanzas of Reinmar's poem elaborate on this paradox and the necessarily split consciousness of the speaker who plays the game of courtly love. Modern anthologies of German poetry rarely include this text, although *Reclams großes Buch der deutschen Gedichte* (Reclam's Big Book of German Poetry; 2007; ed. Heinrich Detering) not only makes space for it, but also gives a complete modern German translation.

In contrast to Reinmar's poem by a male speaker and to Walther's female monologue "Under der linden," we should now look at a dialogue poem in which male and female voices alternate. Heinrich von Morungen's dawn song, "Owê, sol aber mir iemer mê" provides a characteristic example:

> Owê –
> sol aber mir iemer mê
> geliuhten dur die naht
> noch wîzer danne ein snê
> ir lîp vil wol geslaht?
> der trouc diu ougen mîn.
> ich wânde, ez solde sîn
> des liehten mânen schîn.
>   dô tagte ez.

> Owê –
> sol aber er iemer mê
> den morgen hie betagen?
> als uns diu naht engê,
> daz wir niht durfen klagen:
> Owê, nu ist ez tac,
> als er mit klage pflac,
> dô er jungest bî mir lac.
>   dô tagte ez.

> Owê, –
> si kuste âne zal
> in dem slâfe mich.
> dô vielen hin zetal
> ir trehene nider sich.
> iedoch getrôste ich sie,
> daz sî ir weinen lie
> und mich al umbevie.
>   dô tagte ez.

> Owê, –
> daz er sô dicke sich
> bî mir ersehen hât!
> als er endahte mich,
> sô wolt er sunder wât
> mîn arme schouwen blôz.
> ez was ein wunder grôz,
> daz in des nie verdrôz.
>   dô tagte ez.

('Alas, and will her shapely body, even whiter than snow, shine for me ever again in the night? It deceived my eyes. I thought it was the bright moonlight. Then day broke.'// 'Alas, will he ever again await the morning here while night flees from us without our needing to lament: "alas, now it is day," as he lamented while he lay with me recently? Then day broke.'// 'Alas, she kissed me countless times while I slept. Her tears tumbled down. Yet I comforted her so that she stopped weeping and took me in her arms. Then day broke.'// 'Alas, that he has so often loved to look at me! When he removed the covers, he wanted to see my arm bare and unconcealed. It was a great wonder that he never tired of the sight. Then day broke.')

This poem is a dawn song, a genre in which lovers who have spent the night together contemplate the approach of day and the parting that this brings with it. The form entered German literature by way of the French troubadours. Morungen's text takes the form of alternating stanzas sung by each of two lovers, a knight and his lady, a song type found only in the German medieval tradition. The technical term for this genre is "Wechsel." In this type of song, the partners speak in turn, but they do not actually speak to each other. In performance, the alternating stanzas would have seemed more like dramatic monologues. Despite this element of distance between the two lovers, the poem is held together by the common opening of each stanza, "Owê," as well as by the refrain "dô tagte ez." Within the framing opening and closing lines, each stanza consists of two parts: an "Aufgesang" of four lines with alternating rhymes, and an "Abgesang" of three lines held together by a single rhyme. Although there has been some controversy over the order of stanzas, this may not be of great significance, given that, in accord with the "Wechsel" form, the two talk past and not with each other.

As in Walther's "Under der linden," the lovers' intimacy is recounted in retrospect, as an act of memory. Connected with memory is the theme of eyesight as a deceptive mode of perception. The knight's first attempt to describe the radiance of his lover's body is a comparison in which it outshines the whiteness of snow; but later, mistaking it for the light of the moon, he realizes with a jolt that the brilliance of her skin has misled him about the impending dawn of day. When we see the woman's naked body again, it is in the fourth stanza, where we hear her voice. There has been some dispute over whether the words "mîn arme" refer to her arm, or whether the phrase might not mean "poor me." I prefer the first of these alternatives, according to which "arme" is a metonymy for the woman's body as a whole. The color white may suggest a contrast with its use elsewhere in medieval poetry as a trope for purity: the notion of whiteness more dazzling than snow was often used, for example, in connection with the Virgin Mary. This would be consonant with the spiritual dimension that permeates much of Morungen's poetry. It would also cast a somewhat ironic light on the woman's use of the word "wunder" in the final stanza.

Altogether, the lovers' remembered nights together are marked less by fulfillment than by disappointment and sorrow. Constantly anticipating the end of their time together, they cannot fully enjoy their time together. The woman depicts her lover as repeatedly lamenting the imminent break of day, while the man portrays her as not only kissing him again and again, but also weeping almost uncontrollably. The comfort of love-making, indicated in the third stanza, appears as only a brief respite from the cares that continually intrude. The repeated stanza opening "owê" and the refrain "do tagte ez" combine to express this underlying lament. When the woman quotes the knight's lament in the second stanza, "owê, nu ist ez tac," the balance between love and suffering tips toward the negative. While these repetitions create an effect of coherence, the poem contains deep antinomies, as evidenced in the discrepancy between the two views of the man's attitude to the woman's body. The man's claim that vision is deceptive undercuts in advance the woman's opinion that he never tired of viewing her white nakedness. Altogether, the text seems to cast doubt on the alternative space of clandestine trysts and the challenge they pose to courtly *minne* and its high ideals of love from afar.

One of the best-known dawn songs in the German tradition announces itself from the outset as a text of bold metaphors and an unusual deployment of voices and perspective. The poem is not short, so I will comment on it stanza by stanza. Its author is Wolfram von Eschenbach. The opening metaphor forms one of the text's most striking moments:

> »Sîne klâwen
>   durh die wolken sint geslagen,
> er stîget ûf mit grôzer kraft.
> ich sih in grâwen
> taegelîch, als er wil tagen,
>
> den tac, der im geselleschaft
> erwenden wil, dem werden man,
> den ich mit sorgen în bî naht verliez.
> ich bringe in hinnen, ob ich kan.
> sîn vil manigiu tugent mich daz leisten hiez.«

(Its claws have broken through the clouds; it rises up with great power. I see it turning grey, in the way day does when it dawns, the day that will deprive of company the noble man whom, with concern, I let in at night. I shall take him away, if I can. His many great qualities call on me to do so.)

There is almost no way for an English translation to render the boldness and complexity of the original. The poem does not reveal at first whether its first word means "its" or "his": only in line 6 do we understand that "sîne" refers to "der tac." The third-person pronouns that refer to day give way, however, to a third-person pronoun referring to the "noble man." To render the day as "it," as we naturally have to do in English, is to obscure the effect of the complex syntactic structure of this strophe. Indeed, it would not be wrong to write "his claws," given the way in which the dawning day is pictured as some kind of large bird with huge talons. (Some readers have seen it as an animal, or even a hybrid such as a griffin.) The word "taegelîch" means both "daily" and "in the manner of day." We see an event, the first emergence of light in the early morning, which is both thoroughly normal and thoroughly remarkable. Hints of daylight strike through the clouds and then take flight as if they were a bird of prey. The majestic and terrifying image sets the tone for this dawn song.

Wolfram's five dawn songs were an important contribution to the genre. In the Provençal tradition, the watchman took on the task of protecting the lovers from social disapproval. In Wolfram's text, the watchman plays a more significant role: not only does he sing the first and the third stanzas, he also reflects on the position of the male lover, whose reputation demands that his tryst with the woman be kept secret. Throughout most of the poem, the man remains silent, no doubt asleep, though we are not explicitly told as much. One way of understanding the watchman's role, however, is to see it as an expression or even a projection of the male lover's concerns. The watchman's description of the dawning day as a bird of prey mounting into the sky would then be akin to what, in modern poetry, we term an "objective correlative" of the man's fears that his secret may be revealed if he leaves too late in the morning. While he sleeps, the woman rejects the idea that her lover must leave so soon:

»Wahtaer, du singest,
daz mir manige vröide nimt
unde mêrt mîne klage.
maer du bringest,
der mich leider niht gezimt,

immer morgens gegen dem tage.
diu solt du mir verswîgen gar.
daz gebiut ich den triuwen dîn.
des lôn ich dir als ich getar,
sô belîbet hie der geselle mîn.«

(Watchman, what you sing takes many a joy from me and adds to my lament. You bring news that is, alas, not welcome to me, every morning when day breaks. You should keep it from me, I order you, on your honor. I will reward you for that to the extent that I can, so that my companion may stay here.)

The woman's complaint, while formally addressed to the watchman, also expresses a concept fundamental to medieval German poetry: that love brings both pleasure and suffering. The watchman gives expression to social expectations, according to which the male lover's reputation must be guarded above anything else. Daylight brings with it the possibility that the man might be seen by others going about their morning business; it also stands metaphorically for an unseemly revelation of the secret love affair. In the final lines of the poem, we discover that the man is a knight ("rîter," stanza 5). By the norms of courtly love, a knight's desire for a beautiful lady should remain unconsummated: when a knight sings of his love, it is understood that he remains at a distance from the lady. In this instance, however, the watchman has aided the knight in gaining physical access to his beloved. The watchman's argument becomes more insistent in the third strophe:

> »Er muoz et hinnen
> balde und ân sûmen sich:
> nu gib im urloup, suozez wîp.
> lâze in minnen
> her nâch sô verholn dich,
>
> daz er behalte êre unde den lîp.
> er gab sich mîner triuwen alsô
> daz ich in braehte ouch wider dan.
> ez ist nu tac: naht was ez dô
> mit drucken an die brust dîn kus mir in an gewan.«

(He must leave here immediately and without delay. Now let him go, sweet lady. Let him love you later in all secrecy// so that he may retain his honor and his life ["lîp" actually means "body"]. He entrusted himself to my loyalty so that I would bring him here and lead him away again. It is now day: it was night when your kiss and your embrace received him from me.)

Medieval concepts of trust and honor form the backbone of the watchman's argument. The three-way relationship of watchman, woman, and knight is complex. In stanza 2, the woman had expressed her view that the watchman is bound to her in loyalty ("triuwe"). In his response, the watchman points out that he is also bound by "triuwe" to watch over the knight's reputation. The intricate interweaving of this term, understood by the woman as feudal fealty and by the watchman as an ethical principle, determines the dialogue between the two of them. The relationship between them resembles a relay race in which the baton is handed from one to the other, but in which the rules of nighttime are different from the more rational rules of day. The woman continues to beg the watchman to disregard his loyalty to the knight and to continue his song as if society's rules could be broken without harm:

> »Swaz dir gevalle,
> wahtaer, sinc und lâ den hie,
> der minne brâht und minne enpfienc.
> von dînem schalle
> ist er und ich erschrocken ie,
>
> sô ninder der morgenstern ûf gienc
> ûf in, der her nâch minne ist komen,
> noch ninder lûhte tages lieht.
> du hâst in dicke mir benomen
> von blanken armen, und ûz herzen niht.«

(Whatever you please, watchman, sing and leave him here, he who brought and received love. He and I have always been alarmed by your song; even before the morning star rose above him who had come here for love, and when the daylight had not yet shone, you often took him from my white arms but not from my heart.)

The woman's renewed response attempts to bracket the watchman out of the three-way relationship. Indeed, it makes sense to think of the poem as not so much an actual dialogue between the watchman and the woman as a set of intertwined monologues that express the thoughts of these two contrasting figures. In insisting on the reciprocal love between the knight and herself, the woman brushes aside the social expectations to which the knight is also bound. She acts, moreover, as if the watchman's duty were not connected with social mores. Most significantly, she refuses to accept the customary view about when such trysts should come to an end. The threshold between night and day, and by extension between the private and the public realm, is identified differently by the watchman and the woman. Yet although she prefers not to think about the light that will soon emanate from first the morning star and then the rising sun, she does refer to her own "white arms," whose whiteness depends on at least some ambient light. The motif of the woman's bare arms may also be an allusion to the earlier dawn song by Heinrich von Morungen, "owê, sol aber mir iemer mê."

The fifth and final stanza of Wolfram's dawn song departs from the pattern that has been established in which the watchman and the woman exchange views in alternating stanzas. The speaker is now an anonymous narrator who is not one of the characters in the triangular configuration of watchman, woman, and knight. The light motif leads off:

> Von den blicken
> die der tac tet durch diu glas,
> und dô wahtaere warnen sanc,
> si muose erschricken
> durch den, der dâ bî ir was.
> ir brüstlîn an brust si dwanc.
> der rîter ellens niht vergaz;
> des wold in wenden wahtaers dôn:
> urloup nâh und nâher baz
> mit kusse und anders gap in minne lôn.

(As a result of the glances that the day made through the bull's-eye panes, and when the watchman sang his warning, she was compelled to take fright on account of him who was with her there. She pressed her little breasts against his chest. The knight did not forget his manliness, which the watchman's song was trying to take from him. The lovers' parting, which was coming nearer and nearer, gave them a reward for their love with kisses and other things.)

The "blicken" of the day are, of course, the rays of the rising sun; but in accord with the poem's central trope, in which daylight represents the public sphere, they are imagined here as curious eyes peering through the window. The sense of rupture conveyed by the "claws" of day as they burst through the clouds in the opening stanza gives way here to a new recognition: the woman hears the watchman's warning song in a new way that finally takes social constraints into account. The word "erschrecken," which in the fourth stanza referred to the woman's alarm at the imminent break of day, now refers to a renewed understanding of the danger he would run if he took leave of her too late. As the man finally wakes up, the two lovers steal a last moment of pleasure before they take leave of each other.

This final stanza uses to brilliant effect the characteristic division of medieval strophes into "Aufgesang" and the "Abgesang," this time following a different pattern from the one we observed in Morungen's dawn song. These two parts of the stanza were distinguished not only by the rhyme scheme, but also by the fact that each part was sung to a different melody (in chapter 3, we will follow a later development of this form in Luther's hymns). Pivoting on the last line of the "Aufgesang," the poem turns to the couple's love-making before the knight departs. Although the woman has taken fright for his safety, she still induces him to ignore the watchman's warning and, with it, the threat that had been posed at the beginning by the claws of day as it began to rise in the sky. In contrast to the lovers in other dawn songs, this couple, defying daybreak for a moment, wrest erotic pleasure from the very danger of their liminal situation.

This is not the only Middle High German poem of such complexity. Morungen's "Mirror Song," "mir ist geschehen als einem kindelîne," is possibly one of the most challenging and most frequently discussed texts of the period. Often called a "Narcissus poem," it is structured around three key experiences: a moment when, like a child, the speaker tried to grasp his own image in a mirror, a dream of his lady-love, and an allusion to the young man who fell in love with his reflection in a fountain. This is not the place to rehearse the many arguments that have been advanced about this poem, although we should certainly be extremely cautious about applying Freudian concepts to a pre-modern text. The breaking of the mirror in the speaker's childhood and the slightly wounded mouth of the woman in the dream (the text says that her mouth "ein lützel was versêret") imply that something is not right. On one level, the central episode of the dream suggests the problematic nature of the knight's relation to his lady, who is often figured as a mirror for the man. On another level, the poem also explores the complexities of reflection, fantasy, and representation. Confronted with his dream image of the woman with the wounded mouth, the speaker is overcome by fear that her mouth might fade away altogether. The poem seems to ask, what is reality and how can we know it? The question is one that probes to the heart of literature, and the text is not able to answer it. Instead, the speaker recognizes in himself the same shock that Narcissus must have felt when he fell in love with his image in the water. If mirror-images and dreams are nothing but deceptions – deceptions that can lead to harm – what can we say of the song itself, a representation of these experiences? Perhaps the only possible response is one of lament:

> Des hân ich nu niuwer klage begunnen,
> sît mîn herze sich ze sulher swaere bôt,
> daz ich durch mîn ouge schouwe sülhe nôt [. . .]

> (As a result I began lamenting anew because my heart fell into such
> trouble when I saw this misfortune with my own eyes [. . .])

The song-lyrics we have just been discussing were written in the twelfth century, the high point of German medieval literature. In the early thirteenth century, Neidhart (sometimes called "von Reuental," although he never refers to himself that way) invented new forms in which he used village satire to take issue with the concept of courtly love. His way of doing so is intriguing. One of his innovations was an extension of the brief nature descriptions that often occurred at the beginning of love poems. In contrast to the few lines that mention the linden tree and the meadow at the opening of Walther's "Under der linden," Neidhart's poems frequently begin with several stanzas of nature description. The two seasons, summer and winter, engender different types of texts: in his winter poems, for example, the satiric element is stronger and sharper. Unlike post-medieval poems in which the seasons are often considered largely for their own sake, Neidhart's nature descriptions serve as a backdrop for detailed scenes of village life. He presents gaggles of girls planning dances or sledding parties and young men engaged in rough and tumble or even outright brawling. Neidhart even mischievously presents his alter ego, the knight of Reuental, as the object of desire for various young women. In contrast to the courtly love poems of a preceding period, Neidhart's songs bestow names on the characters he presents. Yet although these names might seem to modern readers to suggest individuality, they are really just types. In fact, Neidhart seems to have invented some of the names he uses: the male names, in particular, are designed to suggest the boorishness of the village youths. One point Neidhart makes repeatedly is that the younger generation of the villages desire to be part of courtly culture rather than outsiders to it.

One of Neidhart's summer poems starts with the departure of wintry cold and the arrival of longer days. Here are the first three stanzas:

> Nu ist der küele winder gar zergangen,
> diu naht ist kurz, der tac beginnet langen;
> sich hebet eine wünneclîchiu zît,
> diu al der werlde vreude gît.
> baz gesungen nie die vogele ê noch sît.

> Komen ist uns ein liehtiu ougenweide:
> man siht der rosen wunder ûf der heide;
> die bluomen dringent durch daz gras.
> Wie schône ein wîse getouwet was,
> dâ mir mîn geselle zeinem kranze las.

> Der walt hât sîner grîse gar vergezzen;
> der meie ist ûf ein grünez zwî gesezzen:
> er hât gewunnen loubes vîl.
> bint dir balde, trûtgespil,
> dû weist wôl, daz ich mit einem ritter wil.

(Now the cold winter is quite gone, the night is short, the day begins to
lengthen; a wondrous time begins that gives joy to the whole world. The
birds have never sung more beautifully.// A radiant splendor has come
for our enjoyment: one sees a host of roses on the heath; the flowers
emerge from the earth. How beautifully a meadow was covered in dew
when my young man gathered flowers to make a wreath for me.// The
woods have totally forgotten their gray color; May has perched
upon a green twig: it has brought forth many green leaves. Put your
headscarf on, dear girlfriend! You know that I intend to go out with a
knight.)

This "nature opening" could almost be a poem in itself – but it is not. The
crucial difference between Neidhart's stanzas and the nature poetry of post-
medieval times is the way in which references to village life and the beginnings
of a story are interwoven with the description of natural phenomena. The
speaker, a young woman, tells a friend that they should take advantage of the
beautiful weather (medieval culture distinguished only two seasons, not four)
and go in search of merriment and male company.

Following this opening, the poem shifts to become a dialogue between
the girl and her mother. Shocked by the girl's intention to go dancing, her
mother refuses her the key to the chest where her best dress is kept; but the
girl opens the chest by force. When she returns from the dance, her mother
gives her a beating with the distaff of her spinning wheel. Neidhart frequently
uses this structure – a nature opening followed by dialogue – in his poetry. It
turns his songs into something more like miniature narratives or even brief
dramas.

One of Neidhart's repeated motifs is that of a mirror that his alter ego,
the "Reuentaler," had given a village girl, Vriderun. In numerous poems, the
speaker complains that this mirror has been stolen by a brash young villager
named Engelmar. The mirror motif tends to occur in contexts where the
speaker of a poem laments the decline of the courtly love tradition. Again
and again, Neidhart seems to identify the loss of the mirror with the end of
Minnesang. From this perspective, Neidhart's poems go beyond the critique of
village boorishness by reflecting on the history of Middle High German poetry
from its high point to his own age.

To illustrate this theme in Neidhart, I will now examine a poem that, while
not entirely typical of his work, expresses his dismay at changes that have
taken place in his lifetime. The speaker is someone serving in the crusades,
and although he gives voice to much unhappiness at being away from home,
he nonetheless opens with the coming of summer:

Ez gruonet wol diu heide,
mit grüenem loube stât der walt.
der winder kalt
twanc sie sêre beide.
diu zît hât sich verwandelôt.
mîn sendiu nôt
mant mich an die guoten, von der ich unsanfte scheide.
Gegen der wandelunge
singent wol die vogelîn
den vriunden mîn,
den ich gerne sunge,
des si mir alle sagten danc.
ûf mînen sanc
ahtent hie die Walhe niht. Sô wol dir, diutschiu zunge!

(The meadow is turning green, the wood reveals itself in green leafage.
The cold winter punished them severely. Times have changed. Painful
longing makes me think of the good woman, from whom I cannot bear
to be separated.// Given this transformation, the little birds sing for my
friends, to whom I would prefer to sing myself. The foreigners here pay
no attention to my song. Godspeed to you, German language!)

In these opening stanzas of what is quite a lengthy poem, two changes work
at cross-purposes to each other. On one level, winter is giving way to spring,
but the speaker is not there to see it; instead, he conjures the scene up in his
imagination. The meadow and wood of which he speaks are typical features of
German lands, not of the foreign parts where he currently finds himself. The
little birds sing for his friends at home, substituting for his own song which
cannot reach so far. His longing for his beloved testifies to the distance between
his current location and his home; and by the same token his lament that his
song is not appreciated by those who cannot speak German indicates his desire
to return to German lands. It is believed that the text refers to the disastrous
crusade of 1217–21, in which the crusaders experienced heavy losses. Despite
these historical allusions, the remaining stanzas of the poem are largely carried
by the speaker's imagination. The transition from the opening stanzas runs:
"Wie gerne ich nu sande/ der lieben einen boten dar" (how much I would like
to send a messenger to my beloved). Then, in a bold move, he speaks as if he
were already giving instructions to the imagined messenger. This part of the
poem articulates the message that the messenger is to repeat when he arrives
home. Yet at the same time, the speaker recognizes that the messenger might
not be as speedy as he wishes. In that case, he will go himself, ready to sing

many new songs. Still, that won't be a rapid trip either, since they will have to make a stop in Austria first.

The driving force of the poem is the imagination and, along with it, the "German language" that gives it voice. Implicitly, then, the losses in the crusade and the speaker's sense of exile correlate with the changing times that Neidhart represents in other poems by the loss of Vriderun's mirror. Poetry is the special sphere of the imagination. From this perspective, Neidhart's crusade song can be seen as another reflection on the power of poetry to overcome barriers that exist in reality; at the same time, however, it also mourns the decline of a poetic tradition.

In 1823, Joseph von Eichendorff published in serial form a novella that reworks the tension between simple people and a tradition formerly restricted to the nobility: the narrative was *Aus dem Leben eines Taugenichts* (From the Life of a Good For Nothing). The novella appeared in book form in 1826. The protagonist, a miller's son, is also the narrator. Leaving his father's mill, he sets out to wander in the "wide world," singing songs along the way. Almost immediately, he is captivated by two beautiful women in a beautiful carriage. He falls in love with one of them and invents a song that conveys his feelings about her:

> Wohin ich geh' und schaue,
> In Feld und Wald und Tal
> Vom Berg' ins Himmelsblaue,
> Viel schöne gnäd'ge Fraue,
> Grüß' ich Dich tausendmal.

> (Wherever I walk and gaze, in field and wood and dale, from the mountain to the blue sky, beautiful, gracious lady, I greet you a thousand times.)

This is his first attempt to formulate the song, and at this point it consists of a single stanza. The only inkling that there might be a medieval substratum is the word "Fraue," which echoes the Middle High German "frouwe." Yet like the medieval love poetry we have looked at, this text is a role poem, and of course it is explicitly characterized as a song. In this respect, it is typical of what is termed "medievalism," the use of medieval motifs for modern purposes. Naturally, medievalizing texts tended to present the Middle Ages through rose-tinted and often quite inaccurately calibrated glasses. One way in which they do so is by highlighting what the Romantics saw as the "naivety" of medieval texts. A carefully constructed simplicity is characteristic of this type of medievalism. By the time Taugenichts sings his song a second time, it has acquired additional stanzas and taken on a more "medieval" coloration:

> Wohin ich geh' und schaue,
> In Feld und Wald und Tal,
> Vom Berg' hinab in die Aue:
> Viel schöne, hohe Fraue,
> Grüß ich Dich tausendmal.
>
> In meinem Garten find' ich
> Viel' Blumen, schön und fein,
> Viel' Kränze wohl draus wind' ich
> Und tausend Gedanken bind' ich
> Und Grüße mit darein.
>
> *Ihr* darf ich keinen reichen,
> Sie ist zu hoch und schön,
> Die müssen alle verbleichen,
> Die Liebe nur ohnegleichen
> Bleibt ewig im Herzen stehn.
>
> Ich schein' wohl froher Dinge
> Und schaffe auf und ab,
> Und, ob das Herz zerspringe,
> Ich grabe fort und singe,
> Und grab' mir bald mein Grab.

(Wherever I walk and gaze, in field and wood and dale, from the mountain down to the meadow, beautiful, noble lady, I greet you a thousand times.// In my garden I find many flowers, lovely and fine, I weave many wreaths from them and bind together a thousand thoughts, with greetings intertwined.// I cannot give her any of them, she is too noble and beautiful, all of them must fade, only peerless love remains forever in my heart.// I look as if I'm happy and work at this and that, and even though my heart might break, I dig on and sing, and will soon have dug my grave.)

Although the poem has no exact counterpart in the Middle High German canon, it picks up images familiar from some of the best-known medieval love songs. Much like medieval nature openings, the first stanza of the Taugenichts' song speaks generically of field, wood, and dale. The word for meadow, "Aue," is rooted in the Middle Ages. The motif of the wreath in the second and third stanzas alludes to such poems as Walther's "Nemt, frouwe dîsen kranz." The beautiful lady, addressed in the first version by the more modern term "gnädige Frau" has now become a "high" or noble lady whom the speaker can only adore from afar. In Middle High German courtly love poetry, the fact that the speaker's love for the lady would necessarily go unrequited was generally taken as given. There are, to be sure, examples where the singer claims that he will die of his love. In a poem by Heinrich von Morungen, the unrequited lover exclaims: "die liebe und die leide/ diu wellen mich beide/ fürdern hin ze grabe" (love and suffering will bring me to my grave). Taugenichts' version of this motif, however, is distinctly more lugubrious as he conjures up an image of the spurned lover digging his own grave. At the end of the novella, Taugenichts discovers that his situation was not desperate at all: his lady-love turns out not to be from the nobility after all. The gently comic conclusion of the novella shows the lovers planning their marriage, "und es war alles, alles gut" ("and everything, everything was good").

Eichendorff's inspiration for this song was undoubtedly the anthology of "old German songs" assembled by Achim von Arnim and Clemens Brentano under the title *Des Knaben Wunderhorn* (The Boy's Magic Horn; 1805–1808). Together with two other important publications, Karl Lachmann's edition of Walther von der Vogelweide in the original Middle High German and Ludwig Uhland's poetic rendering of Walther's poetry into modern German, *Des Knaben Wunderhorn* was responsible for unleashing a new craze for the medieval period in the nineteenth century. Some of the poems in this anthology were based on fifteenth-century manuscripts in Clemens Brentano's possession. The anthology also included songs from Herder's collection of old folk songs. The status of many poems in *Des Knaben Wunderhorn* is problematic: not all were of Germanic origin, and some had been written by more recent German poets. The approach Arnim and Brentano took to modernizing the older texts varied from gentle retouching and updated spelling on the one hand to radical rewriting on the other. Nonetheless, their anthology met a need for fresh poetic material, and even the generally skeptical Heine wrote in his essay *Die Romantische Schule* (The Romantic School; 1836): "Dieses Buch kann ich nicht genug rühmen" (I cannot praise this book enough).

Des Knaben Wunderhorn includes several dawn songs from Brentano's manuscript collection. In reworking these texts, Brentano did not hesitate to make substantial changes. In some instances, he assembled what had been separate poems to form longer texts of a more narrative character. The inevitable gaps between these assembled parts were often hauntingly suggestive. In other cases, he embellished the fifteenth-century texts in accord with his own preference for rich rhymes and abundant assonance. The effect is often highly contrived, displaying Brentano's own virtuoso handling of language rather than giving an accurate rendering of the poems in his collection.

In contrast, *Des Knaben Wunderhorn* updates other older texts more cautiously. This is the case, for example, with the ballad about Tannhäuser, a medieval poet about whom very little is known. The version included in *Des Knaben Wunderhorn* is conservatively updated. In its fifteenth-century version, "Der Tannhäuser" used a popular ballad form: four-line stanzas with alternating four-beat lines and three-beat lines, where only the second and fourth lines rhyme. Heine was one of several nineteenth-century poets who wrote his own version of the poem; other writers, such as Tieck and Eichendorff, turned the material into prose novellas. Heine's 1836 version, "Der Tannhäuser: Eine Legende" (Tannhäuser: A Legend), stays very close to the medieval version and its updating by Arnim and Brentano. In the last part of the poem, however, Heine takes advantage of Tannhäuser's return from a visit to Pope Urban in Rome to develop an entirely new, anachronistic side-trip through various parts of nineteenth-century Germany. This allows Heine to compose thumbnail sketches of such cities as Dresden, Berlin, and Hamburg, and to satirize contemporary culture and several poetic rivals.

Heine's interest in the Middle Ages had already begun a few years earlier. His *Buch der Lieder* (Book of Songs; 1827), especially the section headed "Romanzen" (romances), includes several poems that nostalgically conjure up the medieval period. "Die Minnesänger" (Minnesingers) is one of these. The speaker visualizes a competition among medieval poets by comparing them to jousting knights:

> Zu dem Wettgesange schreiten
> Minnesänger jetzt herbei:
> Ei, das gibt ein seltsam Streiten,
> Ein gar seltsames Turnei.
>
> Phantasie, die schäumend wilde,
> Ist des Minnesängers Pferd,
> Und die Kunst dient ihm zum Schilde,
> Und das Wort, das ist sein Schwert.

> (Minnesingers hasten now to the singing competition: Oh, what strange fighting it produces, a very strange tournament.// Fantasy, foaming and wild, is the Minnesinger's horse, and art serves as his shield, and the word is his sword.)

The perspective on the competition is a modern one that attempts to understand a cultural event that is no longer familiar. The present tense is simply a way of making the scene vivid. In the stanzas that follow (there are five in all), the speaker's explanation for the singers' contest is colored by modern sentimentality. Knightly tournaments are presented as combat between contestants in good health, whereas the singing contest is one to which the participants bring a "Todeswund[e]," the wound of unrequited love. The winner, as the final stanza explains, is the singer whose song succeeds in forcing "Liederblut aus Herzensgrund" (the blood of song from the bottom of his heart). Although the speaker does briefly identify with the competing poets (he speaks in stanza 4 of "wir Minnesänger"; we Minnesingers), his song is essentially a vignette of a bygone era that valued poetry in a manner foreign to the modern reader.

Heine's earlier ballad "Lorelei" (1823/24), perhaps his most famous imitation of older poetic forms, is inspired by nostalgia for a past that never was the way we imagine it to have been. From the beginning, the speaker acknowledges his split perspective on the "Märchen aus alten Zeiten" (fairy tale from olden times) that will not leave his mind. Whatever relationship Heine's poem might bear to the "old German songs" of *Des Knaben Wunderhorn*, the tale of the Lorelei is not actually a remnant of the past. On the contrary, it was an invention of Clemens Brentano, who first introduced it in his wild and woolly novel *Godwi* (Baron Karl Godwi; 1801). Eichendorff, in his own novel *Ahnung und Gegenwart* (Premonition and Presence; 1815), reconfigured Brentano's Lore Lay into a demonic figure of seduction. The story is thus not "ein Märchen aus alten Zeiten," but a modern construction that conspicuously refrains from specifying the nebulous past to which it refers. The fiction of the tale's ancient provenance undergoes a significant twist in the final stanza, when the speaker claims uncertainty about how the story ends: "Ich glaube, die Wellen verschlingen/ Am Ende Schiffer und Kahn" (I believe that in the end the waves swallow up the sailor and his boat). This uncertainty intensifies the distance between the time to which the legend supposedly belongs and the present time when the speaker recalls it. While conjuring up the aura that surrounded "old Germany" in the Romantic imagination, Heine's ballad also summons the reader to engage it with a measure of skepticism. Twenty years later, Heine distinguishes in *Deutschland: Ein Wintermärchen* (Germany: A Winter's Tale; 1844) between the historical period, "Das Mittelalter [. . .],/ das wahre, wie es gewesen," and the hybrid fantasy of "gotischem Wahn und modernem Lug,/ das weder Fleisch noch Fisch ist" (Gothic mania and modern falsehood,/ that is neither fish nor fowl). The phrase "wie es gewesen" derives from Leopold von Ranke, the founder of an approach to history that would take into account only reliable sources. In alluding to Ranke, Heine begins to take his leave of Romantic fantasies about the Middle Ages.

While the mania for things medieval largely vanished with the nineteenth century, allusions to medieval motifs do not disappear entirely. Paul Celan, for example, uses the story of Tristan and Isolde in his poem "Matière de Bretagne" (Matter [Stories] of Brittany; 1958) and quotes the medieval mystic Meister Eckhart in "Du sei wie du" (May you be like you; 1969). Yet these allusions and citations appear as fragmentary relics of the past in a world that is itself fundamentally broken and incoherent.

Chapter 3

Devotional poetry

To attend to religious poetry is not merely to observe the ways in which Martin Luther reinvented the German language, though this is an important part of the story. It is also to open up an unusually fecund period in the history of the German lyric, one that resonates throughout much of its subsequent development. Decisive for the emergence of a new type of poetry in Germany at this time was the struggle between the Catholic Church and the Reformation, the latter beginning with Luther and continuing with Calvin. Somewhat later, Pietism, another Protestant movement, was to play a significant role for German literature. In this chapter, we will begin with the Reformation, and follow the poetic impetus initiated by Luther in the early sixteenth century into the period known as *Empfindsamkeit* (the Age of Sensibility in the late eighteenth century), when a focus on specific aspects of dogma yields to a poetic sensibility somewhat closer to our own. Finally, we shall look briefly at some of the ways in which this tradition modulates into mysticism during the Romantic era and into a more general kind of spirituality in our own day. We will conclude by looking at a post-Holocaust poem that poses serious questions about divine benevolence.

The church hymn, or "Kirchenlied," was among the most popular lyric forms in sixteenth- and seventeenth-century Germany. In part, this was the result of the reformers' need to spread their new understanding of the gospel. To facilitate this process, they frequently took up familiar melodies and set new words to them, continuing a practice known as "Kontrafaktur" that had been current during the Middle Ages. This meant that in many instances a worldly song tune became the foundation for a devotional poem. Martin Luther was almost forty years old when he composed his first hymn to commemorate and protest against the murder of two of his fellow reformers in July, 1523. Distributed in the form of a flyer, this song was fittingly titled "Ein neues Lied wir heben an" ("We strike up a new song"). His subsequent hymns emerged from his desire to create a new liturgical practice for his new belief; but they also sparked the composition of hymns by members of the Counter-Reformation, who quickly grasped what a powerful influence communal song could exercise.

Adapting a medieval form, Luther gave his hymns simplicity, familiarity, and a solidity that established them in circles well beyond the Lutheran community. Although his first hymn was a protest song, many of the others were versions of the Biblical psalms of David. Calvin and his followers composed musical versions of the psalms only, not of other texts, because they believed that in this way their liturgy would remain closer to the word of God. Regardless of denomination, these hymns with their strong and easily remembered melodies were a potent way of helping the new beliefs to enter the breath and pulse of the singers. Although later generations may regard these standardized forms as remote from the lyric, or, as Robert Lowell puts it in his poem "Walking Early Sunday Morning" (1967), "stiff quatrains shoveled out four-square," we need to take a step back from our present notions of the poetic to understand the motivation behind the composition of such relatively inflexible verses. Their purpose was precisely to consolidate particular habits of thought, not to make them more subtle or nuanced.

Luther's best-known hymn, "Ein feste Burg ist unser Gott," was first published in 1529. The hymn has been translated into many languages; its most familiar English versions are by Thomas Carlyle, who renders its first line as "A Safe Stronghold our God is Still," and Fredrick H. Hedge, whose more powerful version "A Mighty Fortress is Our God" is perhaps more widely disseminated. Here is the first stanza in Luther's spelling:

> Ein feste burg ist unser Gott,
> Ein gute wehr und waffen.
> Er hilfft uns frey aus aller not,
> die uns jtzt hat betroffen.
> Der alt böse feind
> mit ernst ers jtzt meint,
> gros macht und viel list
> sein grausam rüstung ist,
> auff erd ist nicht seins gleichen.

> (Our God is a solid fortress, a good defense and weapon. He helps us out of all distress that has now afflicted us. The old evil enemy means things seriously now; great power and much cunning is his terrible armor; there is nothing equal to him on earth.)

The hymn bears the marks of its early modern origins not only in its language but also in its form. Based on medieval Meistersang, each stanza consists of an *Aufgesang* made up of two *Stollen* (sections of the poem set to the same melody) followed by an *Abgesang* (a section set to a different melody). In music, this structure is known as the A-A-B form, and, in more complex guises, it has had significant influence on the structure of post-medieval music. Anyone who has sung the hymn will recognize this form in the repetition of a single melody for lines 1–2 and 3–4; the melody changes in lines 5–9. Luther makes effective use of this structure in his development of the antitheses between God and the devil, Christ and man, the worldly and the spiritual. In addition to these basic thematic oppositions, a structure of statement and counterstatement shapes both the syntax and the argument of the hymn.

Inspired by Psalm 46, Luther's hymn is not a simple paraphrase or elaboration of the Biblical text. The relation of hymn to psalm has been the subject of extensive critical debate. Luther eliminates the imagery of roaring waters and shaking mountains, retaining only the slenderest vestige of the "Weltuntergang" motif that plays a prominent role in the Biblical original. Nor does he include the motif of the Lord's city with its refreshing springs. It seems almost perverse that Luther would abandon those elements of the psalm that would appear to lend themselves best to poetic treatment. Even more strikingly, Luther also omits a verse of the Biblical psalm in which God speaks in his own voice: "Seid stille und erkennet, daß ich Gott bin. Ich will Ehre einlegen unter den Heiden; ich will Ehre einlegen auf Erden." (In the King James version, "Be still, and know that I am God: I will be exalted among the heathen, I will be exalted in the earth.")

We can turn these seeming discrepancies into some sort of consistency by highlighting two aspects of Luther's hymn that are significant for both its contemporary meaning and its present-day relevance. The omission of the speaking God allows the hymn to address the congregation more explicitly: once the plural speaker "we" becomes the prime bearer of the message, Luther's notion of communal song as a pedagogical instrument moves into the foreground. His use of the "we" form allows a certain flexibility in our understanding of the poem, which can be understood, on the one hand, as an expression of humankind in general, and, on the other, as the stance of those who supported Luther's call in his own time. It is easy to see why Luther would want to emphasize the communal aspect of his hymn, but more troublesome to explain why he would reject the psalm's fundamental message of potential rejuvenation. One way to understand this second problem is to regard the hymn as a call for solidarity against those who oppose the Reformation. The two phrases "alt böse feind" in stanza 1 and "der Fürst dieser Welt" (the Prince of this world) in stanza 3 are traditional designations for Satan, whose influence, the hymn claims, has now reached a critical juncture. Thus it is perhaps not accidental that Luther's opening lines cast the struggle between the faithful and the forces of evil in terms of a medieval battle in which God performs the dual role of "burg" on the one hand, "wehr und wappen" on the other, and Satan is clothed in the "grausam rüstung" of his own cunning. Upon this metaphorical battlefield, Jesus appears as "der rechte man" (the just man) who fights for us against the devil and who will thus ensure our victory. Luther's insertion of Jesus' name as a synonym for the Lord Zebaoth (the Hebrew term for the lord of hosts) is clearly part of his desire to bring the Old Testament text into accord with the Christian era.

Perhaps the most significant moment in the arc of the poem is the concluding line of stanza 3: "ein wörtlein kan in fellen" (a little word can topple him [i.e. the devil]). With this notion that a word can become a deadly weapon against evil, Luther asserts his claim that the Bible, not the Pope, is the only infallible source of religious authority. The final stanza of the hymn presents the word of God as unassailable because its gifts are those of the spirit. Those who oppose the Lutherans will not be victorious: try as they might, they cannot overturn the true word ("und kein danck dazu haben" means "whether they wish it or not"). Thus, Luther's followers should not despair over loss of worldly goods, honor, or family, for the spiritual kingdom of God ("das reich" in the poem's final line) will belong to them in the end rather than to their opponents.

Another way of approaching the differences between Luther's hymn and the Biblical psalm (which Luther after all also translated into German) is to regard the hymn as a running commentary on, and engagement with, the psalm. While the first and third stanzas pick up a number of elements from the psalm – the notion of God as our refuge and the exhortation to remain fearless in the face of possible destruction – the second and fourth stanzas move away from the Biblical text almost entirely. Seen in this way, the hymn consists of two sets of stanzas in which ideas and phrases from the psalm are first recapitulated and then put into question. The final stanza of Luther's hymn, which allows for the possibility of profound loss of personal possessions and honor, would thus come closer to his contemporaries' feeling of helplessness in a period when it would have been hard to claim, as the psalm text does, that God has banished war for all time.

It goes without saying that this key text in the Lutheran canon has been the subject of many different readings. Even its generic assignment has fluctuated. Over the course of time, the hymn has been regarded as a folk song (in 1806, Arnim and Brentano included it in their anthology *Des Knaben Wunderhorn*), as an expression of the struggle between Lutherans and Catholics, and, by extension, as a special anthem for the Protestant movement. Brecht's "Hitler Choral V" (1933) is a contrafacture of "Ein feste Burg" that mocks Hitler's attempt to acquire pseudo-divine stature. The text of Luther's hymn has been adapted to suit such diverse purposes as the attempted revolution in 1848, the Socialist movement, and protests against the atomic bomb. Its presence in modern hymn-books testifies to its remarkable staying-power.

In addition to "Ein feste Burg," the most influential hymn in Luther's collection has been "Der Psalm De Profundis," his rendering of Psalm 130, a text often assigned to the category of "penitentiary prayers." For Luther, the Biblical text was what he termed a "Pauline psalm," by which he meant that it seemed to anticipate St. Paul's doctrine of salvation by faith. In his commentaries on the psalter, for example, Luther reads Psalm 130 as evidence that the psalmist David believes in divine grace as the only means for forgiveness of sin. Little wonder, then, that Psalm 130 was one of Luther's personal favorites. What struck him most forcefully was the voice of the penitent with which it spoke: "Aus der tieffen/ Ruffe ich Herr zu dir. Herre höre meine stimme/ Las deine Ohren mercken auff die stimme meines flehens" (Luther's translation); (in the King James version, "Out of the depths have I cried unto thee, O Lord. Lord, hear my voice: let thine ears be attentive to the voice of my supplications"). In the hymn version, these verses become:

> Auß tieffer not schrey ich zu dir,
> herr got erhör mein rüffen,
> Dein gnedig oren ker zu mir
> und meiner pit sie öffen.

> (From deep distress I cry to you, Lord God, hear my cry; turn your gracious ears toward me and open them to my plea ["pit" = "Bitte"].)

With this opening, the psalm also seemed to accord with Luther's view that no one could fully come to God without having first descended to the depths of despair. Whether or not Luther inserts the word "not" for metrical reasons, it has the effect of transforming the Biblical phrase "the depths," which generally refers to the waters of the underworld and primordial chaos, into a personal situation. We should not go too far in giving this change a psychological reading, however, since the subsequent argument of the hymn makes clear that the "tieffer not" of the speaker is only the first part of a larger argument about human sinfulness, which is described as present "auch in dem besten leben" (even in the best of lives). We are all sinners, and we must simply wait penitently for divine forgiveness, however long it may take to arrive. Here, too, Luther shapes the psalm to correspond with his conviction that good works could not help the human sinner obtain God's grace.

Psalm 130 opens in the first person but ends with an assertion of community: "Jsrael, hoffe auf den Herrn! denn bey dem Herrn ist die Gnade und viel Erlösung bey jm. Und er wird Jsrael erlösen aus allen seinen Sünden" (Luther's translation); "Let Israel hope in the Lord: for with the Lord there is mercy, and with him is plenteous redemption. And he shall redeem Israel from all his iniquities" (King James translation). In part for this reason, present-day Biblical scholars hesitate between regarding Psalm 130 as an individual lament or as a theological reflection. When he transformed the psalm into a hymn, Luther intensified this shift from the individual to the communal by introducing the first-person plural pronoun ("uns") in the first line of the final stanza, thus including the worshippers singing in the hymn's overall line of thought: "Ob bey uns ist der sünden vil,/ bey Got ist vil mer gnaden" (Though there is much sin among us, there is even more grace with God). In this way, it is as if the ancient community of Israel finds its continuation in the congregation of Luther's day.

The Hebrew verb "to cry" in the first verse of Psalm 130 can be understood as either a completed action or one that continues in the present. Luther's decision to use the present tense in his hymn gives the text a special intensity. The hymn's more extended form adds to this effect, despite the somewhat preachy tone of the second and third stanzas, in which Luther elaborates his doctrine of salvation by God alone. One may speculate, in fact, that it is the forceful opening of the hymn that has ensured its long-lasting appeal even beyond the boundaries of the Lutheran church.

Luther's successor in the German hymn-writing tradition, Paul Gerhardt, achieved an even more widespread ecumenical reception, however. Although Gerhardt was a Lutheran with little tolerance for other Protestant denominations (he was a vehement opponent of Calvinism), his tendency to stay close to the Biblical texts that inspired his hymns enabled their acceptance by the Pietists in the eighteenth century and their inclusion in today's *Evangelisches Kirchengesangbuch* (Hymnal of the Protestant Church in Germany). To some extent, however, this is also the result of selection and pruning that has eliminated some of Gerhardt's more pronounced anti-Calvinist sentiments. His poetic treatment of Psalm 146, "Du meine Seele singe" (1653), is one of his best-known hymns. Unlike Luther's hymns, where fixed meter often overrides natural speech rhythms, Gerhardt's devotional poetry abides by the metrical reform proposed by Martin Opitz in his *Buch von der deutschen Poeterey* (1624). Opitz argued that the German language tended to rely on an alternation of stressed and unstressed syllables: for this reason, dactylic and the anapestic meters were to be avoided in favor of iambic or trochaic ones. Although Gerhardt did not use the six-stress German alexandrine that Opitz promulgated, he did adhere to the idea of alternating strong and weak stresses. Shaped by his preference for simple language, an emphasis on lived experience, and a rich admiration for nature as the work of the Creator, Gerhardt's poetry has remained accessible to a wide range of readers over the centuries since it was first published.

Gerhardt's most frequently anthologized poems are "Abend-Lied" (Evensong; 1648), "Sommer-Gesang" (Summer Song; 1653), and "An das Angesicht des Herrn Jesu" (On the Visage of the Lord Jesus; 1653/56. His "Abend-Lied" is a fine example of his characteristic method. Following the aesthetic theory of his contemporary, August Buchner, Gerhardt structures the poem so that each stanza encompasses a single thought. The first three stanzas begin with natural description – the peaceful woods and fields, the absence of the sun, the appearance of stars in the night sky – and move to a religious idea that emerges from the experience of these natural phenomena. In essence, what Gerhardt gives us here is a way of reading the "book of nature" as a sign of God's presence and promise. The beauties of nature are not important in and of themselves, but as signs for something beyond. By selecting evening as the setting of his poem, Gerhardt emphasizes the importance of spiritual understanding, which allows us to see beyond the sensory apparatus of the human eye and ear. Quiet has descended on the world, and now the speaker of the poem can engage in contemplation and reflection (the slashes in this poem are a contemporary way of indicating commas):

> Nun ruhen alle Wälder/
> Vieh/ Menschen/ Städt und Felder/
>   Es schläfft die gantze Welt:
> Ihr aber meine Sinnen/
> Auf/auf ihr solt beginnen
>   Was eurem Schöpffer wol gefält.

> Wo bist du Sonne blieben?
>   Die Nacht hat dich vertrieben/
> Die Nacht des Tages Feind:
> Fahr hin/ ein andre Sonne
> Mein Jesus/ meine Wonne/
>   Gar hell in meinem Hertzen scheint.

(Now all the woods are at rest; cattle, people, cities and fields, the whole world is asleep; but you, my senses, up, up, you should begin to do what is pleasing to your Creator.// Where have you gone, sun? The night has driven you away, the night, enemy of day: go on your way, another sun, my Jesus, my delight is shining very brightly in my heart.)

Addressing his "Sinne" in line 4 of these opening stanzas, the speaker instructs them to set to work interpreting the sights before his outer eye in terms of divine creation. The departure of the sun is understood in stanza two as a sign of Jesus' death, which causes a quite different light to shine in the heart of the observer. Similarly, in the third stanza, the sparkling stars in the sky remind the speaker of his own ultimate destination, the Christian heaven where he will stand in splendor after death (here again, the slashes are the equivalent of commas):

> Der Tag ist nun vergangen:
> Die güldnen Sternlein prangen
>   Am blauen Himmels-Saal:
> So/ so werd ich auch stehen/
> Wann mich wird heissen gehen
>   Mein Gott aus diesem Jammerthal.

(Day is now over: the little golden stars shine splendidly against the blue hall of heaven; so, just so I will also stand when my God tells me to leave this vale of sorrow.)

Although nature is seen here as a manifestation of the divine, it is not understood in a pantheistic, but rather in an allegorical, manner. Each stanza, composed of two tercets with an end-rhyme linking the first with the second, reflects this way of seeing that moves from the outer world of phenomena to the inner world of the spiritual.

As the poem shifts from nature to the human body in stanzas 4 to 7, it continues this simple parallelism. Methodically, attention to the body as a whole gives way to specific parts of the body: head, feet, hands, and limbs, followed by the eyes, traditionally understood as the windows on the soul. The stages by which we prepare for sleep have their equivalents in the speaker's reflection on the afterlife. The final stanzas (8 and 9) depart from this scheme, however, as they address first Jesus and then the speaker's loved ones. The speaker's care for his family as well as for himself – indeed his decision to conclude the poem with a prayer for those close to him – is characteristic of the period in which Gerhardt writes. Instead of the congregation that gives Luther's "Ein feste Burg" its larger meaning, here it is family with whom the speaker wishes to share his experience of God's promise and for whom he calls on God's blessing.

Matthias Claudius's similarly titled "Abendlied" of 1779, inspired by Gerhart's poem, is also written in stanzas consisting of two tercets linked by a common rhyme. Claudius's poem moves us even further into the bourgeois family world. His evensong was written against the backdrop of a far-reaching effort to modernize older hymns and bring them into line with Enlightenment thought. To be sure, there has been something of a debate about the degree to which Claudius can be seen as a representative of the Enlightenment or a critic of it. Perhaps the best way to resolve this puzzle is to recognize the deliberately naïve posture Claudius adopts in all his writings, his essays and reviews as well as his poems. For his reviews in the newspaper *Der Wandsbecker Bote*, Claudius invents a simpleton named Asmus, whose foolishness the more sophisticated reader was supposed to recognize. This enabled Claudius to speak his mind by indirection, letting his readers believe that they had come to the desired opinion by themselves. The speaker of "Abendlied" is not the ludicrous Asmus, however; rather, it is someone who uses simple language while also being familiar with modern forms of knowledge. This speaker takes an ambivalent approach to recent ideas and discoveries: on the one hand, he knows and accepts the fact that we can only see one side of the moon (stanza 3), but on the other, he doesn't approve of many modern concepts and new-fangled scientific developments (stanza 4). Johann Gottfried Herder's decision to include the poem in his collection of folk songs, *Volkslieder* (Folk Songs; 1778–1779), seems to ignore this complexity, although it also needs to be said that he eliminated the last two stanzas of the poem, possibly in order to avoid touching upon the topic of death. In explaining his decision to include the poem in an anthology of folksongs, Herder is obviously well aware of the musical setting of "Abendlied." Thus he observes that "Das Gesangbuch ist die Bibel des Volks, sein Trost und seine beste Erholung" (The song book is the Bible of the people, their consolation and their best recuperation). In Herder's view, it mattered less that the poem had an individual author than that it provided the kind of comfort people needed. With their measured rhythms, the first two stanzas brilliantly achieve this aim:

> Der Mond ist aufgegangen,
> Die goldnen Sternlein prangen
>   Am Himmel hell und klar;
> Der Wald steht schwarz und schweiget,
> Und aus den Wiesen steiget
>   Der weiße Nebel wunderbar.

> Wie ist die Welt so stille,
> Und in der Dämmrung Hülle
>   So traulich und so hold!
> Als eine stille Kammer,
> Wo ihr des Tages Jammer
>   Verschlafen und vergessen sollt.

(The moon has risen, the little gold stars shine splendidly, bright and clear in the sky; the woods stand dark and silent, and from the meadows white fog rises wondrously. // How quiet the world is, and in the veil of dusk, so familiar and lovely! Like a quiet chamber where you can sleep away and forget the troubles of the day.)

Perhaps the most important point to make about these stanzas is that they do not present an untouched world of beauty and innocence. To see the poem this way would be to privilege the concept of nature at rest in the first stanzas and to overlook the reference to "des Tages Jammer" in line 11. Indeed, even the second tercet of stanza 1 subtly suggests that there may be something troubling in this seemingly peaceful scene. Beneath the moon and the glittering stars, the forest "steht schwarz und schweiget" as if to indicate some dark portent that remains unarticulated. The prominent alliteration draws our attention to the unsettling nature of this silence. We might also dwell a little – as the verse itself does – on the adverb "wunderbar" at the end of this stanza, with its touching placement of a secondary stress on the final syllable ("wúnderbàr"). What does "wunderbar" actually mean here? The word has a large range that includes not simply the admirable, but also the extraordinary and the mysterious. Especially in connection with natural phenomena, "wunderbar" can have an almost religious aura. In Claudius's "Abendlied," the word certainly indicates the almost mysterious beauty of the fog rising from the meadows; but it may not be entirely wrong to see the white fog as a ghostly apparition, a sort of emanation that emerges from nature as nighttime begins to take hold. The secondary stress at the end of the stanza suggests an element of lightness, of lift-off, as it were, in the direction of a world beyond that of the earthly. In this context, the description of the world at dusk as "so traulich und so hold" is not a bourgeois sentiment, but an almost spiritual expression. Certainly, the "stille Kammer" with which it is compared retains some of the flavor of German pietism: nature here becomes a comforting space appropriate to reflection and prayer.

Once we see these hints of a – still somewhat vague – religious feeling that infuses the natural scene, the shift to the more hortatory third stanza is more readily intelligible. With its opening line, "Seht ihr den Mond dort stehen?" (Do you see the moon up there?), this stanza suddenly reveals how different this situation is from that of later German lyric poetry, notably since Goethe. Here, a single observing subject immersed in the wondrous spectacle of nature. Instead, external reality becomes a prop for moral reflection. In this sense, Claudius continues the allegorical readings of nature that we have seen in earlier devotional poetry from Luther to Gerhardt. Unlike Gerhardt, however, Claudius is not reading here from the "book of nature," but is using science as a source for his allegory. If we know and accept the fact that we can never see the other side of the moon, why do we reject the notion that there are other things in nature that are invisible to us? These things, of course, are spiritual, as stanza 5 makes clear: it is divine salvation that we need to "see," even though it is not openly present in the world around us. In our fascination with abstract philosophy ("Luftgespinste") and modern science ("viele Künste"), we regard ourselves as making progress, but in fact we are moving away from the true goal, which is of course belief in God. Everything earthly is transient, as stanza 5 makes clear: we should place our trust not in such vanities, but in the hope of eternal salvation. The Christian ideal explains why we should become as children, approaching nature with simplicity and untroubled piety. The term "einfältig" (simple) in stanza 5 refers to a genuine innocence born of Christian faith. It is important to understand that the poem does not advocate abandoning the earthly, but instead urges that we approach the world in a way that recognizes its inextricable connection with the spiritual. This part of the poem reaches back to the opening stanza, where the apparent divide between heaven and earth (each accorded its own tercet) is incipiently overcome by the rising fog.

Modern readers often find the poem's final stanzas troubling. In particular, the seventh stanza has been a stumbling block for many. Why does the poem end with a reference to a sick neighbor who has not been mentioned anywhere in the earlier parts of the poem? To the modern mind, it seems like an afterthought. Yet within the culture of Claudius's day, the neighbor is at once an individual and a type. In the course of the poem, we have seen what appeared at first to be a single speaker contemplating nature alone, then addressing a group of others who are also observing the scene; as the address becomes plural, however, it expands to encompass human beings altogether. The "wir" who laugh at what cannot be seen in stanza 3 become "wir stolze Menschenkinder" (we proud human beings) in stanza 4. (By the way, the word "eitel" in the phrase that follows – "eitel arme Sünder" – is an old way of saying "nothing but"). As the poem continues, this expansive "wir" contracts somewhat. In stanzas 5 and 6, it is the "wir" of communal prayer, but by the final stanza, the group is addressed more familiarly in terms of "brothers." With the concluding prayer on behalf of the sick neighbor, the poem recalls the Christian obligation to love one's neighbor while also suggesting that all of us may know a specific individual who has need of our prayers. In this sense, Claudius returns to life on earth, fragile and frightening as it necessarily is, but now at the end of the poetic meditation, imbued with Christian ideals. The cold evening breeze serves as a reminder, especially given its divergent stress pattern: "kált ist der Ábendhaùch" (cold is the breath of evening). Removing the last stanza, or even the last two stanzas, as Herder did, turns the poem into something it is not. Above all, it ignores the ingenious way in which Claudius adapts the binary structures of the traditional church hymn, moving throughout between the heavenly and the earthly, the general and the individual. In terms of literary history, this poem opens up the hymn tradition without yet quite embarking on the personal lyric that Goethe had already initiated in the mid-1770s. The musical setting composed by Johann Abraham Peter Schulz has become a well-known secular song.

The texts we have examined thus far constitute only a minuscule sampling of the German hymn tradition as it developed in the wake of the Reformation. There is much else that might be discussed. We might consider later poets who, like Luther, engage with Biblical texts. The cry "from the depths," for example, is a motif that recurs in a number of different contexts. Still, not all poems that employ this phrase are in fact inspired by either Luther's hymn or the Biblical psalm on which the hymn is modeled. Clemens Brentano's "Frühlingsschrei eines Knechtes aus der Tiefe" (A Laborer's Spring Cry from the Depths; 1816; the "Knecht" is a miner trapped in a flooded shaft), an important poem from the Romantic movement, uses the phrase "aus der Tiefe," but is in fact a lengthy gloss on Psalm 96, not Psalm 130. Still, it does use Luther's technique of elaborating on a psalm text, in this case rendering the anguish expressed by the speaker in seventeen four-line stanzas. Two Expressionist poems that use the Latin tag may not be directly related to Psalm 130 at all: Johannes R. Becher claimed that he wrote his "De Profundis Domine" (1913) without any knowledge of the psalm; and Trakl's "De Profundis" (1912) adapts the notion of "the depths" to the rape and murder of a young woman. Rainer Maria Rilke, in the opening lines of the *Duineser Elegien* (Duino Elegies; begun 1912 and completed in 1922), alludes to the cry from the depths when he writes: "Wer, wenn ich schriee, hörte mich denn,/ Aus der Engel Ordnungen" (Who, if I cried out, would hear me/ among the orders of angels). A study of any of these connections would be a fruitful way to link Luther's writing with works of later periods.

Another way to think about how the tradition is continued would be to explore poetry that combines a more conventional approach to religion with a mystic tradition that reaches back to the medieval writer Meister Eckart. Luther himself was, in fact, not untouched by mysticism, although this is not evident in his hymns. Many of his followers, furthermore, repudiated this streak in his writings. In tracing this strand, we might begin with the religious poetry of the Baroque period, notably the strophic hymns of Angelus Silesius (Johannes Scheffler), *Heilige Seelen-Lust, oder geistliche Lieder der in ihren Jesum verliebten Psyche* (The Soul's Sacred Delight or Spiritual Songs of the Soul in Love with Jesus; 1657), which owes much to the work of the mystic Jacob Böhme (1575–1624). Silesius spent most of his life as a Lutheran, but converted to Catholicism in his last years because he was unhappy with other Lutherans' rejection of mystical thought. The brevity of his two-line sets of *Alexandriner* contributes to their allusiveness and intensity; the pointed rhymes pull opposites together or sharpen the paradoxes at the heart of the epigrams; and the central motifs – the rose, for example – reveal the poems' indebtedness to the Neoplatonic tradition. These are poems for contemplation and meditation, poems that ask the reader to use them as starting-points for further thought.

The mystic tradition takes a different form in the strikingly innovative *Hymnen an die Nacht* (Hymns to Night; 1797–1800) of the Romantic poet Novalis (Friedrich von Hardenberg). Inspired by the early death of Novalis's fiancée Sophie in 1797 and informed by the thought of Jacob Böhme, the classical myth of the Golden Age, and the philosophy of Kant and Fichte, these six hymns were first composed in verse, but were eventually published as an extended prose poem with several verse sections that mark the more ecstatic moments in the sequence. Identifying the night as the time when ordinary logic gives way to higher visions, the speaker of the poems aims for an *unio mystica*, not only with the dead beloved, but also with Christ. The final poem, composed entirely in verse, develops the notion that union with the transcendent is possible only through an inward turn that also, by virtue of the paradoxical thought structures characteristic of mysticism, encompasses the external world. A final descent into the depths of the earth enables a vision of infinity and its mysteries. *Hymnen an die Nacht* does not belong so much to the genre of church hymns intended for communal worship as to a broader category of hymns that also include those of classical antiquity. Indeed, Novalis himself had not wanted to call these poems "hymns" at all, but to title them simply "An die Nacht." He did, however, also write some poems in the hymn tradition that he explicitly called "Geistliche Lieder" (spiritual songs). Novalis's sister reported that her father had been singing one of them shortly after his son's death when he happened to ask who wrote it; he was deeply moved when he heard that the writer was his own son. "Was wär' ich ohne dich gewesen" (what would I have been without you) appears in a number of anthologies.

I should like to conclude this glance at the afterlife of the church hymn tradition with a brief discussion of Paul Celan's poem "Tenebrae" (1959). Inspired by a performance of François Couperin's "Leçons des Ténèbres" (Lessons of the Shadows; 1714), the poem creates at one and the same time an idiosyncratic view of the relation between man and God and a blend of Jewish and Christian motifs. Unlike Luther's hymns, which were glosses on the psalms of David, Couperin's composition uses text from the Lamentations of Jeremiah. The Lamentations are customarily read in the

Catholic liturgy for Holy Week, when candles are extinguished one by one (hence the reference to darkness in the title of Couperin's piece). The Biblical text begins with Jeremiah's lament over the destruction of Jerusalem by the Babylonians:

> [1] How doth the city sit solitary, that was full of people how is she become as a widow she that was great among the nations, and princess among the provinces, how is she become tributary. [2] She weepeth sore in the night, and her tears are on her cheeks: among all her lovers she hath none to comfort her: all her friends have dealt treacherously with her, they are become her enemies.
>
> (King James Bible, *Lamentations* 1: 1–2)

We do not know if Couperin wrote more than one section of his planned composition: only the setting of the first chapter is extant. Couperin designed it to be performed on Ash Wednesday. The opening lines of Celan's poem "Nah sind wir, Herr,/ nahe und greifbar" (we are near, Lord, near and palpable) may be linked to Rilke's *Stundenbuch* (1905), which – in the aftermath of Nietzsche's proclamation of the "death of God" – posits a dependence not of man on the divine, but of the divine on mankind; see, for example, the poem "Du Nachbar Gott" (You, Neighbor God) in which the speaker reassures God with the words, "Ich bin ganz nah" (I am quite near). The concept of the *deus absconditus* (the God who has hidden himself from human beings) undergoes a reversal in which God is consoled for a loss of human supporters. In Celan's poem, God is invited to pray to us: "Bete, Herr,/ bete zu uns/ wir sind nah" (Pray, Lord, pray to us, we are near).

Here is the poem in its entirety:

> Nah sind wir, Herr,
> nahe und greifbar.
> Gegriffen schon, Herr,
> ineinander verkrallt, als wär
> der Leib eines jeden von uns
> dein Leib, Herr.
>
> Bete, Herr,
> bete zu uns,
> wir sind nah.
>
> Windschief gingen wir hin,
> gingen wir hin, uns zu bücken
> nach Mulde und Maar.

Zur Tränke gingen wir, Herr.

Es war Blut, es war,
was du vergossen, Herr.

Es glänzte.

Es warf uns dein Bild in die Augen, Herr.
Augen und Mund stehn so offen und leer, Herr.

Wir haben getrunken, Herr.
Das Blut und das Bild, das im Bild war, Herr.

Bete, Herr.
Wir sind nah.

(We are near, Lord. Near and graspable.// Clasped already, Lord, clawed
into one another, as if the body of each one of us were your body, Lord.//
Pray, Lord, pray to us, we are near.// We went leaning into the wind, we
went to bow down to hollows and craters.// We went to drink, Lord.// It
was blood, it was what you had spilled, Lord.// It shone.// It reflected
your image to our eyes, Lord. Eyes and mouth are so open and empty,
Lord.// We have drunk, Lord. The blood and the image that was in the
blood, Lord.// Pray, Lord. We are near.)

Celan's "Tenebrae" interweaves invocations with more descriptive sketches
and rudimentary hints of narrative. Human bodies are "ineinander verkrallt,"
recalling the gas chambers of Nazi concentration camps, where victims were
found desperately clasping one another in their final throes. Leaning against
the wind, victims make their way toward hollow ground and lakes that nestle
in the craters of ancient volcanoes ("Maare") – a landscape remote from
the comforting pastures of the good shepherd in Psalm 23. Here, the hollow
ground suggests a mass grave site, and the volcanic lakes recall the past violence
of nature and presage the human violence that is about to occur. Like cattle
innocently going to drink at a water-hole, the victims have no suspicion of what
is about to happen to them; but we know that they are about to be massacred.
As the poem explains, the blood spilled in their slaughter is also that of the Lord:
the sacrament of the bread and wine celebrated in Christian liturgy has become
an act of murder, and Christ's eyes and mouth have been emptied of meaning.
In the final exhortation to the Lord to pray because "wir sind nah," we can
hear an accusation of the God who permitted the violence of the Holocaust to
happen. This is not the God of Easter, who promises us resurrection through
the passion of Christ and its representation in the transubstantiation of bread

and wine: it is a dark God, one no longer in a position to forgive our sins, but who should himself pray to us for forgiveness.

Celan's "Tenebrae" has moved a long way from a tradition that, in Luther's time, saw despair as a prerequisite for obtaining the divine grace that would surely come to those with faith. It has also travelled far from Nietzsche's declaration of the "death of God." The "we" of its final line is neither a congregation of believers nor a group of questioners, but those who know about the Holocaust and are appalled that it was possible.

Chapter 4

The rhetoric of passion

Are powerful feelings compatible with strict poetic rules? The question suggests that they are not, and yet some writers have felt that passion requires the constraints of regulated form. Indeed, one could even argue that the conflict between overwhelming emotion and regulated expression can intensify the reader's empathy. One crucible for this issue in German literature was the Thirty Years' War (1618–1648), which brought devastation on a previously unimaginable scale. For Andreas Gryphius, one of the most important poets of the time, the defining experience was the shocking destruction of Freystadt (in Bavaria) by fire that he witnessed in 1632. In a poem several pages in length, "Über den Untergang der Stadt Freystadt" (1637; On the Destruction of the Town of Freystadt), Gryphius paradoxically sees the obliteration of the city as disabling the poetic faculty itself. Here are the relevant lines in the original spelling and punctuation (in Baroque poetry, slashes are the equivalent of commas; orthography is often inconsistent, but the versions given below have been slightly normalized):

> Wir schauen derer Noth/ die in den Flammen braten/
> Und schauen keinen Rath. Ihr Musen! ach umsunst!/
> Auch euer Schatz vergeht.

> (We watch the agony of those burning in the flames, and find no solution. You muses! oh, in vain! Your treasure dies as well.)

The conflict between agonizing events and their expression in verse is one that was to mark a great deal of his poetry as well as that of his contemporaries.

In his most famous sonnet, "Thränen des Vaterlandes: Anno 1636" (Tears of the Fatherland in the Year 1636; published 1643), Gryphius expresses outrage over the devastation in more general but more powerful terms. His choice of the sonnet form allows him to counterbalance hyperbolic phrasing with measured rhythms and contrastive structures. The force of the poem sweeps us along from its exclamatory opening line to an apocalyptic picture of desecration:

Wir sind doch nunmehr gantz / ja mehr denn gantz verheeret!
  Der frechen Völcker Schaar / die rasende Posaun
  Das vom Blutt fette Schwerdt / die donnernde Carthaun /
Hat aller Schweiß / und Fleiß / und Vorrath auffgezehret.
Die Türme stehn in Glutt / die Kirch ist umgekehret.
  Das Rathaus ligt im Grauß / die Starcken sind zerhaun /
  Die Jungfern sind geschänd't / und wo wir hin nur schaun
Ist Feuer / Pest / und Tod / der Hertz und Geist durchfähret.
  Hir durch die Schanz und Stadt / rinnt allzeit frisches Blutt.
  Dreymal sind schon sechs Jahr / als unser Ströme Flutt /
Von Leichen fast verstopfft / sich langsam fort gedrungen
  Doch schweig ich noch von dem / was ärger als der Tod /
  Was grimmer denn die Pest / und Glutt und Hungersnoth
Das auch der Seelen Schatz / so vilen abgezwungen.

(We are now totally – indeed more than totally – destroyed! The band of bold nations, the blaring trumpet, the sword greasy with blood, the thundering cannon, have consumed all sweat, diligence, and provisions. The towers are on fire, the church has been toppled, the town hall lies in ruins, the strong are maimed, virgins have been raped, and wherever we turn our gaze nothing but fire, disease, and death pierces hearts and minds. Here through the fortifications and the city fresh blood runs repeatedly. Three times six years ago the waters of our rivers, almost stopped up with corpses, slowly made their way. Yet still I do not speak of what is worse than death, more horrible than the plague and fire and famine: that the treasure of the soul has been taken from so many).

Parallel constructions work rhetorically to compound the terrifying effects of the piled up images of destruction. Confronted with a scene in which fortress and city are constantly running with blood, the reader does not even pause to ask what it might mean to be "more than totally destroyed." Focusing on the disaster, we tend not to notice the orderliness of the verses. Only at the end of the octave, when the proliferation of disasters yields to more abstract thought, do we have time to reflect that the destruction is not restricted to material objects and buildings like towers, church, and town hall.

Although it would be simplistic to regard the experience of war as the sole motivation for the Baroque poets' insistence on the fragility and transitory nature of life, it did heighten their belief that one could not count on anything one might possess in earthly existence: riches, happiness, and health were all subject to the vagaries of fortune. When poets directly addressed war and politics, they often turned to religion for confirmation that life in this world is transient. Here, the toppled church and the apocalyptic imagery of fire, pestilence, and death prepare for the explicit turn to religious issues in the final tercet. Beginning with the rhetorical device of praeterition (claiming not to speak about something that one does in fact mention; here, "doch schweig ich noch"), it goes on to explain that damage to human souls is worse than any other danger the country faces.

The force of the poem resides not in its argument alone. Rhetorical strategies, such the use of lists and parallel constructions, give the sonnet its persuasive power. Most striking is the piling up of strong, often one-syllable, nouns. The description of what the enemy cannons have destroyed: "Schweiß / und Fleiß / und Vorrath" and the catalogue of disaster all around: "Feuer / Pest / und Tod / der Hertz und Geist durchfähret" are characteristic examples of an emphatic use of monosyllabic nouns. In his use of this technique, Gryphius might be compared with John Donne, whose *Holy Sonnets* (1633) employ similar strategies: the first quatrain of one of Donne's best-known sonnets runs:

> Batter my heart, three person'd God; for you
> As yet but knocke, breathe, shine, and seeke to mend;
> That I may rise, and stand, o'erthrow mee, and bend
> Your force, to breake, blow, burn and make me new.

There is an important difference, to be sure: whereas Donne's struggle has to do with his sense that religious belief was at odds with personal experience, Gryphius's has to do with the contrast between outer and inner devastation. Unlike Donne, Gryphius did not have inner conflicts about religion, although as a Protestant, he was forced to flee several times from places where Catholicism was more entrenched.

Another sonnet on the Thirty Years' War, Georg Rudolf Weckherlin's "An das Teutschland" (To Germany; 1641), refrains from evoking suffering and destruction in favor of a call to political action. Writing from England, where he was working as a scribe in the service of the Protestant cause, Weckherlin urges the Germans to abandon the internal divisiveness that has weakened their moral fiber. Here is the first quatrain of his poem:

> Zerbrich das schwere Joch / darunter du gebunden /
> O Teutschland / wach doch auff / faß wider einen muht /
> Gebrauch dein altes hertz/ und widersteh der wuht /
> Die dich / und die freyheit durch dich selbs überwunden.

> (Break the heavy yoke beneath which you are bound, O Germany, wake up, summon your courage again, use your old heart and resist the fury that has overcome you and freedom by your own means.)

In the tercets, his sonnet exhorts its readers to follow those princes who cleave to the right faith, arguing that this will strengthen the hand of God and vanquish their enemies. Its interest for today's readers, however, is more historical than aesthetic: it is an important document, but in terms of poetic power, it simply cannot vie with Gryphius's "Thränen des Vaterlandes." Its significance lies in the posture he takes toward the war. Knowing it only second hand, he speaks in a distanced and abstract way about tyranny and freedom.

A very different argument in opposition to the Thirty Years' War is evoked by Georg Philipp Harsdörffer. In his four-stanza poem "Friedenshoffnung bey Nochschwebender Handlung zu Münster und Oßnabruck: Der Kriegsmann wil ein Schäfer werden" (Hope for Peace during the Still Unresolved Negotiations in Münster and Osnabrück: The Soldier Wishes to Become a Shepherd; 1647), Harsdörffer evokes the Arcadian tradition, with its emphasis on an idealized image of pastoral life, to engender hope after long years of battle and frustrating attempts to secure peace. The treaty of Westphalia, which put an end to the exhausting conflict, was not signed until 1648, one year after Harsdörffer first published this poem. Instead of instruments of war, the speaker – a soldier who is weary of battle – urges that fields and woods, trees and gardens become the new means of ensuring security. In what appears to be an allusion to Gryphius's "Thränen des Vaterlandes," he proposes that wine and poetry take the place of tears and suffering. Conjuring up a vision of return to the Golden Age, Harsdörffer's poem is not a sonnet, but a kind of song. That is not to say that the poem is not strictly organized in terms of meter, rhyme scheme, and stanza structure. Yet dactyls and anapests, short-lined sections in each stanza, and an often humorous use of rhyme create lyric effects that conjure up the delights of the "guldenen Frieden" (golden peace) of which the poem speaks. The pastoral scenes permit the inclusion of such non-Christian elements as an allusion to the altar of Ceres, the naiads of the rivers, and the muses. The gauzy texture and melodic cadences of this poem testify to Harsdörffer's virtuoso handling of the German language. It stands as a reminder that not all poetic production during the Thirty Years' War was preoccupied with pain and suffering.

Indeed, concerns about war did not obscure other poetic themes and traditions. Love poetry, for example, took up topics from classical antiquity and from the Italian Renaissance. The Latin poet Catullus became a point of reference for poetic celebration of erotic exuberance, and Petrarch and his imitators provided an entire vocabulary of metaphors for describing the beloved and the experience of love. Figures from classical mythology – muses, nymphs, and dryads – make appearances in many of the more light-hearted love lyrics (it also should be noted that some poems in this category were written in Latin).

Even when they treat what appear to be personal topics, Baroque poems are not personal in the sense in which we understand the term today. These writers are not allowing their readers to "overhear" their intimate concerns, but using first-person forms to provide models for others to emulate. Paul Fleming's "An Sich" (To Himself; published posthumously in 1641) may help us understand this posture:

> Sey dennoch unverzagt. Gieb dennoch unverlohren.
> Weich keinem Glücke nicht. Steh' höher als der Neid.
> Vergnüge dich an dir/ und acht es für kein Leid/
> hat sich gleich wider dich Glück'/ Ort/ und Zeit verschworen.
> Was dich betrübt und labt/ halt alles für erkohren,
> Nimm dein Verhängnüß an. Laß' alles unbereut.
> Thu/ was gethan muß seyn/ und eh man dirs gebeut.
> Was du noch hoffen kanst/ das wird noch stets gebohren.
> Was klagt/ was lobt man doch? Sein Unglück und sein Glücke
> ist ihm ein ieder selbst. Schau alle Sachen an.
> Diß alles ist in dir/ laß deinen eiteln Wahn/
> und eh du förder gehst/ so geh' in dich zu rücke.
> Wer sein selbst Meister ist/ und sich beherrschen kan/
> dem ist die weite Welt und alles unterthan.

(In spite of all, do not be discouraged. In spite of all, do not give up. Do not yield to any stroke of happenstance. Put yourself above envy. Take pleasure in yourself and do not regard it as suffering if fortune, place, and time seem to have conspired against you all at once. Consider as chosen everything that depresses you and consoles you; accept your fate. Do not regret anything. Do what must be done and before anyone asks you to do it. What you can still hope for may still come to pass. Why do people lament or praise? Misfortune and fortune are within each person. Look at everything. All this is in you. Let go of your vain delusions and before you proceed further, turn within yourself. He who is a master and can control himself is above the whole wide world and all things.)

Fleming puts the sonnet form to brilliant use here. Following Martin Opitz's metrical reform, which insisted on regular alternation between stressed and unstressed syllables, Fleming uses the six-beat German Alexandrine (*Alexandriner*) to support the sense of determination expressed in the four short imperative sentences. In the opening lines, the caesura, or brief pause following the third stressed syllable, is especially clear. Here is the first line with its stresses indicated:

> Sey dénnoch únverzágt. ‖ Gieb dénnoch únverlóhren.

This line has a clear central caesura or pause (indicated in the scansion by the double bar line); but caesuras do not have to be so strongly marked: even when not divided into two separate sentences, as in this case, every line of this sonnet has a caesura at its mid-point. Sometimes a period or comma indicates the caesura, as in lines 1 and 3. At other times syntactical structures suggest a bi-partite division, as in line 4, where the first half of the line ("hat sich gleich wider dich") is set off against a conspiracy of hostile forces composed of "Glück'/ Ort/ und Zeit". Line 14, although unmarked by punctuation, divides after "Welt" and before "und."

The *Alexandriner* permitted masculine (one-syllable) or feminine (two-syllable) rhymes. Fleming's "An Sich" uses an embracing rhyme scheme in the quatrains, with lines 1 and 4 rhyming on two syllables ("unverlohren" and "verschworen"), while lines 2 and 3 rhyme on a monosyllable ("Neid" and "Leid"). Although German could not always compete with the Romance languages, which had strict rules about the total number of different rhymes that could occur in a single sonnet, Fleming does achieve considerable unity here by employing the same rhyme in lines 1, 4, 5 and 8. Even the apparent shift from rhymes in "-eid" in the first quatrain to rhymes in "-eut" in the second quatrain would have been considered at the time as a continuation of the same rhyme. In at least two other poems by Fleming, "Wie er wolle geküsset seyn" (How he wishes to be kissed; 1646) and "Mag denn kein Rath und Trost mir lindern meine Pein" (Even if no advice and comfort assuage my pain), words with the diphthong *ei* are used as rhymes for words with the diphthong *eu*. (In fact, many poets beyond the Baroque period used these as full rhymes.) In the sestet of "An Sich," Fleming creates a subtle effect by employing, in addition to the rhymes in *-ücke*, one set of rhymes in *-an* (with a short *a*) and another set in *-ahn* (with a long *a*). Although we shall look at other German poems that do rival the fluidity achieved in the Romance sonnet, or "resounding poem," too much fluidity in this particular text might undermine the desire of Fleming's speaker to remain firm and steadfast.

Philosophically, "An Sich" adopts a neo-Stoic posture. Like other poems of the period, it builds on ideas developed by the Flemish humanist Justus Lipsius in the late 16th century. Reviving and reconfiguring ideas drawn from the Roman Stoic philosopher Seneca, Lipsisus was able to make a link between ancient Roman Stoicism and Christian belief in the necessity of enduring suffering. "An Sich" presents a compelling argument for the neo-Stoic position. It advises against giving way to passions, either negative or positive. To be sure, the prime emphasis is on negative passions such as envy, suffering, regret, discouragement, and depression, the poem argues, should not be overvalued. Even positive emotions like hope or reassurance may prevent us from accepting what fate brings.

Self-discipline is crucial, and in contrast Senecan Stoicism, this new form requires the individual to look inside himself: "so geh' in dich zu rücke." Although some other Baroque poems frame this injunction in Christian terms, Fleming does not do so here. On the contrary, his sonnet argues against the Christian notion that suffering can be productive. Self-discipline is hard work, as the penultimate line suggests by repeating the same thought in both halves of the verse.

Poems addressing a "you" can be read in two ways: either as speaking to another person such as a friend, lover, or reader in general, or as a form of self-address. Fleming's "An Sich" does both at once. On one level, it gives advice to the reader, urging him not to give up in the face of adversity but to draw on inner strengths instead. On another level, the speaker himself is reinforcing his own firmly held principles by summoning up the courage to put them into practice. The sonnet's two-track address permits it to rise above personal expression and acts as a model for the reader. The emphasis on steadfastness is bolstered by the form, with its careful control of meter, rhyme, and syntax. At the same time, these formal features never become mechanical: after all, alertness is necessary for self-control. Thus, the two-sentence structure of the opening lines is quickly broken up, and obstacles to contentment pile up in the threesome "Glück'/ Ort/ und Zeit" at the end of line 4. The speaker catches himself when he deviates too far from strict symmetry of form or thought; yet he also finds a variety of ways to pace the oppositions he describes, sometimes positioning them into the two halves of a line, sometimes putting them into a single compact phrase. Enjambment is deftly employed in lines 9–10, which mark the turn of thought from the octave to the sestet as the focus shifts to the inner character of the individual himself. Following these subtle variations as the poem unfolds, the final two lines function almost like an apothegm. Notice, though, that what looks on the page like a rhyme is not a true rhyme at all ("kan," with a short "a," and "unterthan," with a long one). Nonetheless, this two-line conclusion has all the clinching power of a Shakespearean rhymed couplet:

> Wer sein selbst Meister ist/ und sich beherrschen kan/
> Dem ist die weite Welt und alles unterthan.

Like Fleming's "An Sich," Gryphius's "Thränen in schwerer Kranckheit" (Tears in Grave Illness; 1643) is also not a poem of personal reflection, even though its author seems to have used an actual illness as an impulse for writing it:

Mir ist ich weiß nicht wie / ich seuffze für und für.
Ich weyne Tag und Nacht / ich sitze in tausend Schmerzen;
Und tausend fürcht ich noch / die Krafft in meinem Hertzen
    Verschwindt / der Geist verschmacht / die Hände sincken mir.
    Die Wangen werden bleich / der muntern Augen Zir
Vergeht / gleich als der Schein der schon verbrannten Kertzen.
Die Seele wird bestürmt gleich wie die See im Mertzen.
    Was ist diß Leben doch / was sind wir / ich und ihr?
Was bilden wir uns ein! Was wündschen wir zu haben?
Itzt sind wir hoch und groß / und morgen schon vergraben:
    Itzt Blumen morgen Kot / wir sind ein Wind / ein Schaum /
Ein Nebel / eine Bach / ein Reiff / ein Tau' ein Schaten.
Itzt was und morgen nichts / und was sind unser Thaten?
    Als ein mit herber Angst durchaus vermischter Traum.

(I feel I know not how, I sigh over and over. I weep day and night, I
suffer from a thousand pains and fear a thousand more. The strength in
my heart vanishes, my spirit pines away, my hands sink down. My
cheeks turn pale, the cheerful adornment of my eyes passes away like the
light of burned-out candles. My soul is assailed by storms like the ocean
in March. What is this life, then, and what are we, I and you? Now we are
high and mighty, and tomorrow we are buried: now flowers, tomorrow
dung, we are wind, foam, fog, brook, frost, dew, shadow. Now
something and tomorrow nothing, and what are our deeds? Like a
dream mixed through and through with bitter anxiety.)

Although the description of this sickness does include bodily symptoms, it
is not primarily a physical phenomenon. Rather, it is characterized from the
outset by sighing and weeping; emotional and spiritual decline is indicated
by the references to "Hertz" (heart) and "Geist" (mind or spirit). The title
word "Thränen" (tears) was a commonplace of the time for any strong form of
suffering; Gryphius's "Thränen des Vaterlandes: Anno 1636" uses the term to
designate the effects of devastation wrought by the Thirty Years' War. According
to seventeenth-century medical theory, the emotions directly affected physical
states. Thus, although the speaker's cheeks turn pale and his eyes lose their brilliance, these are actually signs of spiritual agitation: "Die Seele wird bestürmt
gleich wie die See im Mertzen." The last line of the octave and the first line
of the sestet formulate issues that have given rise to this distress: fundamental questions about earthly life, our position within it, and the problematic
nature of fantasy and desire. The mutability of life and its transitory nature,
including the deeds by which we hope to make a mark, give the lie to the sense
that we hold a special place in the vast scheme of things. The similes of the

octave – the light of burned-out candles and the storm-tossed ocean in March – give way to abbreviated metaphors that pile up in the sestet, forming a short-hand statement about the character of earthly phenomena. The examples in line 11 – flowers that turn to dung – and line 12 – wind, foam, fog, brook, frost, dew, shadow – present an allegory of human life from its first flourishing to its ultimate decay. The speaker's spiritual state is one in which faith in the divine order, in other words an order that culminates in resurrection, is overshadowed by questioning, disbelief, and despair. We should not confuse this state with what we call melancholy today. Rather, this is the sin of *acedia* or torpor of the soul. The sonnet's final line does not reinforce this listlessness, but rather concludes by reminding us that earthly life is but an illusion ("Traum") in comparison to the life we must anticipate after death and resurrection. The sonnet's ending is not a wistful reflection but the exact opposite: recognition that troubles here on earth are temptations to which we must not succumb.

The sonnet form is well suited to this argument because of the contrastive nature of its two main parts, the octave and the sestet. From this perspective, we can see more clearly the difference between the questions of line 8 and that of line 9. Whereas the octave ends with an expression of distress about the meaning of life and our role in it, the sestet opens with an exclamation over the illusory character of our understanding about these matters. Unlike Fleming's "An Sich," Gryphius's "Thränen in schwerer Kranckheit" does not mobilize the bi-partite structure of the *Alexandriner* in support of binary oppositions. Instead, it deploys the Baroque interest in lists to express the urgency of the speaker's situation. Exaggeration, such as the "thousand pains" the speaker suffers, serves to underline this urgency; and yet the poem does not go to the extremes of some poems of the period. It treads a careful line between spiritual distress and logical argument. This may be one of the reasons why it continues to fascinate readers today.

The differences between the German Baroque mentality and the modern period can also be gauged by exploring a poem on a topic that, since the Romantic period, has been relegated to the sphere of nature poetry. Once again, this is a poem by Gryphius: his sonnet "Der Abend" (Evening; 1650). It opens with a splendid image:

> Der schnelle Tag ist hin / die Nacht schwingt ihre Fahn /
> Und führt die Sternen auff. Der Menschen müde Scharen
> Verlassen Feld und Werck / wo Thir und Vögel waren
> Traurt itzt die Einsamkeit. Wie ist die Zeit verthan!
> Der Port naht mehr und mehr sich zu der Glider Kahn.
> Gleich wie diß Licht verfil / so wird in wenig Jahren
> Ich / du / und was man hat / und was man siht / hinfahren.

Diß Leben kömmt mir vor als eine Renne-Bahn.
Laß höchster Gott / mich doch nicht auff dem Lauffplatz gleiten /
Laß mich nicht Ach / nicht Pracht / nicht Lust nicht Angst verleiten!
   Dein ewig-heller Glantz sey vor und neben mir /
Laß / wenn der müde Leib entschlägt / die Seele wachen
Und wenn der letzte Tag wird mit mir Abend machen /
   So reiß mich aus dem Thal der Finsternüß zu dir.

(The rapid day is done; night waves its banner and leads the stars
onward. The tired groups of people leave field and tasks behind. Where
animals and birds were, solitude now grieves. How time has been
wasted! The harbor comes closer and closer to the boat of human limbs.
Just as this light dimmed, so in a few years I, you, and what one has and
what one sees will have vanished. This life appears to me like a
race-track. May I not, highest God, slip on the course; do not let woe,
nor glory, nor desire nor worry lead me astray. May your bright eternal
light be ahead of me and beside me, When my weary body goes to sleep,
may my soul awake, and when the last day creates evening for me, then
tear me from the vale of darkness to you.)

Gryphius's image of night waving its flag and leading a starry phalanx forms
a powerful contrast to the departure of "rapid day" (rapid in contrast to God's
eternity). The dramatic battle metaphor is deployed here in connection with
an everyday occurrence: workers leaving their tasks at the end of the day. In
the workaday world, birds and animals would still be left in the field after
human workers have gone home to rest; but this is not evening in the ordinary
sense. In the context of the sonnet, it becomes an allegory for the transitory
nature of earthly life. This is why thoughts of death emerge in the second
quatrain: the genitive metaphor "der Glider Kahn" stands in for the physical
body, which will ultimately be transported to its heavenly resting place. The
speaker presses the allegory home by asserting the transience of human beings,
human possessions, and human perceptions of reality.

In a typically Baroque manner, the speaker now introduces another simile,
as if the previous ones were not enough. This is the image of the race-track,
which can so easily cause a person to slip or to be misled from the true way. The
temptations that can have this influence are articulated in standard Baroque
fashion in the form of a list. The monosyllabic character of the potential
temptations – "ach," "pracht," "lust" and "angst" – adds weight to their allure
for the human soul. The race-track image carries over from the octave into the
sestet, but the emphasis in the latter is on the speaker's prayer not to be led
into temptation. The triple repetition of the imperative "Laß" at the beginning
of three lines in the sestet hammers this point home. As the final tercet shifts

to the contrast between the weary body and the awakening soul, the speaker articulates the Christian understanding that the "evening" of individual human life is only the beginning of life in the radiance of God. The ich-du connection of line 7, which refers to ordinary human beings, is transposed at the end of the poem into a relation between the speaker of the poem and the addressee (God), who will resolve the contradictions of earthly life.

The Latin term *vanitas* is often used to refer to the theme of transience in Baroque texts. Seventeenth-century German employed the word *Eitelkeit* to refer to the ephemeral nature of earthly experience (note that the word has changed its meaning in modern German). Gryphius's sonnet "Es ist alles eitel" (All is transient; 1643) explores the problem of *vanitas* by means of a series of metaphors that build on a passage from the Biblical book of Ecclesiastes:

> Du sihst/ wohin du sihst nur eitelkeit auff erden.
>   Was dieser heute bawt/ reist jener morgen ein:
>   Wo itzund städte stehn/ wird eine wiesen sein
> Auff der ein schäffers kind wird spilen mitt den heerden.
> Was itzund prächtig blüht sol bald zutretten werden.
>   Was itzt so pocht undt trotzt ist morgen asch und bein.
>   Nichts ist das ewig sey/ kein ertz kein marmorstein.
> Jtz lacht das gluck uns an/ bald donnern die beschwerden.
>   Der hohen thaten ruhm mus wie ein traum vergehn.
>   Soll den das spiell der zeitt/ der leichte mensch bestehn.
> Ach! was ist alles dis was wir für köstlich achten/
>   Als schlechte nichtikeitt/ als schaten staub und windt.
>   Als eine wiesen blum/ die man nicht wiederfindt.
> Noch wil was ewig ist kein einig mensch betrachten.

> (Wherever you look, you see nothing but transience on earth. What this man builds today, that man tears down tomorrow: where cities now stand, there will be a meadow on which a shepherd's child will play with the herds of animals. What now blossoms splendidly will soon be trodden down. The beating heart, the defiant will is ash and bone tomorrow. Nothing lasts forever, neither bronze nor marble. Now fortune laughs, now troubles thunder down on us. The fame of great deeds must pass away like a dream. How can that toy of time, the fragile human being, survive? Alas, what is all this, which we regard as precious, other than a poor nothingness, shadow, dust, and wind. Like a meadow flower that one cannot find again. Yet no single person wants to consider that which is eternal.)

In some versions, Gryphius himself prefaced the poem by the Latin version of the Biblical passage: "*Vanitas vanitorum*, omnia vanitas" (Vanity of vanities;

all is vanity; King James Bible, Eccl. 1:2). In the sonnet itself, he draws on Luther's translation: "Es ist alles ganz eitel, sprach der Prediger, es ist alles eitel" (Prediger 1: 2). The preacher in the Biblical passage adduces several examples of the vanity of earthly life: man sees little profit from all his labor, one generation is replaced by another, the sun rises and sets, the wind blows now one way and then another, rivers run into the sea and yet the sea does not grow larger. The flower in the meadow (the "wiesen blum" of Gryphius's line 13) alludes to Psalm 103: "Ein Mensch ist in seinem Leben wie Gras, er blüht wie eine Blume auf dem Feld; wenn der Wind darüber geht, so ist sie nimmer da, und ihre Stätte kennt sie nicht mehr"; in the King James translation: "As for man, his days are as grass: as a flower of the field, so he flourisheth. For the wind passeth over it, and it is gone; and the place thereof shall know it no more." (Psalm 103: 15–16) While alluding to these Biblical examples of transience, Gryphius adapts them to the Baroque stock of metaphors: "schaten staub und windt" (line 12), for instance, did not need to be explained to seventeenth-century readers, who already recognized them as allegories of transience. In contrast to Luther, whose hymns were versions of the psalms designed for community singing, Gryphius is writing for an educated reader who appreciates the virtuosity of his skills in imitation and variation.

Parallelism and antithesis, rhetorical structures common in the Baroque period, are deployed with subtle modulations in "Es ist alles eitel." The sequence of clauses beginning with "was" in the opening part of the sonnet is interrupted by a "wo"-clause in line 3. The list of parallel examples is broken up by enjambment and elaboration in lines 3–4. Human achievements like the construction of houses or cities are interwoven with elements from nature like the flower. And in his references to bronze and marble as things that do not last forever, Gryphius also alludes to Horace's famous claim that art is a "monument more lasting than bronze." If everything is transient, Gryphius suggests here, why would art be more enduring? The reader is forced to keep thinking along with the speaker of the poem rather than accept the superficial impression of repetition. With typical Baroque delight in exaggeration and excess, the speaker continues to heap up metaphors for transience well beyond the usual point where we would expect a turn in thought. Not until the final line does a new idea intervene: that of God's eternity. For the modern reader, this conclusion may seem abrupt. In the Baroque period, however, such a delay was not uncommon. Here, the final line challenges us to think beyond the sonnet's ending and contemplate the eternal verities.

Hoffmannswaldau's "Vergänglichkeit der Schönheit" (Transience of Beauty; published posthumously in 1695), takes a different approach to the theme of transience by blending it into the Petrarchan tradition that provided the

German Baroque poets with their vocabulary for love poetry. We do not know exactly when Hoffmannswaldau composed this sonnet, which for unknown reasons he did not include in the collection of his translations and poems he assembled during his lifetime (he died in 1679). "Vergänglichkeit der Schönheit" is addressed to an unnamed beloved woman, whom the speaker does not hesitate, however, to confront with the prospect of her own death in the very first line:

> Es wird der bleiche tod mit seiner kalten hand
> Dir endlich mit der zeit umb deine brüste streichen/
> Der liebliche corall der lippen wird verbleichen;
>   Der schultern warmer schnee wird werden kalter sand/
>   Der augen süsser blitz/ die kräffte deiner hand/
> Für welchen solches fällt/ die werden zeitlich weichen/
> Das haar/ das itzund kan des goldes glantz erreichen/
>   Tilgt endlich tag und jahr als ein gemeines band.
> Der wohlgesetzte fuß/ die lieblichen gebärden/
> Die werden theils zu staub/ theils nichts und nichtig werden/
>   Denn opfert keiner mehr der gottheit deiner pracht.
> Diß und noch mehr als diß muß endlich untergehen/
> Dein hertze kan allein zu aller zeit bestehen/
>   Dieweil es die natur aus diamant gemacht.

(Pale death with his cold hand will, in the end, stroke your breasts for the final time; the lovely coral of your lips will fade; the warm snow of your shoulders will turn to cold sand; your eye's sweet flash, the strength of your hand will yield to time, before which all things submit; your hair, which now rivals the shine of gold, will be erased by days and years like a common ribbon. Your well-formed foot, your lovely gestures, will turn in part to dust, in part to nothing at all; for no one will pay homage any more to the divinity of your splendor. This and much more than this will finally pass away; your heart alone can survive for all time because nature has made it of diamond.)

Formally, this sonnet is much lighter in tone than those of Gryphius, in part because the syntax tends to play down the caesuras or even eliminate them entirely (as in "corall der lippen," line 3). Even more than in Gryphius's "Es ist alles eitel," Hoffmannswaldau's "Vergänglichkeit der Schönheit" reduces the antithetical structure of the alexandrines and continues the sequence of metaphors through to the third-last line. But although the fluidity of form is characteristic of a love poem, this address to a beloved woman does not rest content with enumerating the various attributes that comprise her beauty.

The sonnet opens with a favorite motif of the Baroque, the *memento mori* or injunction to bear death in mind. The sinister idea that death will one day caress the lady's breasts seems at first glance an unappealing theme for a love poem. Instead of using the Petrarchan stock of comparisons to exalt the woman's beauty – coral for her lips, snow for her white shoulders, gold for her hair – the speaker deploys these images to insist that her lovely physical form will vanish with her death. And instead of contenting himself with the notion that the living body turns in the end to dust, the speaker emphasizes the fact that his lover will become nothing at all ("nichts und nichtig"). The conclusion takes an unusual turning, however, when it claims that the woman's heart will survive because it is made of diamond. How is this final line to be understood? On one level, it may be saying that one part of the lovely woman will survive, namely her heart, the seat of her emotions. On another level, though, it may be that the speaker is reproaching her for being hard-hearted. The sonnet seems to play off the threatening figure of Death against the woman whose beauty has made her a kind of pagan goddess worshipped by admiring men. That may be another part of the speaker's reproach to the woman. Certainly, the word "diß" (= *dieses*) could refer to her loss of "divine" status just as much as it refers to the entire catalogue of beautiful features. If so, the speaker is criticizing his mistress, or more specifically her unwillingness to consummate their relationship physically. The *carpe diem* (seize the day) that was also a favorite of Baroque poets takes on a less carefree attitude than is usually the case in poems on that topic. The light tone appears to be at odds with the uncomfortable message. Yet precisely this dual aspect makes the poem so remarkable. It takes up a motif that Gryphius had developed in a poem about a dead woman whose bones had been disinterred, "Über die Gebeine der ausgegrabenen Philosetten" (On the Bones of Disinterred Philosette; 1643) and turns it into something completely different. The speaker of Gryphius's sonnet is horrified to find, in the dreadful sight of Philosette's bones, the absence of those features that once made up her physical beauty: her golden hair, her snowy brow, her rose-red mouth. Lacking ears, eyes, and nose, the skull is terrifying to behold, and the bony nose ridge that has now become visible "could not be compared with ivory before," as the speaker grimly comments. In Gryphius's poem on Philosette, Petrarchan conceits have been nullified in death. Hoffmannswaldau, by contrast, allows the familiar metaphors to retain their flavor as gestures of male gallantry toward beautiful women, while at the same time reminding us that they will ultimately vanish away. This double strand running through in the poem not only gives it depth, but also a somewhat grim wit that caps the poem at the end.

Still, like the other Baroque sonnets we have considered in this chapter, Hoffmannswaldau's "Vergänglichkeit der Schönheit" is not an expression of personal emotion. For its contemporary readers, the poem's achievement lay in the virtuosity with which it took up familiar themes – death and transience, on the one hand, and the poet's frustration with his resisting lady, on the other – and turned them into an entirely new composite. The reader was expected to appreciate the technical mastery with which the poet took up this challenge.

After the intense interest in sonnets during the seventeenth century, the form fell into eclipse for a good deal of the eighteenth. When it picked up again in the last decades of the eighteenth century, most poets still used the *Alexandriner* as their favored meter. Soon, however, August Wilhelm Schlegel ushered in a new fascination with the sonnet form, giving it a fresher and more flexible aspect by employing iambic pentameter with feminine (two-syllable) rhymes. Eschewing the energetic fervor of Gryphius's sonnets, the Romantic poets were special admirers of Paul Fleming. One poem of Fleming's that appealed in particular to their sensibilities was his sonnet "An den Ort/ da Er Sie erstlich umfangen" (On the Place where He first Embraced Her; posthumously published, 1646). As the title indicates, it is a poem about erotic love. Its opening lines depict a *locus amoenus*, the beautiful spot in nature where lovers traditionally meet. Yet in a brilliant imaginative gesture, the landscape also seems to take the shape of a beloved body: bushes, flowers, pearly dew, and fountains bear the aspect of head, face, breast, and womb. It is as if two images were superimposed. For the lover, it is a sacred grove, attended by muses and inhabited by hamadryads and other denizens of the woods, and he concludes by exhorting others to protect the lovely place. The light tone of Fleming's love poetry, its mellifluous rhymes, relative avoidance of strong caesuras, and emphasis on natural settings clearly attracted the Romantic poets, who looked to him as a precursor. Followers of A. W. Schlegel's fluid approach to form began to produce a flood of sonnets in a mode that aimed to rival the use of resonant rhymes familiar from the Romance languages. *Sonettenwut* (sonnet craze) was the term introduced by Gottfried August Bürger to describe the new fashion that swept through the groups of Romantic poets in the early years of the nineteenth century. Ludwig Tieck, Joseph von Eichendorff, and Clemens Brentano were all prolific writers of sonnets. Goethe experimented with the form in 1807/8, creating a sonnet-cycle that first appeared in 1815 and was extended in 1827. He even adopted the term "Sonettenwut" in his poem "Nemesis" (1815), the eleventh sonnet in his sequence. Reminding the reader that one can avoid catching influenza if one doesn't attend social events, the speaker of "Nemesis" regrets his failure to follow this maxim in the case of the sonnet craze (the reader is supposed to think at this point of the second sense of the Italian word "influenza," meaning "influence"). Having allowed himself to be exposed to love and literature, he finds himself pursued by the Furies in the guise of "Sonettenwut und Raserei der Liebe" (the craze for sonnets and the ravings of love).

Another poem, "Ihr liebt, und schreibt Sonette!" (Sonnet 14 in Goethe's sequence), is a playful critique of the craze in which he was himself participating in the very act of writing this text. Here Goethe presents a complex response to the problem of representing passion in structured language. This poem begins with a humorous expression of astonishment: "Ihr liebt, und schreibt Sonette! Weh der Grille!" (You're in love, and writing sonnets! What a silly whim!). The sonnet is divided between a group of speakers called "the doubters," who question whether powerful feelings can be adequately expressed in a regulated form like the sonnet, and the "lovers," who believe that passion can help break through the rigidity of prescribed poetic rules:

> *Die Zweifelnden*
> Ihr liebt, und schreibt Sonette! Weh der Grille!
> Die Kraft des Herzens, sich zu offenbaren,
> Soll Reime suchen, sie zusammenpaaren;
> Ihr Kinder, glaubt, ohnmächtig bleibt der Wille.
> Ganz ungebunden spricht des Herzens Fülle
> Sich kaum noch aus: sie mag sich gern bewahren;
> Dann Stürmen gleich durch alle Saiten fahren.
> Dann wieder senken sich zu Nacht und Stille.
> Was quält ihr euch und uns, auf jähem Stege
> Nur Schritt vor Schritt den läst'gen Stein zu wälzen,
> Der rückwärts lastet, immer neu zu mühen?
>
> *Die Liebenden*
> Im Gegenteil, wir sind auf rechtem Wege!
> Das Allerstarrste freudig aufzuschmelzen,
> Muß Liebesfeuer allgewaltig glühen.

(*The doubters:* You're in love, and writing sonnets! What a silly whim! The heart's power of expression should seek rhymes and pair them up with one another? Children, believe me, the will is powerless.// Quite without form, fullness of heart can still scarcely speak: it wants to maintain itself; then storms drive through all the strings, and then they drop down again into night and silence.// Why do you torment yourselves and us, rolling up a steep path, step by step, the heavy stone that pulls backward, only to start over again?// *The lovers:* On the contrary, we're on the right track; in order joyfully to melt the stiffest substance, the fire of love must glow all-powerfully.)

Goethe cleverly delays the turn of thought until the second tercet, apparently giving the doubters more space. Yet the doubters' argument is complex, and thus in a sense justifies the greater number of lines they take. While they doubt whether the highly wrought sonnet can be a fitting vehicle for passion, the doubters also recognize that abandonment of form scarcely enhances articulation. Passion, they argue, repeatedly breaks through even the most sketchy structures. Form and passion are incompatible, and in the conflict between the two, words must ultimately yield to silence. In the end, the process is Sisyphean: each time we attempt to give expression to powerful emotions, we are stopped short by the sheer resistance of linguistic form. The poem does not merely address this problem, it also demonstrates it. Embedded words break up the flow of the first quatrain ("sich zu offenbaren"; "glaubt"), an enjambment spills over in the second quatrain, and the first tercet presents significant syntactical complexities. The relative clause "der rückwärts lastet" qualifies "der Stein," but it is positioned in such a way that it breaks up the symmetry between the verbal forms "zu wälzen" and "zu mühen." These two verbs describe two related aspects of the torment created when one attempts to express strong emotions in verse.

The lovers' response is more straightforward – and above all, much more compact. It begins with an exclamation and ends with a two-line explanation: strong passions, the lovers argue, are the best way to make rigid structures more flexible. One might almost say, as a corollary, that the articulation of passion might be the best thing that could happen to the sonnet. To be sure, the lovers' reply is linked to the doubters' conclusion by the rhyme scheme, since each line of the second tercet completes a rhyme from the first. At the same time, however, it is as if the complications in the first tercet are resolved by clearer exposition in the second. In the final analysis, the supposed conflict between feeling and form is revealed as a pseudo-problem. Like several other – but by no means all! – poems in Goethe's sonnet cycle, this dialogue-sonnet demonstrates how well the sonnet lends itself to wit and irony.

Lightening up the sonnet and making it more flexible was the most tangible result of the "Sonettenwut." Even after the craze had died down, the sonnet form did not completely fade away. The late Romantic August von Platen and the turn-of-the century poet Hugo von Hofmannsthal are among its most adept practitioners. Tracing these developments would burst the bounds of this chapter. Nonetheless, no consideration of the sonnet in German could be complete without attention to Rilke's reinvention of the form in his two-part sonnet-sequence *Sonette an Orpheus* (Sonnets to Orpheus; 1922). These poems, which burst forth in a single month after his completion of the *Duineser*

Elegien, are even more airy than the sonnets of the Romantics: indeed, air is one of their dominant motifs. Intended as a "monument" for a young ballet dancer who had died young, they hark back to Mallarmé's "tombeaux" or tombstone poems, most of them written in memory of other famous poets (though one is a memorial to his young son). Like Mallarmé's "tombeaux," Rilke's *Sonette an Orpheus* are also poems about poetry, in particular about its status as something both material and immaterial. "Atmen, du unsichtbares Gedicht!" (Breathe, you invisible poem!) begins the second part of Rilke's sequence (*Sonette an Orpheus* II, 1). And breathing is exactly what these sonnets do, sometimes by inserting dashes and marks of ellipsis, sometimes by shortening a line at a crucial moment, and sometimes by adopting meters foreign to the pentameter lines that had become customary in German-language poetry in the wake of A. W. Schlegel. The sequence begins with a sonnet about Orpheus, the classical precursor of the modern poet, and continues with a sonnet about Wera Ouckama-Knoop, thus positioning the sequence as a celebration of poetry itself as well as an expression of mourning for the young dancer. The third sonnet of the first part illustrates very well the complexities of this posture:

> Ein Gott vermags. Wie aber, sag mir, soll
> ein Mann ihm folgen durch die schmale Leier?
> Sein Sinn ist Zwiespalt. An der Kreuzung zweier
> Herzwege steht kein Tempel für Apoll.
>
> Gesang, wie du ihn lehrst, ist nicht Begehr,
> nicht Werbung um ein endlich noch Erreichtes;
> Gesang ist Dasein. Für den Gott ein Leichtes.
> Wann aber *sind* wir? Und wann wendet *er*
>
> an unser Sein die Erde und die Sterne?
> Dies *ists* nicht, Jüngling, daß du liebst, wenn auch
> die Stimme dann den Mund dir aufstößt, – lerne
>
> vergessen, daß du aufsangst. Das verrinnt.
> In Wahrheit singen, ist ein andrer Hauch.
> Ein Hauch um nichts. Ein Wehn im Gott. Ein Wind.

(A god can do it. How, though, tell me, shall a man follow him through the narrow lyre? His direction is ambivalence. At the fork of two heart-roads stands no temple for Apollo.// Song, as you teach it, is not desire, nor wooing of something finally attainable; song is being. An easy thing for a god. But when *are* we? And when will *he* turn// the earth and sun toward our being? The fact that you love, young man, is not it, even though that's when your voice opened your mouth, – learn// to forget

that you sang out. That trickles away. To sing in truth is another breath.
A breath about nothing. A blowing in the god. A wind.)

Apollo is the god of poetry (or song, to use the classical term that Rilke
employs here). Orpheus, the most famous singer in ancient mythology, had
received his first lyre from Apollo. Inspired by a stone relief he had seen in
Naples, Rilke had already retold the story of Orpheus in his poem "Orpheus.
Eurydike. Hermes" (Orpheus. Eurydice. Hermes; 1904; the periods between the
three names are meant to imitate the inscription on the stone). In the *Sonette
an Orpheus*, Rilke returns to the myth of Orpheus's attempt to bring his wife
Eurydice back from the underworld by using his extraordinary musical powers
to charm the god of the underworld. When Orpheus secured her release but
was not successful in bringing her up to the earth, he mourned her loss in songs
that, according to classical tradition, made the whole of nature bow down in
reverence. Only a god, Rilke's sonnet declares, can descend into the underworld
and return: hence the opening words of the sonnet, "Ein Gott vermags" (a god
can do it). But the moment when Orpheus forgets the instruction not to look
back while Eurydice follows him up from the underworld – the moment when
he turns around to check if she is still behind him – is interpreted in this sonnet
as a sign of Orpheus' dual heritage. The "Kreuzung zweier Herzwege"(line 3)
refers to this moment when Orpheus loses Eurydice and she must turn back
while he is compelled to go on alone. Life in the world involves desire, Rilke's
poem tells us, and Orpheus' longing to retrieve Eurydice from Hades is part
of that all-too human emotion. The address to an unnamed "Jüngling" (line
10) encompasses both Orpheus himself and any human youth who might
read this sonnet. The unidentified pronoun "*er*" in line 8 presumably refers to
Apollo. Other unidentified pronouns, the "du" and "ihn" of line 5 (possibly
Apollo and Orpheus respectively), as well as an extremely abstract mode of
expression, make the ideas developed in lines 5–12 highly complex and difficult
to unravel. One point common to both the second quatrain and the first
tercet has to do with desire. "Begehr" is a strong word that implies, in Rilke's
usage, the desire for possession. The later sections of Rilke's innovative prose
work *Die Aufzeichnungen des Malte Laurids Brigge* (The Notebooks of Malte
Laurids Brigge; 1910) introduce the concept of "intransitive love," in other
words love that is not object-directed. Twelve years after the completion of
the *Aufzeichnungen*, Rilke picks up this idea again in connection with poetry,
which the *Sonette an Orpheus* present as something beyond ordinary human
passions. "Dies *ist* nicht, Jüngling, daß du liebst, wenn auch/ die Stimme dann
den Mund dir aufstößt" (lines 10–11): not every song that seems inspired is free
from human desires, which are always attached to an object and connected

with the possibility of possession. There is also a purer form of song, the kind that Orpheus learned from Apollo and that is not inflected by human motivation. This other, non-earthly poetry is defined in the last line of the sonnet: "Ein Hauch um nichts. Ein Wehn im Gott. Ein Wind." In this final line of the sonnet, as elsewhere in the sequence, Rilke completely reconfigures the *vanitas* motif of the Baroque sonnet. Whereas the worldly for Gryphius and his contemporaries is "nothing" in the sense that everything it comprises is transient and subject to decay, for Rilke in his Orpheus sonnets poetry itself is a kind of nothing. It is so precisely because it is immaterial, because it subsists in the imagination, and because it transfigures earthly things and feelings. In insisting on the immateriality of poetry, Rilke also reconfigures the notion of inspiration, a word that literally means to breathe something into something else, as when God animated the first human beings by insufflating them with his breath. Poetry, in this new understanding, is the product neither of inspiration by the muses nor of love for a specific human being. Poetry in this sense is a "breath," a "wind," that has neither an identifiable origin nor a specific goal. This ideal of perennially unachievable "pure poetry" marks Rilke's late poetry as an heir to the Symbolist movement of the late nineteenth and early twentieth centuries. Instead of struggling with the problem of representing passion in language, Symbolist poetry aspires to a form of language that comes as close as possible to the non-representational.

A brief consideration of one recent poet who has practiced the sonnet form and another who engages with the Baroque will serve as a coda to this chapter. The first is Günter Grass (b. 1927), better known in the English-speaking world as a novelist, but also a very fine poet. The second is the prize-winning younger poet Durs Grünbein (b. 1962), whose interest in the Baroque goes back to the city of his birth, Dresden. The works at which we shall glance here are relatively recent, but behind them lies in each case a trajectory that focuses on the problem of articulating passion in the widest sense of the term.

In his collection of sonnets *Novemberland* (November Land; 1993), Günter Grass builds on his deep reading in Baroque literature. Grass's first novel, *Die Blechtrommel* (*The Tin* Drum; 1959), had revealed his indebtedness to the Baroque novelist Grimmelshausen, and his later narrative *Das Treffen in Telgte* (*The Meeting at* Telgte; 1979) testified to his close familiarity with other major Baroque writers. The 1979 text centered on a fictive meeting of twenty-one important figures from the period in a Westphalian town just before the end of the Thirty Years' War. Obvious parallels to Gruppe 47, the group of post-World War II writers of which Grass was a member, indicate his profound sense of kinship with his predecessors from the Baroque; indeed, it appears that he saw himself as a latter-day Grimmelshausen. The thirteen sonnets of *Novemberland*, by contrast, make no secret of their debt to Andreas Gryphius. "Thränen des Vaterlandes: Anno 1636" is the model against which Grass's poetic assessment of the country's deterioration must be read. Major themes of Gryphius's poetry – war, violence, and constant reminders of death – are also at the heart of Grass's sonnet collection, along with much of Gryphius's favorite vocabulary. Grass's topic is the rise of neo-Nazism in the recently reunified Germany and the increasing violence toward residents who were not German citizens. An attack on a shelter for asylum seekers in Mölln, where three Turkish women were burned to death, provided the initial impulse for the sonnets in *Novemberland*. Yet although the parallels with Gryphius are central to *Novemberland*, the sonnets themselves do not attempt to vie with the tight structures in which the Baroque poet excelled. The sepia sketches that accompany them create a deliberately messy effect. The sonnets mingle language that alludes to Baroque poetry with terms from modern economics and advertising. The eleventh sonnet, "Nach kurzer Krankheit," rewrites the Baroque metaphor of disease in terms of influenza and the common cold. Trivial though they may seem, these illnesses are also glossed as signs of a "new cult" that has emerged like a reactivated virus. The reference is, of course, to neo-Nazism. Presenting the miseries of flu season as an old song sung to a new melody, this sonnet uses its relation to Baroque poetry to reflect on the character of modern medicine, modern social and political culture, and modern poetry. In the second quatrain, "Hustentropfenzählen" (counting cough drops) replaces the counting of syllables in verse; while this may primarily allude to the regular alternation of stressed and unstressed syllables advocated by Opitz, it presumably also invokes the meters that the speaker of one of Goethe's *Römische Elegien* (Roman Elegies; 1795) taps out on the back of his sleeping lover. Runny eyes and persistent coughing are no longer a reminder that we should take refuge in divine salvation; instead, as the sestet of this sonnet makes clear, they are merely a topic of talk shows that rapidly gives way to other subjects.

That the sonnets in *Novemberland* total thirteen alludes, of course, to the unlucky number of superstition. It presumably also relates to the number of lines in the traditional sonnet, thus indirectly suggesting that the sequence, written at an ominous cultural juncture, deliberately stops short of the traditional number, fourteen, associated with the sonnet form. The sepia sketches indicate each poem's number while also containing its text in small, hasty brushstrokes that contrast with the printed text of the poems beside them. The sketches for the first and thirteenth poems, with bold numerals 1 and 13, suggest grass in the foreground; the first is overwritten in the right front corner by lines from the corresponding poem, while in the sketch for the thirteenth, the grass is more pervasively overwritten by text and marshy land has appeared in the background. The grass motif is a double allusion: first to Grass's name, of course; but secondly to Dürer's watercolor "Großes Rasenstück" (Large [Patch of] Turf; 1503; for more on this painting, see Chapter 10). In the present era, Grass seems to suggest, form is no longer pristine: rather, it is an imperfect overlay on an earlier model.

Durs Grünbein began writing his book *Porzellan: Poem vom Untergang meiner Stadt* (Porcelain: Poem on the Destruction of My City; 2005), in 1992. Born in Dresden in 1962, Grünbein lived there until he moved to West Berlin in 1985. Prior to writing this book, he had already written several poems about his native city, notably his very fine "Gedicht über Dresden" (Poem about Dresden; 1991; see Chapter 9). The publication of *Porzellan* coincides with the completed restoration of the Dresden Frauenkirche in October 2005, to which it briefly alludes. Yet the book takes no part in this celebration: instead, it functions as a "memento" of the firestorm created by Allied bombing of the city in February 1945. The title refers, of course, to one of the products for which Dresden had become famous: its delicate porcelain. It also alludes to the aesthetic character of the city itself, which under the Allies' attack turned out to be no more solid than the teacups and figurines once manufactured there. *Porzellan* consists of forty-nine short, numbered poems, each one differently positioned on its page as if it had been randomly thrown there. The allusion to Mallarmé's *Un coup de dés* (A Throw of the Dice; 1897), with its lines thrown across the pages as if cast from a dice cup, is unmistakeable. As Grünbein also indicates in earlier texts, poetry has become a fragment, akin to a shard of ancient pottery that has remained as a partial witness to the art of a previous time. Similarly, the small poems of *Porzellan* suggest, Dresden's celebrated beauty – its exquisite Baroque architecture gave it the appellation "Florence on the [river] Elbe" – was reduced to fragments in the firestorm of February 1945. The trochaic meter is based on a form frequently used for dialogue in ancient Greek drama. Not for nothing has Grünbein come to be known as a *poeta doctus*, or learned poet (he has done a great deal of translation, especially from classical antiquity). Each poem has only ten lines: they are not sonnets. Willfully ignoring the restoration of the city's famous church, the poems insist on their incomplete character. Similarly, despite the (ironically) pompous genre designation in the volume's subtitle, "Poem," the forty-nine poems do not constitute a coherent "long poem" or even a structured sequence. They remain scattered pieces. In this respect, they stand in distinct contrast to Grünbein's long poem *Vom Schnee oder Descartes in Deutschland* (On Snow or Descartes in Germany; 2003), a forty-two-canto poem in Baroque alexandrines, as appropriate for a narrative of events that take place during the Thirty Years' War. In *Porzellan*, however, Grünbein opts for a compromise solution to the problem of poetic form. Rejecting nostalgia while still paying tribute to his native city, Grünbein takes care to avoid the strong emotions called forth in Gryphius's war sonnets.

Chapter 5

Classical antiquity and modern experience

The notion of creative genius was crucial to a new kind of German poetry that emerged in the period around 1770; it was accompanied by a set of related ideas such as inspiration, originality, authenticity, and spontaneity. The new paradigm involved a distinct shift from the more rule- and form-bound poetry that had preceded it. Although Goethe's poetry of the 1770s was regarded as the apotheosis of the new movement, it could scarcely have come about without Klopstock's development of free verse ("freie Rhythmen") as a powerful organ for poetic expression in German. The impact of Klopstock's long religious poem "Die Frühlingsfeier" (The Festival of Spring; 1759), not solely on Goethe himself but also on the literary community of his time, can be measured by the way he uses a reference to this text as the impulse that sets in motion the plot of his Storm and Stress novel *Die Leiden des jungen Werthers* (The Sorrows of Young Werther; 1774). In addition to Klopstock, Pindar's odes, which Goethe studied intensively in 1773, seemed to reinforce the idea that free verse was the most powerful medium for a new kind of poetic expressivity. With respect to Pindar, this was actually a misunderstanding based on the presentation of his poems in short lines that was common at the time; but it was a view that Klopstock himself had articulated in his poem "Auf meine Freunde" (To My Friends; 1747), where he posed as alternative models the complex strophic form of the Greek ode and the untrammeled outpouring of words he attributed to Pindar, whose songs "taumeln" (tumble) freely from their creator's soul. Increasingly, Goethe's poetry of the early 1770s adopts the gesture of words spilling forth without inhibition. The rebellious formulations of "Prometheus" (most likely written 1774), the ecstatic language of "Ganymed" (probably also written 1774), the incantatory repetitions of "Wanderers Sturmlied" (Wanderer's Storm-Song; probably written 1772), and most strikingly, the impetuous syntax of "An Schwager Kronos" (To Coachman Chronos; composed 1774) are good examples of this mode. As explorations of poetic creativity and its wellsprings, "Prometheus" and "Wanderers Sturmlied" suggest that the poet is not so much, as the Earl of Shaftesbury had put it, a "second maker under God," but a virtual equal of the divine creator. The speaker of "Prometheus" depicts himself as forming human beings "nach meinem Bilde,/ Ein Geschlecht, das mir gleich sei"; and in the final lines of "Wanderers Sturmlied," the speaker claims that "ich schwebe/ Über Wasser über Erde/ Göttergleich." There is, to be sure, an important difference between the first of these two poems, a *Rollengedicht* (role poem) in which Prometheus is the speaker, and the second, where the speaker remains unidentified. "An Schwager Kronos," which Goethe claims to have written in a post coach on October 10, 1774, the voice that urges on the driver seems to speak for the poet himself.

Perhaps the most innovative of Goethe's poems from this decade is "Im Herbst 1775" (In Autumn 1775), retitled "Herbstgefühl" (Autumn Feeling) in 1789:

> Fetter grüne, du Laub,
> Am Rebengeländer
> Hier mein Fenster herauf!
> Gedrängter quellet,
> Zwillingsbeeren, und reifet
> Schneller und glänzend voller!
> Euch brütet der Mutter Sonne
> Scheideblick, euch umsäuselt
> Des holden Himmels
> Fruchtende Fülle;
> Euch kühlet des Mondes
> Freundlicher Zauberhauch,
> Und euch betauen, ach!
> Aus diesen Augen
> Der ewig belebenden Liebe
> Vollschwellende Tränen.

(Green more lushly, you leaves, on the vine lattice here up to my window! Swell more densely, twin berries, and ripen faster and more lustrously full! You are warmed by mother sun's parting glance, moistened all around by lovely heaven's fruiting fullness; you are cooled by the moon's kindly magic breath, and bedewed, oh! from these eyes by eternally revivifying love's full-welling tears.)

Though they are in fact artfully arranged, the opening lines of the poem create the impression of tumbling out helter-skelter. The interpolation of the apostrophe, "du Laub," in the opening sentence makes it hard to recognize at first that the main verb is the unusual compound "heraufgrünen," used as a transitive verb governing "Fenster." The adverb "fetter," placed at the very beginning, is not one that would normally be applied to the greening of leaves, and this, too, causes a moment of disorientation for the reader, who almost needs to parse the sentence before completely understanding it. The verbs "quellet" and "reifet" are more immediately identifiable as imperatives, and thus point backward to confirm the realization that "grüne" is also an imperative. A series of genitive complements placed before the nouns they refer to now sets the reader on a firmer track: "der Mutter Sonne/ Scheideblick," "des holden Himmels/ Fruchtende Fülle," and "des Mondes/ Freundlicher Zauberhauch" all follow a familiar model of poetic expression. They allow us also to understand a similar phrase in the final lines, "der ewig belebenden Liebe vollschwellende Tränen," after the interpolated "ach!" and the placement of "aus diesen Augen" before the actual mention of tears. Complicating the reader's comprehension is the verb "betauet," which we might expect, following the mention of the way in which sun, moon, and sky accelerate the ripening of the grapes, to refer to a natural phenomenon. This effect is not accidental: it is a significant aspect of the poem that the speaker's tears can be virtually equated with dew.

Having taken into account these parallels, we can see more clearly that the imperatives of lines 1–6 are not merely whimsical, but almost have the force of magical incantations. At issue is not merely the growing and ripening of the vine, but the entire complex relationship of the speaker to nature. Looking out of his window, he seems at first to be contemplating a familiar autumn scene. From that perspective, we might imagine that he eagerly awaits the ripening of the grapes and the wine they may eventually become; but this is not a poem in anticipation of autumn's fullness. Nor is it a celebration of a reciprocal interaction between man and nature. Rather, it expresses a deep sense of unease about such tropes.

The poem's original title, "Im Herbst 1775," has led some readers to think of it in biographical terms as an expression of Goethe's distress over the end of his relationship with Lili Schönemann. To regard the poem as an occasional piece, however, would be to limit it unduly; and this may be one reason why he gave it a more general title in the 1789 edition. But it is also not a poem about a vague "feeling" or mood. In fact, it is a poem that directly addresses the problem of creativity. The dynamic character of the text, with its energetic phrasing (not only the imperatives, but also the compound verbs "heraufgrünen" and "umsäuseln" and the comparative adverbs "fetter" and "gedrängter"), suggests that poetic creativity is both like and unlike the creative forces of nature. The somewhat puzzling formulation "Zwillingsbeeren" for grapes seems to be chosen in part because it will ultimately find a near-equivalent in the "twin" tears that well up in the speaker's eyes at the end.

The word "Zauberhauch" marks a crucial moment, since literally, of course, the moon does not "breathe" at all. The term "Hauch" alludes to traditional metaphors of inspiration, but significantly, this inspiration is not attributed to a deity. And although the speaker does utter the word "ach!" – a breath-like word if ever there was one – his final line suggests that tears rather than words are the only proper expression of autumnal emotion. Yet of course, the poem itself consists of words, brilliantly chosen and ingeniously arranged.

In terms of literary history, the poem bears traces of the age of sensibility while owing its dynamics to *Sturm und Drang* (Storm and Stress); at the same time, it voices reservations about the possibility of poetic genius. It musters familiar images proper to the theme of autumn while placing them in a new, unexpected context. It employs the short lines and frequent enjambments that Goethe and his contemporaries believed were characteristic of Pindar, while also using freely alternating dactyls and trochees in the manner of Klopstock's hymns. But while deploying forms reminiscent of earlier poets, it also manages to create an impression of spontaneity. And whereas the poem emphasizes the speaking self situated in a particular moment, the feelings it describes are not so specific that readers cannot participate in the poem's larger gesture.

Not all of Goethe's poems from this period contain the clear temporal reference encapsulated in the title of "Im Herbst 1775." Sometimes an extraneous document testifies to the genesis of a particular poem. Such is the case with the second "Wanderers Nachtlied" (Wanderer's Night-Song; titled "Ein Gleiches" (another one) only because he published it together with a first "Wanderers Nachtlied"), which Goethe scratched into a board on the wall of a hunting cabin in Thüringen on September 6, 1780. We know this because Goethe wrote to his friend Charlotte von Stein the same day, explaining that he had gone there to escape the worries and confusions of Weimar. The term "Erlebnislyrik," derived in part from Wilhelm Dilthey's conception of poetry as an expression of "Erlebnis," was for some time an accepted way of explaining the impression of freshness that Goethe created in his poetry of this period; but it was also frequently misunderstood to refer to the biographical circumstances of composition rather than the more capacious idea that Dilthey had in mind. Certainly, knowing about Goethe's break with Lili Schönemann or his stay in the mountain hut in Thüringen does not dramatically change our understanding of "Im Herbst 1775" or the second "Wanderers Nachtlied." Still, it is important not to regard these poems merely as constructed: what Goethe achieves so brilliantly here is the effect of unconstrained speech, in spite of the verbal, rhythmic, and motivic patterns that give these texts their shape. We have already seen how enjambments both mark and break up the parallels and contrasts that structure "Im Herbst 1775." The second "Wanderer's Nachtlied" creates a sense of spontaneity through complex rhythmic variation:

Über allen Gipfeln
Ist Ruh,
In allen Wipfeln
Spürest du
Kaum einen Hauch;
Die Vögelein schweigen im Walde.
Warte nur, balde
Ruhest du auch.

(Over the hilltops is quiet; in all the treetops you can hardly sense a breath; the little birds in the wood are silent. Wait, soon you will be quiet as well.)

Not everyone will agree on exactly how the poem should be scanned, but we can certainly see that the rhythmic parallel between lines 1 and 3 is broken slightly by the shift from the stressed first syllable of "über" of the first line to the unstressed "in" of the third; and the trisyllabic "Vögelein" (a dactyl) distinctly lightens the third-last line. Some lines begin with unstressed and others with stressed syllables: but what about line 2? Should it be read as an iamb or a pseudo-spondee with a secondary stress followed by a primary stress ("Ist Rúh" or "Ìst Rúh")? What about line 5: how much stress, if any, should "einen" receive? Should it be scanned "Káum einen Háuch" or "Káum éinen Háuch"? It is precisely this sense of natural speech that underlies the poem, working both with and against its more calculated formal devices (notably its use of rhyme), that makes the text seem so unaffected and spontaneous.

Commentators have noticed how the scene is described in an arc from the highest point in the landscape, the mountain peaks, via the treetops and the birds, to the human being who is addressed – or who addresses himself – in the final lines. The conclusion is ambiguous: on the most obvious level, it alludes to sleep that will refresh the wanderer after his long day of walking; but on another level, it hints at death, the fate that befalls everything living. The presence of the word "Hauch" in line 5 is significant. While "Im Herbst 1775" spoke of the way in which "des Mondes freundlicher Zauberhauch" cooled the grapes at night, here the magic emanates from the almost complete lack of "breeze" or "breath" in the landscape. The mastery of the poem lies precisely in its ability to say much while using few words. This, too, is a kind of inspiration.

In Goethe's *Wilhelm Meisters Lehrjahre* (Wilhelm Meister's Apprenticeship Years; 1795/96), the question of originality is broached through Mignon's song of book 3, chapter 1. The three-stanza poem with its slightly varied refrain is printed without introduction at the opening of the chapter, a strategy that allows us to see it first as a completely formed piece. Soon, however, we discover that the poem is not exactly what it seems to be. The singer is the child Mignon, whose freedom Wilhelm has purchased from a gypsy theater troupe. Wilhelm first hears Mignon singing outside his door; when she enters, she sings this song to the accompaniment of a zither. But she does not sing it in German. From an earlier chapter of the novel, we know that Mignon speaks "ein gebrochnes, mit Französisch und Italienisch durchflochtenes Deutsch" (broken German mixed with French and Italian); Wilhelm cannot understand the words of the song completely, and so he writes them down and translates them into German as best he can. "Aber die Originalität der Wendungen konnte er nur von ferne nachahmen" (but he could only faintly imitate the originality of its turns of phrase). The narrator notes what is lost in Wilhelm's translation: "Die kindliche Unschuld des Ausdrucks verschwand, indem die gebrochene Sprache übereinstimmend und das Unzusammenhängende verbunden ward" (the childlike innocence of the expression vanished as the broken language was made harmonious and the disconnected elements unified). She sings the song twice:

> Kennst du das Land, wo die Zitronen blühn,
> Im dunkeln Laub die Goldorangen glühn,
> Ein sanfter Wind vom blauen Himmel weht,
> Die Myrte still und hoch der Lorbeer steht,
> Kennst du es wohl?
> > Dahin! Dahin
> Möcht' ich mit dir, o mein Geliebter, ziehn!
>
> Kennst du das Haus? auf Säulen ruht sein Dach,
> Es glänzt der Saal, es schimmert das Gemach,
> Und Marmorbilder stehn und sehn mich an:
> Was hat man dir, du armes Kind, getan?
> Kennst du es wohl?
> > Dahin! Dahin
> Möcht' ich mit dir, o mein Beschützer, ziehn!
>
> Kennst du den Berg und seinen Wolkensteg?
> Das Maultier sucht im Nebel seinen Weg,
> In Höhlen wohnt der Drachen alte Brut,
> Es stürzt der Fels und über ihn die Flut:
> Kennst du ihn wohl?
> > Dahin! Dahin
> Geht unser Weg; o Vater, laß uns ziehn!

(Do you know the land where the lemon-trees bloom, where golden oranges glow in dark foliage, a gentle wind wafts from the blue sky, the myrtle stands silent and the laurel tall, Do you know it? – There, there I would like to go with you, my beloved!// Do you know the house? Its roof rests on columns, the hall gleams and the chamber glimmers, and marble statues stand and gaze at me: What has been done to you, poor child? Do you know it? – There, there I would like to go with you, my protector!// Do you know the mountain and its cloudy path? The mule picks its way through the fog, the dragon's ancient brood dwells in caves, the cliff drops down and over it the waves: Do you know it? – There, there is where our way leads, Father, let us go!)

The accomplishment and polish of this poem, which appears as a self-sufficient text at the head of the chapter, are evident; yet Wilhelm's frustration with his attempt to render it coherently suggests that Mignon's version is somehow preferable to his. Her words, however, remain inaccessible to us: we only have the poem in Wilhelm's translation. What he calls her "broken language" suggests, furthermore, that the version she sings may not actually be the original. Would the song have been more beautiful if she had sung it in the language in which it was composed (Italian, perhaps)? Or is it more beautiful precisely because of its brokenness, which Wilhelm finds childlike and fresh?

After her second performance of the song, she stops and a little conversation ensues between her and Wilhelm in which the two speak past each other in an amusing way. When she uses the first line of the song to ask Wilhelm a question, "Kennst du das Land?", he replies not by saying whether he has been there, but by saying that "Italy must be what is meant." When he asks her where she acquired the song, she echoes the word "Italy" as if that were its place of origin. But she refuses to answer Wilhelm's question if she has ever been there. Their mismatched questions and answers form a subtle commentary on the complex nature of origins, one that hints at a paradox at the heart of creativity: even when a text may seem to be the quintessence of originality, there is always a longer tradition that informs it, even as it also struggles to break free of tradition. The exchange between the androgynous Mignon and her adoptive father Wilhelm can be seen as representing precisely the transition from an earlier understanding of genius as the spirit of a place to the concept of genius as a special kind of creativity.

Still, Wilhelm's exquisite "translation" of Mignon's only half-articulate song in fact covers up the actual origins of the poem in literary tradition. While Mignon's broken language contains no fragments of English – as far as the narrative informs us – her song has antecedents in English literature, first in Edmund Waller's poem "The Battle of the Summer Islands," with its lines:

> Bermuda, wall'd with rocks, who does not know?
> That happy island where huge lemons grow,
> And orange-trees, which golden fruit do bear,
> Th' Hesperian garden boasts of none so fair

and second, in James Thomson's *The Seasons*, which includes a reformulation of these motifs in its section "Summer" (1727):

> Bear me, Pomona, to thy citron groves,
> To where the lemon and the piercing lime,
> With the deep orange, glowing through the green,
> Their lighter glories blend. Lay me reclined
> Beneath the spreading tamarind, that shakes,
> Fanned by the breeze, its fever-cooling fruit.

What Goethe does with these antecedents is to take set pieces and convert them to lines that come alive when attributed to the mysterious Mignon and her relationship to Wilhelm. Not only do they now express two different versions of nostalgia – the child's longing for a home from which she has been separated and the young man's longing for his own place in literary tradition – they also rapidly lose their idyllic resonance as they acquire two new stanzas that break with the traditional models.

These stanzas retain the external form of the first, but gradually they introduce frightening images that would be out of place in Waller's or Thomson's paradisiacal scenes. The change in tone occurs unexpectedly in lines 3 and 4 of the second stanza, oddly connected by "und" with the radiance of the beautiful villa. The marble statues stare balefully at the poem's speaker, apparently identified as Mignon herself – or at least, so the words "du armes Kind" lead us to believe. The reproach is not directed at her but at those who have brought her to her current condition. And yet Mignon is in another land far away: only the imagination can construct this encounter between her displaced self and the marble statues of what the song suggests was her former home. It is not clear whether the marble statues are remnants or imitations of classical antiquity.

The third stanza includes more worrisome or even fear-inducing images: the cloudy mountain path on which the mule tries to find its way; the caves with their brood of dragons; and the sheer cliff attacked by the ocean. To construe the mountain scenery as part of the route over the Alps that leads back to Italy seems to me far too literal an explanation of this stanza. What happens, rather, is that the paradise imagery is gradually eroded as the poem proceeds: the marble statues look with disapproval on the erosion of tradition in the present day, and the treacherous cliffside setting near which the house is situated suggests that paradise is never truly free from danger. The genitive phrase "der Drachen alte Brut" is more likely to be a reformulation of *et in arcadia ego* (where the speaker is Death). Seen from this perspective, the poem not only expresses regret for a lost paradise, but also suggests that the seeds of Mignon's current distress were already present in the seeming idyll of the home the song recalls so nostalgically.

Reminiscences of antiquity are present in the form of the gleaming house with its columns and the marble statues; but these are most likely filtered through the sixteenth-century architect Andrea Palladio, whose work, especially his Villa Rotonda, Goethe saw and admired during his Italian journey (1786–1788). Classical antiquity is a dominant presence, by contrast, in Goethe's *Römische Elegien* (Roman Elegies; 1795). Most anthologies of German poetry include the fifth elegy, which has come to be the best known of the series (I use the traditional numbering, although scholars now include two priapic poems that frame the sequence as it was originally published, thus changing the familiar number system). Unlike Mignon's song, which looks with nostalgic longing at a place no longer present, Goethe's fifth Roman elegy opens with a reference to time and place:

> Froh empfind ich mich nun auf klassischem Boden begeistert;
> Vor- und Mitwelt spricht lauter und reizender mir.
> Hier befolg' ich den Rat, durchblättre die Werke der Alten
> Mit geschäftiger Hand, täglich mit neuem Genuß.

> (Now, on classical soil, I feel happy and inspired; past and present speak to me more clearly and more delightfully. Here I do as advised and leaf through the works of the ancients with an industrious hand and with new enjoyment every day.)

Despite the reference to "classical soil," Goethe did not write these lines during his stay in Rome: rather, he wrote them retrospectively, after his return to Weimar. As long as we understand that poetry is not necessarily written on the spot, this distinction matters little – though the speaker does suggest, humorously, that attempts to encapsulate the erotic in proper meter may even begin during the aftermath of love-making:

> Oftmals hab' ich auch schon in ihren Armen gedichtet,
> Und des Hexameters Maß leise mit fingernder Hand
> Ihr auf dem Rücken gezählt. Sie atmet in lieblichem Schlummer,
> Und es durchglühet ihr Hauch mir bis ins Tiefste die Brust.

> (Often I started composing verse while in her arms, and counted the hexameter's measure softly with my fingers on her back. She breathes in beautiful slumber, and her breath glows through me into the depths of my bosom.)

If, as the poem suggests, imagination is the key to appropriating and actualizing the classical tradition, this is so in a double sense that applies both to the speaker's experiences in Rome and his attempt to conjure them up in verse. The poem traces the way in which the classical "triumvirate" – the elegiac poets Catullus, Tibullus, and Propertius – provides a model that animates both the sexual encounter and its poetic expression.

In reconnecting with the tradition of the Latin love elegy, Goethe decided to construct his *Römische Elegien* using series of classical distichs (sets of two lines) in the manner of the three late Roman poets he had been reading so attentively. Appropriating the form in German verse is at once a way of measuring and bridging the distance between "then" and "now," as well as between book-learning and practice. As Goethe knew from reading other poets who had experimented with recreating classical meters in the German language, the task was not altogether easy. Each distich consisted of a hexameter line followed by a pentameter line; but these lines are not what we understand in English by "hexameter" and "pentameter." This was because the length-based meters of classical Greek and Latin did not mesh easily with the stress-based word- and sentence-rhythms of German. The classical hexameter had six feet, but not six stresses. By the same token, the classical pentameter had five feet, but not five stresses; an added complexity is that the five feet are arranged in two sets of two and a half. (For more on this topic, see the appendix on metrics.) Recreating verse forms from ancient Greek and Latin in German was a challenge that forced both writer and reader to retune their ears, as it were. For example, if each "long" syllable in the ancient languages had to become a stressed syllable in German, would it be possible to write a spondee? In German, the closest one can come is usually a combination of a primary and a secondary stress. Some German poets proposed that a trochee might also be used to substitute for a spondee. Heated debates broke out about this issue. Some proponents of the trochee permitted it in the first foot of a line, but not, in general, elsewhere. In Goethe's fifth Roman elegy, almost all of the hexameter lines begin with a trochee. An intriguing example is the passage cited above, in which the speaker describes how he taps out prospective verses on the back of his sleeping beloved:

> Ōftmāls| hāb ĭch ăŭch| schōn ĭn| īhrĕn| Ārmĕn gĕ|dīchtĕt,
>   Ūnd dĕs Hĕ|xāmĕtĕrs| Māß|| lēĭsĕ mĭt| fĭngĕrndĕr| Hānd

As indicated by the scansion above, the first foot of the hexameter line can be understood as a spondee (in terms of stress, one would read "óftmàls," to approximate the classical spondee; normally, of course, the word is trochaic: "óftmals"). The third and fourth feet of this line, which in Latin could consist of either a spondee or a dactyl, substitute a trochee that begs to be read as a sort of virtual spondee. But the pentameter line – in which, by an amusing chiasmus, or criss-cross structure, the "Hexameter" is mentioned – is a perfect example of the form. Indeed, Goethe has already used the caesura of the pentameter several times in this poem to illustrate the duality of perception, mental and physical, that underlies the elegy: "Mit geschäftiger Hand, täglich mit neuem Genuß" (l. 4); "Werd ich auch halb nur gelehrt, bin ich doch doppelt beglückt" (l. 6); "Sehe mit fühlendem Aug, fühle mit sehender Hand" (l. 10).

The ease with which Goethe adapts the classical distich throughout the poem testifies both to the inspiration of the beloved, whose breath "durchglühet" his breast, and to the attending presence of the ancient god of love, Amor, whose name, as many commentators have noted, is an anagram of "Roma," the city whose recollection animates the entire poetic sequence. Revivifying the ancient meter is not unlike perceiving marble statues as the sculptural records of once-living bodies, a discovery the speaker wittily uses to justify his interest in tracing with his hand the form of his lover's body (lines 7–8). The poem comes full circle as Amor, thinking of how he had performed this same service for the three Latin elegists, trims the lamp in the final lines. The appearance of the ancient deity in modern Rome – and by extension in the modern world more generally – reunifies sensory and intellectual experience in a way the speaker has not previously known.

When Goethe decided to give his poem-sequence the title "Römische Elegien" (his original manuscript used the title "Erotica Romana"), he was primarily alluding to his Latin precursors, who also employed elegiac distichs as a vehicle for love poetry. Despite the poems' awareness of differences between antiquity and the present, they ultimately proclaim connections that bridge the time gap; thus, the poems are not elegies in the English sense of the word. As German poets appropriated classical meters with increasing fluency, they continued to use them for a fairly wide range of material. Nonetheless, there are some German poems from this period that do use elegiacs to express sorrow or mourning. Schiller's 200-line elegy "Der Spaziergang" (The Walk; 1775) is one of the best examples. In this text, the speaker uses a walk up a mountain as an occasion to reflect on the difference between ancient and modern poetry, a topic Schiller simultaneously explored in his theoretical treatise, "Über naïve und sentimentalische Dichtung" (On Naïve and Sentimental Poetry; 1795/96). The key words in this title have special meanings: "naïv," which he applies to ancient poets, means in direct contact with nature, whereas "sentimentalisch," the category he links with modern writers, means separated from nature and desiring to return to it. "Sentimentalisch" (which is not the same as "senti-mental," a word that also exists in German), is not a pejorative word: rather, the modern writer has a heightened awareness of his distance from his classical precursors and is thus in a position to reflect on the reasons why he cannot simply return to their seemingly more straightforward relationship to the natural world. The speaker of "Der Spaziergang" models this development in a hike that takes him to the outskirts of town and from there into the woodland, where the path begins to mount. As the walker moves through different sorts of vegetation characteristic of their position on the mountainside, he recalls stages in the cultural development of man that seem to find an equivalent in the changing natural surroundings. As he nears the summit, he feels lost and alone; the landscape becomes wild and arid, and he longs for the embrace of the comforting natural landscape he enjoyed lower down. Finally, however, he reaches the peak and realizes that his experience of loss was only a terrifying illusion; in reality, nothing fundamental has changed:

> Immer dieselbe, bewahrst du [= die Natur] in treuen Händen dem
> *Manne,*
>   Was dir das gaukelnde Kind, was dir der Jüngling vertraut,
> Nährest an gleicher Brust die vielfach wechselnden Alter:
>   Unter demselben Blau, über dem nämlichen Grün
> Wandeln die nahen und wandeln vereint die fernen Geschlechter,
>   Und die Sonne Homers, siehe! sie lächelt auch uns.

> (Always the same, you [= nature] retain for the adult man what the
> dandling child and the youth confided to you, you nourish at the same
> breast the multiply changing ages: beneath the same blue, above the
> same green the nearer and the more distant generations walk united,
> and Homer's sun, behold! smiles for us too.)

Thus, while the poem registers and reflects on the losses that come with the passing of time, it also adheres to the traditional scheme of elegy in which loss is made up for by a final consolation.

Schiller's "Nänie" (Dirge; 1799) follows a similar trajectory. This poem, also in elegiac distichs, begins by mourning the fact that beauty must inevitably pass away ("Auch das Schöne muß sterben!"; even the beautiful must die) but ultimately arrives at a more comforting view of this necessity. The title "Nänie" comes from the Latin *naenia*, a lament sung to accompany a funeral procession. The poem's argument is shaped by reference to three moments in ancient mythology when a beautiful person was unable to escape death: first, Eurydice, who nearly became an exception to the iron rule of nature when Orpheus' song softened the heart of Pluto, god of the underworld; second, Adonis, the beautiful youth who could not be saved from death by Aphrodite; and third, Achilles, whose heroic death in battle could not be undone by the plaints of Thetis and the nereids. Although the text provides sufficient information for the reader to identify these mythic references, it also discreetly refrains from mentioning the names of Eurydice, Adonis, and Achilles. As one scholar points out, the poem is moving, after all, toward a conclusion that will elevate the art of mourning poetry as one that remembers those important to cultural tradition: if these figures need to be named, it would be hard to claim that they are permanently etched in cultural memory. The final lines of "Nänie," like those of "Der Spaziergang," thus provide a consolation: in this case, the idea that commemoration in poetry is a splendid thing in its own right, and more than happens to lesser people ("denn das Gemeine geht klanglos zum Orkus hinab"; for what is common goes down to Orcus [= the underworld] unsung). The poem thus reflects on the value of elegy itself ("Klaglied"; lament, l. 13, is another variant of "Nänie") as a medium for preserving beauty in spite of its inevitable passing away. In this respect, it serves as an example of Schiller's argument in "Über naïve und sentimentalische Dichtung" that elegy is particularly appropriate for the kind of poetry he terms "sentimentalisch." Whereas Goethe's "Römische Elegien" aim to revivify classical antiquity by bringing it into the modern world, Schiller's "Nänie," which mentions only ancient examples, has a more epigonal aspect in that it looks back to the past without revivifying the present. Nonetheless, it continues to hold out hope for elegiac poetry as a way of saving the aesthetic.

Classical distichs (or the classical hexameter alone) were not the only vehicle used at this time to hark back to antiquity. Hölderlin's "Heidelberg" (1800), to name just one example, uses a meter derived from ancient Greek odes. Klopstock had already introduced these meters, along with a proliferation of variants of his own invention. Influenced by Klopstock but also drawing directly on his own knowledge of ancient Greek poetry, Hölderlin favored two types of ode strophes: the alcaic and the asclepiadeic; he also wrote one ode in the Sapphic form (see appendix on metrics). Although his poem "Heidelberg" happens to be addressed to the town of that name, a German classical ode does not have to address anything or anyone: what makes it an ode is its use of a Greek ode strophe. Here is a scanned version of the opening stanza:

> Lāngĕ | līeb ĭch dĭch | schōn,‖ mŏchtĕ dĭch,| mīr zŭr | Lūst,
>   Mūttĕr | nēnnĕn, ŭnd | dīr ‖ schēnkĕn eĭn | kūnstlŏs | Līed,
>   Dū, dĕr | Vātĕrlănds|stădtĕ
>   Lăndlĭch|schŏnstĕ, sŏ | vīel ĭch | sāh.

As in the case of the elegiac meters derived from classical antiquity, these marks when used to scan German verse are not indications of vowel lengths (though in the ancient languages, they did indicate syllable length): in German, stressed syllables stand in for the original long syllables wherever practicable. When most of the syllables that were long in the ancient languages are stressed in German, it is a sign of special mastery of this form.

Let us now consider the first two stanzas together:

> Lange lieb ich dich schon, möchte dich, mir zur Lust,
>   Mutter nennen, und dir schenken ein kunstlos Lied,
>   Du, der Vaterlandsstädte
>   Ländlichschönste, so viel ich sah.
>
> Wie der Vogel des Walds über die Gipfel fliegt,
>   Schwingt sich über den Strom, wo er vorbei dir glänzt,
>   Leicht und kräftig die Brücke,
>   Die von Wagen und Menschen tönt.

(I have loved you for a long time, and would like, for my own pleasure to call you mother, and give you an artless song, you, the most country-beautiful town of all I have seen in our fatherland.// As the bird of the forest flies over the mountaintops, so the bridge, light and strong, resounding with carts and people, swings over the river as it shines its way past you.)

The poem's opening stanza establishes a connection between its speaker and the city that is at once aesthetic and psychological. With the neologism "ländlichschön," he evokes in a single rhetorical stroke the beauty of Heidelberg, a city nestled in a landscape that resembles the countryside more than it does an urban environment. In calling it the most beautiful of all the cities he has seen in his native land, he also links Heidelberg through comparison with a larger geography. In keeping with its countrified beauty, he offers the city "ein kunstlos Lied" (an artless song). This is an astonishing claim to make in a poem written in asclepiadeic strophes. Obviously, artistry is at the very heart of this type of poem: it would be difficult just to toss off an asclepiadeic ode in a moment of inspiration. Yet Hölderlin's extraordinary handling of this challenging form almost persuades us that, through artistry, he has achieved a kind of artlessness.

To grasp the imagery of the second stanza, it helps to have seen a picture of Heidelberg with its famous bridge across the river Neckar. In subsequent stanzas, the ode also refers to the partially ruined castle that stands on the steep mountain slopes overlooking the city. For the speaker, the bridge is not static, but in motion. The bird in the simile of stanza 2, the river itself, and the traffic over the bridge are all moving, and the bridge connects the two sides of the river with graceful arches that almost appear to be moving as well. In reality, of course, it is the speaker's eye – or perhaps his mind's eye – that executes this movement. Yet precisely at the moment when architecture seems to fly, the speaker recalls a time when he was brought to a standstill by some inexplicable power:

> Wie von Göttern gesandt, fesselt' ein Zauber einst
>   Auf die Brücke mich an, da ich vorüber ging
>   Und herein in die Berge
>   Mir die reizende Ferne schien
>
> Und der Jüngling, der Strom, fort in die Ebne zog,
>   Traurigfroh, wie das Herz, wenn es, sich selbst zu schön,
>   Liebend unterzugehen,
>   In die Fluten der Zeit sich wirft.
>
> Quellen hattest du ihm, hattest dem Flüchtigen
>   Kühle Schatten geschenkt, und die Gestade sahn
>   All' ihm nach, und es bebte
>   Aus den Wellen ihr lieblich Bild.

(As if sent by gods, a magic spell once held me fast on the bridge as I was crossing it, and charming distance appeared to me from deep in the mountains,// and the youth, the river, traveled far into the plain, sadly happy like the heart when, thinking itself too beautiful to perish from love, it casts itself into the floods of time.// You had given him springs, had given the fleeting one cooling shadows, and the banks all followed him with their gaze, and their lovely image trembled up from the waves.)

The word "Zauber" indicates a phenomenon that Hölderlin sometimes called the eternal moment: an experience of insight when time seems to stand still. In keeping with his use of the Greek ode form, Hölderlin evokes plural gods, as if they too continued to exist in the present. Indeed, the strange optical experience he describes here in which his eye seems to penetrate deep into the mountain while at the same time distance seems to come forward to meet him ("schien" means both "appeared" and "showed itself, or shone forth"), is for him a sign that the divine still inhabits this landscape. Unlike the first two stanzas of the ode, these two are not separated syntactically: instead, the sentence continues sinuously throughout both stanzas. The motif of connection and motion also continues in both the choice of verbs ("vorüberging," "zog," "unterzugehn," "wirft") and dative pronouns of reference ("mir," "sich selbst"). Yet the power of this magical moment is also linked with sadness and even – if only in a simile – self-destruction. These images do not indicate suicidal wishes in the ordinary sense of the word, but rather, they point to the fact that, in becoming one with this beautiful scene, the viewer must temporarily give up his or her individuality. This explains, in part, why the speaker recovers so rapidly from the tug of the river away from the bridge and re-establishes the connectedness of the scene as a whole in the fifth stanza of the ode. Here, the mountain sources from which the river has emerged and the cool shade of the wooded slopes through which the river runs as it passes through Heidelberg contribute to the sense that nature is an interlocking whole. Just as the river itself had been personified as a "youth" in stanza 3, now its banks are personified as their gaze follows the moving river as it moves away from them. The imminent loss represented by their wistful gaze is balanced, however, by the image they see of themselves in the water. Unlike the "Herz" of stanza 4, which might have succumbed to its own Narcissus-like image had it not decided to plunge on with the forward movement of time, the mirror image of the river banks is "lieblich" rather than self-destructive. But the poem does not end with this self-reflective beauty.

> Aber schwer in das Tal hing die gigantische,
>   Schicksalskundige Burg nieder bis auf den Grund,
>   Von den Wettern zerrissen;
>   Doch die ewige Sonne goß
>
> Ihr verjüngendes Licht über das alternde
>   Riesenbild, und umher grünte lebendiger
>   Efeu; freundliche Wälder
>   Rauschten über die Burg herab.
>
> Sträuche blühten herab, bis wo im heitern Tal,
>   an den Hügel gelehnt oder dem Ufer hold,
>   Deine fröhlichen Gassen
>   Unter duftenden Gärten ruhn.

(But the gigantic castle, fatefully knowing, hung heavily right down to the bottom of the valley, ravaged by storms; yet the eternal sun poured// its rejuvenating light over the giant, aging figure, and all around living ivy displayed its green color; welcoming woods rustled down over the mountain.// Bushes bloomed upward to where, in the pleasant valley, leaning against the hill or sweetly disposed to the bank, your happy streets rest among sweet-scented gardens.)

These final stanzas intensify the paradoxical movement that unifies nature and man-made structures. On the one hand, the lowering castle ruin seems to portend some dreadful fate, but on the other, it is drenched in sunlight and rejuvenated by green vines and pleasant trees. Apparent downward motion, like that of the hulking castle as it dominates the deep valley, is balanced by upward motion like that of the growing vegetation. By the same token, the threatening aspect of the castle is counteracted by the happy streets of the city. Adverbs of direction such as "nieder" and "herab" (twice) contrast with the last word of the ode, "ruhn." Objects like the castle ruin and the city streets, as well as growing things like ivy, bushes, woods, and gardens, hover in a strange state of semi-animation. Adjectives like "lebendig," "freundlich," "heiter," and "fröhlich" contribute to this effect. For the reader, progress through the poem has been an intricate movement through space, time, and the emotions. A description of a beautiful town set in lovely country has turned into a journey into human and natural history, but also a complex demonstration of vision in both the optical and poetic sense.

Hölderlin's much-anthologized "Hälfte des Lebens" (Halfway Through Life; 1805) steps away from this complex interconnectedness to give voice to a more profound sense of fracture:

> Mit gelben Birnen hänget
> Und voll mit wilden Rosen
> Das Land in den See,
> Ihr holden Schwäne,
> Und trunken von Küssen
> Tunkt ihr das Haupt
> Ins heilignüchterne Wasser.
>
> Weh mir, wo nehm ich, wenn
> Es Winter ist, die Blumen, und wo
> Den Sonnenschein,
> Und Schatten der Erde ?
> Die Mauern stehn
> Sprachlos und kalt, im Winde
> Klirren die Fahnen.

> (With yellow pears and full with wild roses, the land hangs into the lake, you lovely swans, and drunk with kisses you dip your heads into the sacred-sober water.// Alas, where shall I take, when winter comes, the flowers and where the sunshine and shadow of earth? The walls stand mute and cold, in the wind the weather-vanes clatter.)

Although Hölderlin wrote many poems in classical meters, this one bears only traces – recollections, one might say – of them, notably in the dactyls that break through increasingly as the poem proceeds. And unlike his odes, which take shape dialectically, "Hälfte des Lebens" contains no synthesis or sublation (to use Hegel's term) of the positive and negative images presented in its two stanzas. Yet it would be simplistic to regard the description of late summer, represented by the pears and the wild roses of stanza 1, and the prospective vision of winter, specifically named in stanza 2, as an unalloyed opposition. The fullness of the late-summer scene makes land and water appear as part of a single unity in which the fruit and flowers hang over the lake while the swans drift on the surface of the water but also dip their heads down into it. At the same time, however, this unified vision is also interrupted by the exclamatory address to the swans ("ihr holden Schwäne"; you lovely swans) that bursts forth within a fluid sentence otherwise structured mainly by enjambments. Significantly, the apostrophe breaks into the stanza at its mid-point, line 4, turning what had been a description into an address to the swans. The compound adjective "heilignüchtern" in line 7 tempers the imagery of excess that dominates the first three lines and prepares for the sobering thoughts that open the second stanza. For Hölderlin and his contemporaries, this adjective, while innovative in terms of the German language, also alluded to an idea from classical antiquity, the concept of *sobria ebrietas* (sober drunkenness). Even the mention of swans suggested to the classically educated reader of the time the topos of the poet as swan.

The second stanza shifts to a vision of winter where flowers no longer bloom and nature is largely supplanted by man-made objects such as the wall and the weather-vanes. The wall is described as "sprachlos und kalt," and the sound made by the weather-vanes is nothing but a metallic clattering. Not only is human language lacking in this scene, but poetic language is especially endangered. As in the first stanza, the reader familiar with classical antiquity would understand the search for flowers as also a search for poetic metaphors. In contrast to the late-summer scene of the first stanza, the winter scene of stanza 2 expresses despair about whether poetry can now be written at all. In this sense, the poem articulates a sense of belatedness that longs to restore the rich possibilities of antiquity but regards the modern world as tragically broken. Like Goethe's "Im Herbst 1775," Hölderlin's "Hälfte des Lebens" is a poem in what was thought at the time to be the Pindaric mode. Both poems reflect on the nature of poetic creativity and its necessary preconditions, but for Hölderlin the rupture between tradition and the present day is one that may perhaps not be healed even by poetry.

If distance from classical antiquity was a central problem for poets of the period around 1800, the Goethezeit itself became a kind of lost ideal for many later poets. It would much exceed the limits of this chapter to trace the entire history of this issue. Instead, a poem by Rolf Dieter Brinkmann from 1975 might serve as an apposite coda to the story of tradition and originality. Its title is also part of the poem:

Einen jener klassischen

schwarzen Tangos in Köln, Ende des
Monats August, da der Sommer schon

ganz verstaubt ist, kurz nach Laden
Schluß aus der offenen Tür einer

dunklen Wirtschaft, die einem
Griechen gehört, hören, ist beinahe

ein Wunder: für einen Moment eine
Überraschung, für einen Moment

Aufatmen, für einen Moment
eine Pause in dieser Straße,

die niemand liebt und atemlos
macht, beim Hindurchgehen. Ich

schrieb das schnell auf, bevor
der Moment in der verfluchten

dunstigen Abgestorbenheit Kölns
wieder erlosch.

(One of those classical// black tangos in Cologne, at the end of the
month of August, when the summer is already// quite dusty, shortly
after closing time from the open door of a// dark restaurant that belongs
to a Greek, to hear it is almost// a miracle, for a moment a surprise// to
draw breath, for a moment a pause in this street// that nobody likes and
that makes one breathless, just to pass through it. I// wrote that down
quickly before the moment in the damned// hazy deadness of Cologne
died out again.)

The clever arrangement by which the title also becomes the poem's first
line – the opposite of the more familiar process where the first line is used
to refer to an untitled poem – serves to open the poem with an element of
surprise. The rhetoric used in the title is itself classical in its gesture toward
"one of those things" that is thoroughly familiar; and yet we rapidly discover
that the referent is not anything we might have expected. All we know from
the word "einen" is that the noun will be masculine: it will not be "Gedichte,"
"Elegien," or "Lieder." Still, we are surprised to discover that the classical
item is a "black tango." We assume that the music is coming from a radio
or record player. Suddenly the term "classical" takes on a different meaning.

Tango is believed to have originated with the African people who were taken to Argentina as slaves, and "black tango" is the term used to describe those forms in which the African element appears strongly and distinctively. The brief hesitation at the end of the first line might be seen as recalling, in a very general way, the movement of tango, with its syncopated music and combination of slinky dance steps and sudden stops and starts. When tango is most sharply syncopated, it is known as "hesitation tango." The enjambments of this free verse poem, often placed at critical junctures, imitate this aspect of the dance and its music. For example, the compound word "Ladenschluß" is divided into two, emphasizing the shift from workday to leisure time. In subsequent lines, the text both refers to and echoes the hesitating rhythms of the tango: the words "Überraschung," "Aufatmen" and "Pause" are each connected with the thrice-repeated "Moment" to suggest the brief rests and shifts in the emphasis of the music and dance. Throughout this passage, enjambments continue to mimic the syncopated rhythms. These effects increase the remove from the predictability of classical meters.

Yet a distinctly "classical" idea does arise around the middle of the poem, precisely in the word "Moment." This word recalls the aesthetics of German Classicism and Romanticism, where an epiphanic or privileged moment stands in for a heightened form of insight that cannot be expressed in words. Hölderlin calls this experience the "ewiger Augenblick" or eternal moment; and Goethe's Faust makes his wager on whether or not he will wish to make the fleeting "Augenblick" last longer. Such moments exist in the interstices of poetic artic- ulation, not in the flow of words. By definition, they are elusive: they arrive unbidden and vanish swiftly away. The final lines of Brinkmann's poem reg- ister this brevity in an image of the special moment as a light that is quickly swallowed up by the steamy, dusty atmosphere of the city. The moment creates "eine Pause in dieser Straße." The brevity of the final line leaves the reader with the sense that something is missing. The absent second part of the line is another "pause" in the rhythm of music, city, and poem.

What the speaker experiences in this moment is not, however, identical with the traditional epiphany: he is careful to modify the word "Wunder" by the adverb "beinah." In case the reader might think of the poem as prose cut up to look like verse, "Einen jener klassischen" quickly dispels this delusion. The enjambments of lines 1–3 all emphasize time: "Ende des/ Monats August," "der Sommer schon/ganz verstaubt ist," and "kurz nach Laden/ Schluß." As the surprising tango music is heard, the lines seem to hesitate, hover, and hold time in suspension.

In the final lines of the poem, which constitute its second sentence, the focus shifts to the speaker, who now refers to himself in the first person. Standing alone at the end of line 12, the pronoun "Ich" acquires more stress than it might otherwise have had, so that in effect the speaker contrasts himself with both the Greek man who owns the restaurant and people from fancier districts who disparage this area. By means of this triangulation, the poem comments on multicultural German society of the 1970s, in which a Greek resident unsurprisingly works in a run-down part of town. Both the Greek restaurant owner and the tango music come from elsewhere; but the speaker, whose recognition of the melody as a "classic black tango" marks him in his own mind as culturally sophisticated, is German and presumably lives in Cologne. Is he not perhaps also a little biased in his surprise at hearing the music in this unfashionable location?

This "Ich" is also part of the classical tradition. Like Goethe's lover tapping out classical meters on the back of a sleeping woman, the speaker of Brinkmann's poem jots down his impression of the special moment while it is happening. This gesture suggests a certain spontaneity or immediacy. Yet the poem's last word – in a strikingly amputated line – is the verb that alludes to the extinguishing of the moment's brilliance, "erlosch." The shift to the past tense in the last four lines is a recognition that the momentary experience cannot last.

Finally, we should not pass over the temporal setting of the poem, in the dusty month of August when the summer is almost over and many of those who live in Cologne have gone away on vacation. The life expressed in the tango music is at odds with the "Abgestorbenheit" of the city, a deadness that distresses the speaker of the poem. The main part of the poem is all but tenseless: the description of the tango music coming from the Greek restaurant is dependent on an infinitive, "hören." In particular, the phrases following the colon lack verbs entirely, appropriately for the evocation of a miracle that seems to stop the flow of time. The one present tense verb occurs in the clause that identifies the experience as "beinah/ ein Wunder." At the end of the poem, the verbs shift to the past tense as if to mark the end of the magical moment. The more closely we look at Brinkmann's poem and the art with which it is structured, the more we begin to understand why it appears in anthologies: it is one of those classical ones – a classic for the late twentieth century.

Chapter 6

Romantic poetry and the problem of lyric unity

For many readers, German Romantic poetry is the very essence of lyric expression. This is not only due to the Romantics' own conception of poetry as song, but also to the fact that a large number of Romantic poems were in fact set to music in the course of the nineteenth century. The lyric, in this conception, was a mode of expression that turned fleeting images into a luminous whole. It created a unity between self and world that might last only for a moment, but suggested nonetheless a deeper harmony between subjective and objective reality, past and present. From this perspective, it might appear that a lyric poem can be read as an isolated text without special reference to the context in which it originated. Yet although many Romantic poems lend themselves well to this approach, it does not fully accord with the German Romantics' own poetic practice and the conceptions of poetry that this implies. Often, the Romantics highlighted the problematic aspect of unified form, sometimes to the point of undermining the notion altogether. For this reason, we need to approach this poetry with care, looking for networks of images that help a poem to cohere while at the same time noting moments in the text that put its unity into question.

German Romantic poetry often seems familiar, and thus readily accessible, because many of its stock ideas and motifs have become common coinage, not only in German literature but also – via Coleridge and his contemporaries – in English literature. Many are known in song versions. Love and longing, nature, solitude, and premonitions of death are part of this inventory. Nature, in its German Romantic guise, includes the forest, wind in the trees, the singing of birds, the running brook, and frequently the water mill. The verb *rauschen* means both rushing (as of water) and rustling (as of leaves in the wind); in these acoustic phenomena the Romantics recognized the inchoate voice of nature. Birdsong was the natural model to which poetry aspired. The Romantic poets used these nature motifs in ever-varying combinations to evoke solitude, memory, loss, and lyric expression.

A quintessential German Romantic poem, Clemens Brentano's "Hör, es klagt die Flöte wieder" (Listen, the flute laments once more; 1803), reworks the prototypical soundscape. The rushing water of the brook has been replaced by the sound of a flowing fountain, and birdsong is transposed into the sound of a flute:

> Hör, es klagt die Flöte wieder,
> Und die kühlen Brunnen rauschen.
> Golden wehn die Töne nieder,
> Stille, stille, laß uns lauschen!
>
> Holdes Bitten, mild Verlangen,
> Wie es süß zum Herzen spricht!
> Durch die Nacht, die mich umfangen,
> Blickt zu mir der Töne Licht.
>
> (Listen, the flute laments once more, and the cool fountains gush. Musical tones drift down, golden; hush, hush, let us listen!// Gracious entreaty, gentle desire, how sweetly it speaks to the heart! Through the night that embraces me, the tones' light glances toward me.)

The first stanza evokes an act of listening that becomes, in the second stanza, a merging of listener with sounds heard, and of self with nature. The plaint of the instrument in the opening line suggests the notion of loss, and the first line of stanza 2 joins longing with an unspecified desire. At the end of the poem, the sounds created by human beings transform themselves into the tones of nature itself. To be sure, there is an odd slippage from a plural pronoun ("uns") in the first stanza to the singular pronouns "mich" and "mir" in the second. Originally, the poem was to have been a duet in which lovers, a man and a woman, each sang a pair of lines in turn. Brentano had written it for a *Singspiel* (a form of simplified opera). Compensating for the shift to singular pronouns, the last two lines of the poem intensify the sense of union between nature and the speaking subject ("die Nacht, die mich umfangen"). The synaesthetic formulation "der Töne Licht" (note the genitive construction) situated at the end of the poem's final line pulls together the idea that subject and object are inextricably linked. Poetic unity reflects a deeper unity of self and nature.

A short poem by Joseph von Eichendorff develops a similar set of imagery. The poem began its life as a song in Eichendorff's novella *Aus dem Leben eines Taugenichts*, where it is sung twice. Later, when Eichendorff collected his poems into a single volume (1837), he gave this text the title "Abend" (Evening):

> Schweigt der Menschen laute Lust:
> Rauscht die Erde wie in Träumen
> Wunderbar mit allen Bäumen,
> Was dem Herzen kaum bewußt,

> Alte Zeiten, linde Trauer,
> Und es schweifen leise Schauer
> Wetterleuchtend durch die Brust.

(The loud rejoicing of human beings falls silent: the earth rustles wondrously with all its trees as if in dream [see my discussion below for another way of reading these opening lines]; what the heart is scarcely conscious of – olden times, gentle sorrow; and soft tremors shoot like lightning through one's breast.)

This is one of many poems in the Romantic canon that evokes a transitional moment: in this case, the moment when the noise of the day subsides and sociable life gives way to solitary dreaming. What dreams here, however, is nature itself, whose almost imperceptible noises – expressed by the Romantics' favorite verb "rauschen" – evoke and even instigate a special state of mind in the listener. Nature at evening creates an ambience that at once gives access to emotions that lie just below the surface of consciousness and summons up memories of earlier times that are recalled with sorrow because they are long past. This state of mind is pleasurable, but it also contains a premonition of something troubling or even preternatural, as the final lines of the poem indicate. The unifying reading is thus already one that understands the poem as one that carries a negative undercurrent along with its more positive assertion about the wondrous quality of this moment. The reference to subconscious emotion is placed at the very center of the poem, creating a significant symmetry.

Some moments in the poem, however, do not yield themselves so easily to paraphrase. The unusual word "wetterleuchtend" is one of these. Another is the inversion of the opening line ("Schweigt der Menschen laute Lust"), and another again is the conjunction "und" in the second last line that seems to link with undue ease two parts of the poem that are not entirely consonant. The poem's stock motifs and familiar Romantic scenario are undercut by rifts and inconsistencies.

"Wetterleuchten" describes the way lightning flashes from such a distance that we cannot actually hear the thunder that follows (see Wahrig's dictionary). In Eichendorff's poem, the verb represents a premonition that is not supported by any empirical experience – in this case, the sense of foreboding that accompanies the experience of nature as the light in the sky fades and gives way to images from memory and imagination. The "leise Schauer" felt by the subject are not located in the mental realm, however. Instead, these tremors pass through the human breast and thus by metonymy through the heart (line 7). They are sensations that can be felt, but not fully articulated. The "leise Schauer" thus evoke a central ambition of German Romanticism: to probe the realm of memory and emotion that lies beyond formulation in ordinary language. The Romantic poets believed that poetry could penetrate this realm in ways that other forms of speech and writing could not.

Looking back at the opening of the poem, with its inversion of verb and subject in the first and second lines, we can draw further conclusions about the way in which the world outside the self is represented in this poem. There are two ways of reading these lines. First, they can be understood as constructions using the dummy subject "es," in which case they could be expanded as: "Es schweigt der Menschen laute Lust; es rauscht die Erde wie in Träumen." Second, we could read them as if they consisted of an if- or a when-clause preceding a main clause that follows from this premise, in which case they could be expanded as: "Wenn die laute Lust der Menschen schweigt, dann rauscht die Erde wie in Träumen." It is not at all clear which version gives a better meaning, or if we should even attempt to choose between the two alternatives. Eichendorff, a master of poetic ambiguity, often uses this type of construction.

Finally, we must attend to the word "und" that opens the second-last line and thus introduces the final sentiment of the poem. The conjunction "and" usually links two things that belong together in some way. We can understand how "Trauer" might give rise to dark premonitions. But the mildness of this sorrow ("linde Trauer") is surely not likely to make one tremble. The rhyme between "Trauer" and "Schauer," which suggests that these feelings somehow go together, is supported by the linking word "und" – and yet the two emotions are really quite different in kind. Furthermore, the poem seems to pivot unexpectedly from an experience of nature in its most magical form (indicated by the word "wunderbar" – another favorite of the Romantic poets) to an experience that is not entirely pleasant. There is no grammatical preparation for this shift in mood – no "but," "yet," or "however" – and so we are taken by surprise as we reach the end of the poem.

What are we to make of this? We have a poem that seems, on one level, to flow fairly smoothly and, on another level, to take an unexpected twist. This is in fact one of the characteristic features of German Romantic poetry. In many ways, one might say that this two-level aspect of the poem lies at the very heart of the Romantic conception of consciousness, the human relationship to nature, and poetry as such. By letting the two levels slide uneasily across each other like tectonic plates, the Romantic poet indicates a problematic aspect of its principal subject-matter: the inadequacy of language, even at its most fluent, to articulate what lies beneath the surface of empirical perception and rational exposition.

"The Romantic is itself a translation," says a character in Clemens Brentano's eccentric and all-but-forgotten Romantic novel *Godwi*. For the modern reader, this statement seems counter-intuitive because we think of poetry as the direct expression of individual subjectivity and personal experience. For the Romantics, poetry seemed to emanate from some realm of knowledge that cannot be expressed in ordinary language. Poetry was the vehicle not only for reaching into the sphere of pre-consciousness, but also for transforming what the Romantics understood as the dumb language of nature into human speech.

Joseph von Eichendorff's poem "Wünschelrute" (Divining Rod; 1835) is one of the most compact and compelling articulations of this view:

> Schläft ein Lied in allen Dingen
> Die da träumen fort und fort,
> Und die Welt hebt an zu singen,
> Triffst du nur das Zauberwort.

> (A song slumbers in all things that dream on and on, and the world begins to sing if you find the magic word.)

Underlying this poem is the notion that nature contains its own innate music and that human beings can bring this music to life (make "the world begin to sing") if only they find the magic word that will unlock it. For the German Romantics, the rustling of leaves, the rippling of water, the singing of birds and the entire panoply of sounds that can be heard in a natural setting were what Friedrich Schlegel called "formless, unconscious poetry." The poet was the one who could hear the secret song of nature and translate it into human language. This is why the "things" in Eichendorff's poem are not presented as inanimate, but as dreaming: the secret song of nature is cognate with both the unconscious and the imagination. The address of the poem's final line to a "du" is at once a form of self-address on the part of the speaker and an address to the reader, who is seen as equally capable of finding the "magic word." Here the poem adopts a view most explicitly articulated by Novalis, who believed that everyone was, potentially, a poet. Eichendorff's "Wünschelrute" moves freely across the border between naïve and sophisticated use of language by employing the rhymed four-line stanza familiar from folk ballads while at the same time employing an artful inversion of verb and subject in the opening line and an implied if-clause in the final line. The poem itself enacts the "translation" from the language of sleeping nature to the language of lyric poetry. Its brevity makes it easily memorable, yet it probes the very heart of the relationship between conscious and unconscious, object and subject, nature and art.

One offshoot of this expanded notion of translation was the Romantic generation's interest in folk songs and tales. Achim von Arnim and Clemens Brentano published their collection of songs *Des Knaben Wunderhorn* in 1806 and 1808, and Wilhelm and Jakob Grimm their *Kinder- und Hausmärchen* (Children's and Household Tales) in 1812 and 1815. Not all of this material had actually come from oral sources. Some of the Grimms' fairy tales were retellings of stories from the French, and many of the songs gathered by Arnim and Brentano were drawn from old German manuscripts. *Des Knaben Wunderhorn* also includes variations, adaptations, and re-combinations. The characteristic style ("Märchenton" or fairy-tale tone) of the Grimms' tales and the simple wording of the songs in *Des Knaben Wunderhorn* are in fact the result of the collectors' attempts to create the effect of works that had emanated directly from the people. In this respect, the collections were as much translations, in a capacious sense of the word, as reproductions. The fascination with popular traditions led to a mania for creating modern approximations to the fairy tale and the folk song. In this way, the Romantic writers translated two entire genres into forms that were very much their own.

A proliferation of newly invented ballads, often based on old stories, was an important part of literary production during this period. The Lorelei poems are a good example. Heinrich Heine's version of the legend, "Ich weiß nicht, was soll es bedeuten" (I don't know what it might mean; 1824), is the best known, in part because of Silcher's musical setting, which gained the song long-standing popularity. It was preceded, however, by Clemens Brentano's "Zu Bacharach am Rheine" (At Bacharach on the Rhine; 1802), Eichendorff's "Waldgespräch" (Conversation in the Woods; 1815), and Otto von Loeben's "Die Lorelei" (The Lorelei; 1821). Heine, twenty years younger than Brentano and nine years younger than Eichendorff, highlights the problematic nature of his belated reception of the story. But even Brentano's final stanza tells us that the name "Lore Lay," echoing from the rocks, seems to multiply the modern speaker's personal identity. And Eichendorff, by emphasizing the lateness of the hour when his Loreley – moved to a woodland setting – works her spell on the hapless traveler, also hints at the fact that the speaker himself is a latecomer to a much older poetic tradition. Heine frames his ballad with an explicit reference to the story's ancient provenance; the speaker tells us from the outset that he is overcome with nostalgia for olden times. The story does not exist merely in its older forms, but also – and more importantly – in the speaker's mind. Yet the speaker's knowledge of the tale is imperfect: he confesses in the last stanza that he does not know (or perhaps does not wish to know?) whether the boatman in the old story actually drowns in the end. In this way, Heine puts into question his retelling of the tale and thus the Romantic enterprise of "translating" material from an older period for present use. Indeed, he even hints at a fundamental problem of interpretation in the opening line: "Ich weiß nicht, was soll es bedeuten."

The interest in old ballads and the fascination with translation in its broadest sense were among the reasons why the Romantics were attracted to Mignon's haunting song "Kennst du das Land, wo die Zitronen blühn" (Do you know the land where the lemon trees blossom). In this song, Goethe's protagonist renders into exquisite German what the young girl communicates in broken language (see Chapter 5). In this way, Mignon stands for a primitive state of consciousness that precedes the more sophisticated awareness of her new friend, Wilhelm.

One of the most moving adaptations of the "Kennst du das Land" motif is Joseph von Eichendorff's poem "Denkst du des Schlosses noch" (Do you still think about the villa?; 1859). Familiar anthologies vacillate between two different versions of the poem, one taken from a manuscript by the author, probably from the 1830s, and the other a revision by Eichendorff's son, Hermann, who made significant changes to the final stanza when he published the text in 1859. Here is Eichendorff's original wording:

> Denkst du des Schlosses noch auf stiller Höh?
> Das Horn ruft nächtlich dort, als ob's dich riefe,
> Am Abgrund grast das Reh,
> Es rauscht der Wald verwirrend aus der Tiefe –
> O stille! wecke nicht! es war, als schliefe
> Da drunten unnennbares Weh. –
>
> Kennst du den Garten? – Wenn sich Lenz erneut,
> Geht dort ein Fräulein auf den kühlen Gängen
> Still durch die Einsamkeit
> Und weckt den leisen Strom von Zauberklängen,
> Als ob die Bäume und die Blumen sängen,
> Von der alten schönen Zeit.
>
> Ihr Wipfel und ihr Brunnen, rauscht nur zu!
> Wohin du auch in wilder Flucht magst dringen:
> Du findest nirgends Ruh!
> Erreichen wird dich das geheime Singen,
> In dieses Sees wunderbaren Ringen
> Gehn wir doch unter, ich und du! –

(Do you still think about the villa on the silent hill? Each night the horn sounds there as if calling you; near the abyss, the deer grazes, the forest rustles confusingly from the depths – O hush! don't awaken! it was as if

an unnamable grief were sleeping down there.// Do you know the
garden? – When spring renews itself a young lady walks there in the cool
pathways silently through its solitude and awakens the gentle stream of
magical sounds as if the trees and flowers were singing of the beautiful
olden days.// You treetops and you fountains, keep on rustling!
Wherever you may go in your wild flight: you will never find rest! The
secret singing will reach you, in this lake's wondrous turmoil let's go
under, I and you! –)

The first words of the second stanza, "Kennst du den Garten," are the clue
that links this poem to Mignon's "Kennst du das Land," and when we look
back from this line to the beginning of the poem, we can hear a rhythmic echo
of Mignon's song. Many of the themes and motifs in this poem are familiar
from other Romantic poems. The rustling forest and the gushing fountain,
the sound of the horn, the magic tones that emanate from trees and flowers,
and the notion of a secret song ("das geheime Singen") in nature belong to
the Romantic stock in trade. As in other texts from the period, nature seems
to invite the listener to enter its most intimate recesses and understand its
mysterious and bewitching language. The poem's coherence derives from this
cluster of motifs, and its appeal depends on the nostalgia it conveys – again,
in accord with Romantic thought patterns – for a shared earlier time ("die
alte schöne Zeit") that comprises not just childhood but also a deeper and less
personal past. By giving the poem the title "Heimat" and adding a subtitle
informing us that the poet's brother is its addressee, Hermann Eichendorff
substantially narrows the poem's scope of reference. The villa (this "Schloß"
is not a castle) and its surrounding garden allude to more than the real home
where the boys grew up; they also mean "home" in the sense of human beings'
primal belonging to nature and the deepest reaches of consciousness that
underlie this relationship and its poetic expression.

Hermann Eichendorff evidently found the apparent death wish at the end
of the poem embarrassing, and changed the last two lines to read:

Ach, dieses Bannes wunderbaren Ringen
Entfliehn wir nimmer, ich und du!

(Oh, we will never escape the wondrous turmoil of this spell, I and you!)

Although the speaker and his addressee are still trapped in the magic spell
wrought by nature, they are, at least, perhaps still alive. By substituting
"Bannes" for "Sees," Hermann avoided the metrical necessity of reading the
latter as a two-syllable word, smoothing over any hint of metrical tension. And
by avoiding the final invitation to self-destruction ("Gehn wir doch unter, ich

und du! –"), Hermann also eliminates an intriguing ambiguity in the original ending, which configures suicide by drowning as a voluptuous surrender to the secret singing of the lake waters.

Finally, we need to think about a grammatical problem that troubles the surface of the poem: the transitive verb "wecke" seems to be used in an intransitive sense. Scholars have long puzzled over this curious usage. We might resolve this problem by reading "wecke nicht!" as an arrested moment in a thought that will ultimately be completed with the words "ein unnennbar Weh":

> O stille! wecke nicht! es war, als schliefe
> Da drunten ein unnennbar Weh.
>
> (O hush! Don't awaken! it was as if an unnamable grief were sleeping down below.)

This reading would make "Weh" both the subject of "schliefe" and the (unspoken) object of "wecken." "Wecken" is, after all, a transitive verb; as such, it invites the reader to look for a direct object. This is a remarkable rhetorical figure, one that comprehends something that cannot be articulated in ordinary language. It is as if the poet were to say "Don't awaken – what? I can't say – I fear to say – what it is that I dread you might awaken." Parsing the sentence in this way identifies "ein unnennbar Weh" as the hidden object of "wecken." Yet even as the speaker claims not to be able to name what he dreads, he does know, and is able to say, that he feels as if an unnamable grief were sleeping down below. These lines, through their transgressive grammatical structure, articulate the ambiguities of the Romantic understanding of a form of consciousness that lies just below what can be properly grasped in language.

Frequently, Romantic poems were first published as inset songs in novels and stories. Within these narrative surroundings, they were attributed to specific characters and presented as part of the interaction of these characters with nature and with other people. In the later part of the Romantic period, some writers began to gather their poetry together in volumes of "collected verse." Such collections wrenched the poems from their place in novels and novellas and reorganized them under various thematic rubrics.

Sometimes quite astonishing shifts occur when poems that first appeared as part of a novel are loosened from their narrative moorings. One striking example is Eichendorff's poem "Frische Fahrt" (Setting Out), which began its life as an inset lyric in his novel *Ahnung und Gegenwart*. Today, this novel is the province of specialists; most readers know the poem only as an independent text. Still, it is informative to see how the poem functions within the context of *Ahnung und Gegenwart*. In the novel Countess Romana, confined by her mother to the family villa and its protected garden, sings it as an expression of protest. Unfortunately, the high-spirited young woman is an incipient adventuress who rapidly embarks on a course that will bring her to moral ruin. One night, she sets her ancestral home on fire and kills herself with a shotgun. Her reluctance, in the final lines of the song, to ask where her wild flight might end anticipates this ghastly conclusion. From this perspective, the poem implies that the energizing power of spring is a mere delusion that distracts us from its potential to lure us into a dark abyss.

The poem acquired a more positive sense when Eichendorff used it as the opening piece in his collected poems of 1837. Placed in this position, the lyric expresses the promise of new beginnings and a desire to merge the self with nature. The warm air of spring, the sound of horns in the forest, the energy lent by wind and water blend together to create an invigorating and inspiring effect:

> Laue Luft kommt blau geflossen,
> Frühling, Frühling, soll es sein!
> Waldwärts Hörnerklang geschossen,
> Mut'ger Augen lichter Schein;
> Und das Wirren bunt und bunter
> Wird ein magisch wilder Fluß,
> In die schöne Welt hinunter
> Lockt mich dieses Stromes Gruß.

> (Mild blue air flows in, spring, spring, that's what it is! The sound of horns moves toward the forest, the bright light of bold eyes; and the confusion, increasingly manifold, becomes a wild, magic river, whose greeting tempts me down into the beautiful world.)

The second and final stanza intensifies the identification of self and world and the sense of promised ecstasy:

> Und ich mag mich nicht bewahren!
> Weit von Euch treibt mich der Wind,
> Auf dem Strome will ich fahren,
> Von dem Glanze selig blind!
> Tausend Stimmen lockend schlagen,
> Hoch Aurora flammend weht,
> Fahre zu! ich mag nicht fragen,
> Wo die Fahrt zu Ende geht.

> (And I can't rein myself in! The wind drives me far away from you. I want to journey on the river, blissfully blinded by its bright reflections!

A thousand voices call seductively; High up, Aurora wafts, flaming;
Drive on! I do not care to ask where this journey will come to an end.)

At the end of the poem, the speaker comments on the rising sun ("Aurora"), which corresponds implicitly to the awakening of spring at the beginning of the poem and concludes with an enthusiastic admonition to take up the invitation and plunge into the enticing wider world.

Still, the poem includes a number of expressions that are at odds with this enthusiasm. The impressions received from the outside world are perceived as "Wirren," the river is described as "magisch wild," and the speaker sees the desire to go out into the world as a seductive power ("locken"). The opening of the second stanza suggests an inability to resist this seduction ("Und ich mag mich nicht bewahren!"); and the overwhelming effect of light on water or in the air makes the speaker feel not just blissful, but also blind ("selig blind"). To be sure, we could read a word like "Wirren" as a sign of the intricate interconnectedness of things, the verb "locken" as an invitation to let go of everyday constraints, and the phrase "selig blind" as an articulation of poetic ecstasy. But this complex of words and phrases also implies something more disturbing, a hint of dangers to come.

Where does this poem really stand? There is no easy solution to the problem of these two conflicting tendencies in the text. The standard answer to the question is that Eichendorff's poetry frequently presents an ambivalent view of the relation between self and world. His poem "Zwielicht" (Twilight; 1815), for example, has become a textbook example of Romantic ambivalence. But this poem also comes from *Ahnung und Gegenwart* and, like "Frische Fahrt," it is sung by Romana. Should we defer to the original context of these poems? Might we not say that they become more complex and more interesting when they are freed from the novel? For Eichendorff and his contemporaries, poems could be seen from different angles, they could be framed and defined by larger narrative structures at one time and removed from those contexts at another. Poetry was infinitely variable, ever able to reveal yet another aspect of its complex personality. The fact that we want the poems to "stay put" in one mode or another is the result of our own (perhaps problematic) attachment to the concept of aesthetic unity.

To be sure, a unified view of the world was one of the Romantics' greatest aspirations, and literature was the medium destined to project this vision. Yet all along, the Romantics questioned the possibility of achieving this kind of synthesis. All poetry could do was to present an approximation to a holistic model that could never be fully realized in human thought or language. The German Romantic philosopher Friedrich Schlegel wrote much of his work in the form of "fragments" that pointed toward an imagined, but unarticulated, whole. His contemporary Friedrich von Hardenberg, known by his pen name, Novalis, also espoused this idea. Novalis's "Wenn nicht mehr Zahlen und Figuren" (When numbers and diagrams are no longer; 1800), for example, proposes a world in which everything is harmoniously interconnected, yet set in an indeterminate future time:

> Wenn nicht mehr Zahlen und Figuren
> Sind Schlüssel aller Kreaturen,
> Wenn die, so singen oder küssen,
> Mehr als die Tiefgelehrten wissen,
> Wenn sich die Welt ins freie Leben
> Und in die Welt wird zurückbegeben,
> Wenn dann sich wieder Licht und Schatten
> Zu echter Klarheit werden gatten,
> Und man in Märchen und Gedichten
> Erkennt die wahren Weltgeschichten,
> Dann fliegt vor Einem geheimen Wort
> Das ganze verkehrte Wesen fort.

> (When numbers and diagrams are no longer the key to all creatures, when those who sing or kiss know more than the wisest scholars, when the world returns to free life and back into the world, when light and shadow unite once more to engender genuine clarity and people recognize in fairy tales and poems the true stories of the world, then the whole topsy-turvy business will take flight in the face of a single secret word.)

Underlying this poem is a tripartite conception of temporality developed in different forms by many of the German Romantic philosophers and poets. Novalis believed that the Reformation and Enlightenment had destroyed a community of feeling and unity of thought that characterized society during the Middle Ages. To restore the harmony he attributed to medieval culture, Novalis argued for renewed attention to emotion, intuition, and imagination. The tools of modern science – numbers and diagrams – needed to be replaced by the expression of feeling. Poetry, understood as a mystical force, was the medium that would enable a third age to come into being.

The utopia sketched in the if-clauses that make up most of "Wenn nicht mehr Zahlen" is one in which feeling has won the victory over reason and poetry has won over history. The modern world, with its emphasis on scientific knowledge and enlightened thought, is pictured as a distortion of a truer reality that will ultimately emerge through the power of a single "secret word." The speaker can imagine the way in which this future world will transcend the dualities of reality as we know it, revealing what we perceive as opposites – light and darkness – in the form of "echter Klarheit." The mysterious word that will unlock the hidden unity of nature remains, however, unknown and hence unspoken.

For many Romantic poets, this "word" was to arise in the first instance from nature itself. Brentano's early poem "Sprich aus der Ferne" (Speak from the Distance; 1801) presents the idea of a secretly unified world in a simple rhymed stanza that forms the poem's beginning and ending:

> Sprich aus der Ferne
> Heimliche Welt,
> Die sich so gerne
> Zu mir gesellt.

> (Speak from the distance, secret world that so willingly comes to keep me company.)

Like Novalis's "Wenn nicht mehr Zahlen," Brentano's "Sprich aus der Ferne" suggests a series of possibilities. In Brentano's poem, the unified vision comes about at moments when the sharp contrasts of daytime are no longer visible: after the sun has gone down, under the gentle light of the moon, or at the dark of midnight. At such times, divisions and distinctions are no longer apparent, as everything blends into a single harmonious form:

> Alles ist freundlich, wohlwollend verbunden,
>   Bietet sich tröstend und trauernd die Hand.
> Sind durch die Nächte die Lichter gewunden,
>   Alles ist ewig im Innern verwandt.

> (All things are connected in friendship and good will, all things offer their hand consolingly and mournfully. Just as each night is interwoven with light, everything is inwardly related to everything else.)

This final stanza of the poem, preceding the concluding refrain that repeats the opening quatrain "Sprich aus der Ferne," is relativized in the novel where it first appeared (*Godwi*) by a discussion between the protagonist and his friend, who cannot agree about whether there really is a "secret world" that underlies and gives coherence to the disparate elements of visible nature. In Brentano's collected poems, by contrast, the poem speaks clearly and affirmatively for a conception of the world as intimately interconnected.

Yet Brentano's late poem "Was reif in diesen Zeilen steht" (Whatever is ripe in these lines; 1838), often understood as a kind of poetic testament, can only bring things together in a set of symmetrically arranged oppositions:

> O Stern und Blume, Geist und Kleid,
> Lieb, Leid und Zeit und Ewigkeit!
>
> (O star and flower, spirit and garment, love, suffering, and time and eternity!)

Body and spirit, reality and imagination, temporality and eternity have become no more than so many linguistic ciphers. The terms are evocative, but although their arrangement hints at completion and resolution, the gesture of sheer naming ultimately suggests that some things cannot be fully elaborated.

Even before this late text of Brentano, Heinrich Heine's brilliant free-verse poem "Abenddämmerung" (Evening Twilight; 1825) had mocked the theme of nature's secret language. The speaker of this poem from his North Sea cycle presents himself, in a wonderful combination of everyday and Romantic vocabulary, as "gedankenbekümmert und einsam" (troubled by thoughts and lonely). As the sun sets over the sea and the waves roll in toward the shore, he seems to hear

> Ein seltam Geräusch, ein Flüstern und Pfeifen,
> Ein Lachen und Murmeln, Seufzen und Sausen,
> Dazwischen ein wiegenliedheimliches Singen –
>
> (A strange noise, a whispering and whistling, a laughing and murmuring, sighing and soughing, and in between a secret lullaby-like singing –)

With this heterogeneous and exaggerated collection of sound effects, Heine shows his skepticism toward the secret song of nature. Rhythmically, the neologism "wiegenliedheimliches" recalls the dactyls of classical German verse while also harking back to the more awkward polysyllable "gedankenbekümmert" (though a dactyl glimmers even in that more uncomfortable phrase). Yet the poem does not conclude by disparaging the Romantic: instead, it concedes an element of mystery that retains its fascination even once we have experienced disillusionment. In the poem's final lines, the speaker recalls himself as a little boy, crouching by the house door with his young friends and observing older girls:

> Während die großen Mädchen,
> Neben duftenden Blumentöpfen,
> Gegenüber am Fenster saßen,

Rosengesichter,
Lächelnd und mondbeglänzt.

(While the big girls sat next to fragrant pots of flowers opposite us by the window, rosy faces, smiling and lit by the moon.)

This final image evokes precisely what the central part of the poem finds laughable. There is an affinity between the girls, with their "Rosengesichter," and the blooming flower pots beside which they sit. Mysteriously smiling and illuminated by the moon (that perennial Romantic requisite), they seem to possess some kind of secret knowledge that cannot be specified.

The Romantic vision of a unity of world and self came increasingly undone in the mid nineteenth century. One of Mörike's most often cited lyrics echoes Brentano's "Hör es klagt die Flöte wieder" (1803), which we have already examined in this chapter. The madrigal "Er ist's" was first published in 1828 without a title (the latter was added a year later):

Frühling läßt sein blaues Band
Wieder flattern durch die Lüfte;
Süße, wohlbekannte Düfte
Streifen ahnungsvoll das Land.
Veilchen träumen schon,
Wollen balde kommen.
– Horch, von fern ein leiser Harfenton!
Frühling, ja du bist's!
Dich hab ich vernommen!

(Spring lets its blue ribbon flutter once more through the air; sweet, familiar scents drift expectantly through the countryside. Violets are already dreaming: they plan to emerge soon. – Listen, the soft sound of a harp from afar! Yes, spring, it's you! I've heard you!).

The synaesthetic effects of Brentano's poem – the merging of color and sound, for example – are not present in Mörike's text. The speaker does not employ that characteristic verb of the Romantic movement, "rauschen," with its suggestion of sound whose components cannot be isolated from one another. In "Er ist's," the senses of sight, smell, and hearing are kept distinct: the speaker notices the blue spring sky, smells the scents of the new season, and hears the sound of a distant harp. The coming of the violets is of course only imagined, but this element of inwardness is also an important ingredient in the poem. Although the verb "vernehmen" primarily means "to hear," it also means to experience through the senses. It is precisely the specific attention to sight, smell, and hearing that permits the speaker to capture the earliest appearance of spring.

In this attention to the finest of sensory impressions, "Er ist's" can be described as a poem in the wake of the Romantic movement rather than as a Romantic text proper (see Chapter 7).

Many elements of the Romantic vision had a long afterlife. They are picked up repeatedly in early twentieth-century modernism, in the period following World War II, and even in the present day. The Expressionist Georg Trakl alludes to the Romantic heritage in the final stanza of his "Verklärter Herbst" (Transfigured Autumn; 1912):

> Es ist der Liebe milde Zeit.
> Im Kahn den blauen Fluß hinunter
> Wie schön sich Bild an Bildchen reiht –
> Das geht in Ruh und Schweigen unter.
>
> (It is the gentle time of love. In the boat going down the blue river, how beautifully one image joins another – All that goes under in peace and silence.)

Here we can see that the motif of the flowing river has been reduced to its most elementary principles. The formulation "Bild an Bildchen" suggests that these loosely linked images are perceived as a tidy sequence of unspecified miniatures. The tension between fullness and loss, in Romanticism a confused tangle of inseparable and complex emotions, is now neatly divided between "der Liebe milde Zeit" and the silent destruction of the images as they drown in the river. The verb "untergehen" does not mean that the images are drowned out, in a metaphorical sense: rather, it suggests shipwreck (with respect to the boat) and death by water (with respect to the idyllic scene). The poem is imbued with nostalgia for a sense of wholeness that cannot be recovered. Other poems by Trakl address the problem of the loss of harmony more radically, enacting it through more poignantly disjointed poetic structures and, after the start of World War I, connecting it with larger social disruptions (see Chapter 8). In such texts, poetic unity is recognized as a problem.

For the most brilliant poet of the late twentieth century, Romanticism remains only in the form of disconnected images and ideas that no longer fully cohere. Paul Celan's poem "Fadensonnen" (Thread Suns; 1967) can be read as an almost direct reworking of Eichendorff's "Wünschelrute," or at least of related ideas in the Romantic repertoire:

> Fadensonnen
> über der grauschwarzen Ödnis.
> Ein baum-
> hoher Gedanke

greift sich den Lichtton: es sind
noch Lieder zu singen jenseits
der Menschen.

(Thread suns above the grey-black wasteland. A tree-high thought
grasps for the light tone: there are still songs to be sung beyond human
life.)

The setting of the poem suggests some kind of wasteland, perhaps even
terrain destroyed by war. Apart from the "Fadensonnen" (a word that does not
easily yield up its meaning, but that suggests at least on one level that sunlight
does not fully penetrate this sinister landscape), there is only the gray-black
desert. A tree is only present in the form of a metaphor, a thought which,
reaching toward the sun, seems to rise upward like a tree. It does, however,
grasp or attain a kind of goal, seen as if through the synaesthetic imagination
of the Romantics as a combination of light and music. What follows the
colon is the content of that thought: the recognition that, even after so much
destruction, there is still a place for "song" or poetry. Yet this place is not here
in this world: it is elsewhere, "beyond" human existence. The magic word of
Eichendorff's "Wünschelrute" is missing here, and Eichendorff's assumption
that the language of nature can somehow be translated into human language
has become a threadbare and fragile notion at best.

When twentieth-century poems take up motifs from the Romantic repertoire, they almost always imply an inability to recreate the atmosphere in which
these motifs originated as characteristically "poetic" images. At the same time,
they extend and elaborate tensions that already existed in Romantic poetry
between the desire to create a unified poetic text and the sense of rupture and
loss that constantly worked against the fulfillment of this desire.

Chapter 7

The self and the senses

While Heine's characteristic irony is born of his position between a longing for Romantic unity and a profound skepticism about its possibility, two
post-Romantic poets, Eduard Mörike and Annette von Droste-Hülshoff, were
less willing to resolve this tension using the strategies of distancing that we
observed in Heine's "Abenddämmerung" (see Chapter 6). Heine's inclusion of
everyday or traditionally non-poetic language, his flexible deployment of free
verse, and his complex presentation of time and consciousness in this poem
and the *Nordsee* cycle in general adumbrate a kind of poetry that will recur
during the nineteenth century. His development of a meditative form that
takes close account of shifts and disparities, contradictions and ambiguities in
thought and feeling, sets the stage for some of the most significant poetry of
a period that tended to prefer prose narrative to the lyric. In large measure,
Mörike's and Droste's approach emerged from their new understanding of
the relationship between self and world: Romantic thinking about how creativity functions was being supplanted by new attention to the processes of
sensory perception. When Mörike and Droste write about nature, there is no
self-evident recognition of a secret voice that emanates from the natural world
and makes itself accessible for "translation" into poetic language. Instead, the
experiencing subject takes a less active posture to the world outside, registering with intricate subtlety the ever-fluctuating impressions that play upon the
psyche. At first, this poetry appears diffuse and at times even resistant to ready
comprehension: proliferating imagery suggests deep-seated uncertainty, and
language itself seems somehow incapable of providing resolution. Where is the
source of this confusion: in the speaker of the poem or in the external world?
This question is the nub of the problem for the poets as they wrestle with the
unsettling character of sensory perception.

In order to situate this issue in Mörike and Droste, this chapter will go
further back in literary history, beginning with what was known as *Empfindsamkeit* (equivalent to and influenced by the Age of Sensibility in English
literature). Emerging in the 1740s and 1750s, this movement was both acutely
sensitive and concerned with sense perception: unchecked emotionality was

coupled with, and even triggered by, close attention to small details. Goethe's novel *Die Leiden des jungen Werthers*, though usually considered as a work of *Sturm und Drang*, also bears many of the distinguishing marks of *Empfindsamkeit*. The chapter will end with a consideration of another phase of German poetry which continues the trajectory begun in the mid eighteenth century: the impressionist strain in Hofmannsthal and the early Rilke in the period around 1900.

The backdrop to this entire swathe of poetry focusing on sensory perception can be located in the years that led up to *Empfindsamkeit*. When Barthold Hinrich Brockes explored sensory perception in his collection of poems about nature, *Irdisches Vergnügen in Gott* (Earthly Pleasure in God; 1721–1748), his aim was to demonstrate that the fine details of nature do not exist for their own sake but as testimony to the ingenious hand of the Creator. In keeping with the tradition that nature was a book open for reading by anyone willing to pay careful attention, Brockes focuses mainly on the visual. A frog, a butterfly, a hyacinth, but also a pumpkin, as well as rain, clouds, and ice drifting on the surface of a pond are all – among many other items – the subject of poetic description that attends to the sheer variety of color, shape, and markings that characterize these objects. For the speaker of Brockes' poems, the things of nature stand in a special relationship to man because through them we are able to appreciate the power of God. By observing the specific individuality of natural objects, we come to understand the complexity of the world around us. Yet as he points out in his poem "Der Gold-Käfer" (The Gold-bug), sensory impressions are strictly speaking nothing at all. What we see, hear, smell, taste and feel is fleeting: when there is no light, for example, we cannot see colors. "Ohne Gott, den Brunn des Lichts,/ Sind wir, und ist alles, nichts" (without God, the fount of light, we – and everything – are nothing). As a poet of the Enlightenment, Brockes uses scientific knowledge about the senses to underpin a larger argument about the relation of the phenomenal world to the divine. Our search for stability in the world of sensations is in vain: whenever we try to pin things down, we behave like the poet's little son, who cries when the gold-bug he has caught in his hand flies away without leaving a trace. In the often anthologized poem "Kirschblüte bei der Nacht" (Cherry Blossom at Night; 1727), the astonishing whiteness of cherry blossom in the moonlight cannot compare with the bright white starlight that penetrates the speaker's soul when he realizes that the delicate petals are but a poor reflection of divine light:

> Wie sehr ich mich an Gott im Irdischen ergetze
> Dacht' ich, hat Er dennoch weit grös're Schätze.

Die gröste Schönheit dieser Erden
Kann mit der Himmlischen doch nicht verglichen werden.

(However much I delight about God in earthly things, I thought that he
has far greater treasures yet. After all, the greatest beauty on earth
cannot be compared with heavenly beauty.)

Brockes was a Deist: in other words, his belief in God was independent of
specific church dogma. His attention to the fleeting and fragile character of
the small things in nature is the anchor for his argument about the constancy
of the divine. At the same time, however, his special sensitivity to the sheer
multiplicity of earthly phenomena showed the way for a more effusive kind
of poetry. Friedrich Gottlieb Klopstock's free-verse poem *Die Frühlingsfeier*
(The Festival of Spring; first version 1759) owes much to Brockes' *Irdisches
Vergnügen in Gott*. In Klopstock's *Frühlingsfeier*, the speaker discovers that a
lowly worm is no less significant in nature than a powerful thunderstorm:

Aber, du Frühlingswürmchen,
Das grünlichgolden
Neben mir spielt,
Du lebst;
Und bist, vielleicht –
Ach, nicht unsterblich!

(But, you little spring worm, golden green, playing beside me, you live;
and are, perhaps – oh, not immortal!)

The troubling thought that the worm might not be immortal (because in
traditional theology it has no soul) is implicitly undercut by the anacoluthon
following "vielleicht" and the sigh of disappointment expressed in the ejacu-
lation "Ach." Looking for evidence of God's presence in nature, the speaker of
this poem would clearly like to find it in the worm that bears the characteristic
color of nature on its body. As the poem proceeds, the speaker recognizes God
in the sound of thunder, yet at the conclusion also in the calm that follows the
storm.

When the protagonist of Goethe's novel *Die Leiden des jungen Werthers*
alludes to this poem in the context of a thunderstorm that interrupts a social
gathering, he reveals his acceptance of the notion that we apprehend the divine
through our sensory impressions. Even before this striking scene, Werther –
not unlike the speaker of Klopstock's *Frühlingsfeier* – perceives the presence
of the Almighty in the tiniest details of nature, such as the teeming world
of worms and insects he observes while lying in the grass; yet his narcissistic

self-involvement is ultimately quite different from the more regulated, if also sentimental, approach to nature characteristic of *Empfindsamkeit.*

A good hundred years separates the nature poetry of Mörike and Droste from that of Brockes, and even the *Empfindsamkeit* of Klopstock's *Frühlingsfeier* and Goethe's *Werther* lies well in the past. Goethe was a significant influence on Mörike, but the latter's early poetry, beginning in 1822, also overlapped with the later phase of the Romantics. Some of his most significant poems were written at a time when the Romantics were presenting a polished image of their texts in compilations of their complete works. The notion of Mörike as an epigone or latecomer – a view that dominated scholarship for some time – is not entirely correct. Rather, we can observe Mörike's poetry emerging from what was still in large measure a Romantic world, but testing it against a more finely calibrated set of responses to Romantic conceptions of self and nature.

We have already seen (in Chapter 6) how a poem like Mörike's "Er ist's" differs from the inchoate soundscapes of Romantic nature in its more nuanced rendering of sensory perceptions. Let us turn to another early poem by Mörike on the same theme, the more complex meditative poem "Im Frühling" (In Spring; 1828). As in "Er ist's," sensory perception is paramount, but here it functions less well to hold world and self together:

> Hier lieg ich auf dem Frühlingshügel:
> Die Wolke wird mein Flügel,
> Ein Vogel fliegt mir voraus.
> Ach, sag mir, all-einzige Liebe,
> Wo *du* bleibst, daß ich bei dir bliebe!
> Doch du und die Lüfte, ihr habt kein Haus.
>
> Der Sonnenblume gleich steht mein Gemüte offen,
> Sehnend,
> Sich dehnend
> In Lieben und Hoffen.
> Frühling, was bist du gewillt?
> Wann werd ich gestillt?
>
> Die Wolke seh ich wandeln und den Fluß,
> Es dringt der Sonne goldner Kuß
> Mir tief bis ins Geblüt hinein;
> Die Augen, wunderbar berauschet,
> Tun, als schliefen sie ein,
> Nur noch das Ohr dem Ton der Biene lauschet.
> Ich denke dies und denke das,
> Ich sehne mich, und weiß nicht recht, nach was:
> Halb ist es Lust, halb ist es Klage;

Mein Herz, o sage,
Was webst du für Erinnerung
In golden grüner Zweige Dämmerung?
– Alte unnennbare Tage!

(I lie here on the spring hill: the cloud becomes my wing; a bird flies on
ahead of me. Oh tell me where you are, all-encompassing and unique
love, so that I can stay with you! But you and the winds have no home.//
My mood is open like a sunflower, longing, expanding in love and hope.
Spring, what do you intend? When will I be satiated?// I see the cloud
wandering and the river; the sun's golden kiss penetrates deep down
into my bloodstream; my eyes, wondrously intoxicated, act as if they
were falling asleep; my ear alone listens to the sound of the bee. I think
of this and that, I feel longing but don't know exactly what for: it is half
desire and half sorrow; my heart, tell me: what memories do you weave
in the dusk of golden green branches? – Old, unnameable days!)

In contrast with Romantic poetics (at least in broad outline, if not in every
individual realization), this text struggles with the problem of articulating the
message of nature. Auditory and visual impressions from the natural world
awaken the speaker's senses but bring no fulfillment. The sounds and sights
of nature – a bird whose flight he longs to follow, breezes that never seem to
settle, a floating cloud, a moving river, the warmth of the sun and the buzzing
of a bee – give no answer to the question he asks about his own relation to the
manifestations of spring; nor can he give clear shape to the perceptions that
crowd in on him. In the end, what has presented itself as a present experience
reveals itself as a web of inarticulate memories: "alte unnennbare Tage." If the
world described in the poem has any coherence, it is not intrinsic to nature
but supplied by human memory.

Furthermore, although the poem introduces numerous details from nature,
they are not only evanescent, but pull in different directions. The first line
seems to name a location, but what is this "Frühlingshügel" actually? The
unusual compound word draws attention to the strange combination of the
concrete and the imaginary that characterizes the text as a whole. We may
quite reasonably suppose that the cloud, bird, river, and bee are somehow
"there" in the scene on the hill, but they are constantly in danger of becoming
mere ciphers. The sunflower subsists on a different plane from these other
natural objects, not only because sunflowers do not bloom in the spring, but
more importantly because the speaker designates it as a metaphor for his own
psychological state: "der Sonnenblume gleich steht mein Gemüte offen." Yet
nature does not respond, let alone satisfy his longing. And although the words
"all-einzige Liebe" suggest the possibility of an all-embracing wholeness that

might contain but not usurp his individual existence, the landscape does not appear to provide this. The speaker asks numerous questions (one of them, in line 5, an indirect question) to which no answers come apart from the odd "reply" in the final line that seems to be more of a sigh than a response. The questions, furthermore, have disparate addressees: love, spring, and the poet's own heart.

Even what sometimes seem like awkward expressions in this poem have a part to play in the whole. "Im Frühling" is about transitions, and transitions are not only fleeting and hard to grasp, they are frequently not smooth. Although the poem is rhymed, the line length varies, often quite strikingly, as in the case of the participles in the second section ("Sehnend,/ Sich dehnend"). The last line of the poem, " – Alte, unnennbare Tage," adds a third rhyme word to a scheme that has otherwise consisted of pairs; technically, one might regard this line as superfluous, but within the context of the poem it strengthens the rhyming pair to which it harks back ("Klage," "sage") while providing the response that nature has not given. This kind of set-off line with a supernumerary rhyme is characteristic of the madrigal form. As a formal and thematic conclusion, though rather vague in reference, it mitigates the hesitant opening of the final section: "Ich denke dies und denke das." With its prosaic formulation, this line at first seems like a filler, yet its function is to highlight the speaker's distracted, indecisive mood. Even at the outset of the poem, the sequence of thought is not logically tight. It does not help, for example, to press too hard on the coherence of the imagery involving the cloud and the bird: "Die Wolke wird mein Flügel,/ Ein Vogel fliegt mir voraus." What these lines present is a sketch, not a fully formed picture. The point is not to delineate a scene in nature, but to illustrate the disjunctive nature of the speaker's responses to it. As the speaker's eyes, "wunderbar berauschet," begin to close, hearing takes over as he listens to the sound of the bees. The poem invites its readers, as it were, to put themselves into the same drowsy state as its speaker, a state in which the different senses blend over into one another. Yet even this state is formulated with a strange precision: he is not actually falling asleep, though his eyes "tun, als schliefen sie ein." Interior and exterior are complexly interwoven, yet how exactly this takes place cannot be fully articulated. Despite the speaker's request, "Mein Herz, o sage," the heart is not an organ that can speak. The ethereal metaphor of memories woven in the branches is suggestive rather than strictly explanatory. In this respect, sensory perception in Mörike's "Im Frühling" functions quite differently from sensory perception in Brockes, where it is used as a precisely honed instrument for discerning the divine in nature.

Another early poem by Mörike, "An einem Wintermorgen, vor Sonnenaufgang" (On a Winter Morning before Sunrise; composed 1825 but first published in 1833), shares many of the characteristics of "Im Frühling" while shaping a more definitive conclusion. A transitional moment, contradictory impressions of the natural world, and vacillating psychological responses on the part of the speaker are common to both poems.

"An einem Wintermorgen" opens in the last moments of darkness before sunrise. The compound adjective "flaumenleicht" (light as down) in the opening line suggests the lightness of snowflakes – it is a winter morning, after all – but it is actually a transferred epithet, describing the transitory nature of a moment that seems almost weightless. Snow, even the possibility of snow, is not mentioned at all; its essential attribute merely hovers in the background. The fragility of this moment suggests that ineffable bliss may be near at hand. This is the hope that motivates the poem. Opening himself to impressions, the speaker compares his soul or psyche in with a "Kristall" (crystal; line 5). Though we might think of snow crystals in this wintry context, the image seems rather to be a gem-like prism. But what does it mean that that this crystal has not been touched by a "falscher Strahl des Lichts" (false ray of light)? Only gradually do we recognize what is at stake here: the speaker's desire to remain in the downy state of that special time before sunrise. From the perspective of this fragile darkness, light seems like a traitor eager to put an end to a magical moment. This magic stems from the Romantic belief in the power of night: the word "Wollust" (delight or sensual pleasure) would have reminded contemporary readers of Novalis's *Hymnen an die Nacht* (1800), notably of the following lines from part 4:

> Hinüber wall ich,
> Und jede Pein
> Wird einst ein Stachel
> Der Wollust sein.

(I shall pass over, and every torment will be a spur to pleasure.)

As long as the speaker of "An einem Wintermorgen" is held in the last moments of darkness, the rules of Romantic thinking obtain, according to which true enlightenment is only possible when rationality is suspended. From this point of view, daylight (symbolizing reason) is a false temptation, as opposed to night (seen as a mode of access to mystical truths). In Mörike's poem, the weightlessness of early darkness causes the speaker's psyche to vacillate between fluidity and stasis:

> Zu fluten scheint mein Geist, er scheint zu ruhn,
> Dem Eindruck naher Wunderkräfte offen,

Die aus dem klaren Gürtel blauer Luft
Zuletzt ein Zauberwort vor meine Sinne ruft. (lines 7–10)

(My spirit seems to flow, it seems to rest, open to the impression of
imminent wondrous powers which at last are summoned to my senses
by a magic word from the clear sash of blue air.)

Today, the compound word "Zauberwort" is best known from Eichendorff's
"Wünschelrute", a poem that seems to sum up the program of German Romanticism, postulating nature as the repository of a latent voice to which the poet
will give expression. That Mörike's earlier "An einem Wintermorgen" contains
the same word reminds us of the inherent complexity of literary periodization.
Despite their differences in form and style, Mörike and Eichendorff invoke a
common vocabulary for the relation between poetry and nature and respond
to common questions about the process of creativity. Yet in Mörike's "An einem
Wintermorgen," the magic word does not stand at the conclusion of the poem:
instead, it is part of a transitional stage in a complicated process. Indeed, the
notion of the "Zauberwort" is hedged in with reservations that emphasize the
subjectivity of this stage. The repeated verb "scheint" coupled with the noun
"Eindruck," invites a certain degree of skepticism about what may only seem to
be reality (lines 7–10). Wondrous powers appear to be at hand, but might they
perhaps be illusory? This section of the poem gives no decisive answer to this
question. Although a new section begins, its opening (lines 11–12) echoes these
hesitations. Increasingly, doubts surface about the validity of the experience.
A cluster of words referring to lightness and brightness ("hell," "licht," and
"glänzend") come together in puzzling ways. Can his eyes really be bright and
alert if he has to close them to hold on to a vision that he now calls a "Traum"
(dream)? Is the word "Feenreich" (fairy realm) to be understood positively or
negatively? By what logic does the throng of images and thoughts that at first
seem to be milling around at the gate of his heart suddenly become a school
of fish-like creatures in his bosom? The bizarre concatenation of metaphors
draws attention to the difficulty of grasping these ideas, which seem to have
been insinuated into the speaker's mind by someone else (see the pronoun
"wer" that opens the question formulated in lines 14–17).

Section 4 of the poem draws on two different traditions to give expression to
his puzzling state of mind: the sound of shepherds' flutes at the birth of Jesus
alternate with drinking songs as at an ancient Dionysian festival. Again, as in
the previous section, the speaker wonders if these auditory impressions might
be attributed to someone outside himself. Of course, they come from memories
of reading or perhaps modern approximations to these sacred traditions. The
two questions beginning with the pronoun "wer" in sections 3 and 4 suggest

a degree of dissociation in which his own mental content appears somehow separated from himself.

Yet it seems that these questions, permitting him to see his own mind as if from outside, also make possible an entirely new turn. Fresh strength and courage seem to course through him as he rises to the heights of ecstasy; yet almost immediately, he feels plunged into inexplicable melancholy:

> Die Seele fliegt, so weit der Himmel reicht,
> Der Genius jauchzt in mir! Doch sage,
> Warum wird jetzt der Blick von Wehmut feucht?
> Ists ein verloren Glück, was mich erweicht?
> Ist es ein werdendes, was ich im Herzen trage? – (lines 27–31)

> (My soul soars as far as the heavens extend, the spirit rejoices within me! But tell me, why is my eye moist with melancholy? Is it a lost happiness that softens me? Is it happiness to come that I bear in my heart?)

The German word "Genius" does not mean the same thing as "genius" in present-day English: it has, rather, the older sense of a spirit – here perhaps not so much the spirit of a place as the spirit of a time: the early-morning darkness before sunrise – that rejoices within the speaker. The shift from joy to sadness is not really as negative as it may at first appear: after all, the ecstatic moment of poetic inspiration is by definition both expansive and fleeting.

Looking back at the first four sections, we recognize that virtually everything is interior: we see not so much the wintry morning as the reflections it calls forth in the speaker. Yet we are not told what images and thoughts crowd the speaker's mind; all we know is that they are constantly moving and changing like a goldfish in a pond. Like the metaphor of the crystal, the fish-pond metaphor serves not to clarify the scene but to highlight the way it permits imagination to take over.

This flickering quality of the speaker's responses finds a parallel in the poem's form. After an opening quatrain in five-stress lines with embracing rhymes, the rhythm becomes less predictable and the rhyme scheme more varied. First an eye-rhyme creeps in: "Luft" and "ruft" (lines 9–10). Although full rhymes predominate throughout the poem, one rhyme is tripled in the fourth section ("Klänge," "Lustgesänge," "Gedränge"; lines 18–21) and in the sixth section, the full rhyme "reicht" and "erweicht" is joined by the half-rhyme "feucht" (lines 27–30). The rhymed couplet beginning with " – Hinweg, mein Geist!" (lines 32–33) is reminiscent of the ritornello of a madrigal, but it does not stand here at the end of the poem, as would be the case in that form. Another two-line sentence does conclude the poem (lines 38–39), but although there is a clear pause before it, the rhyme scheme integrates it with the rest of the final section.

The dash of line 32 separates the last phase of the poem from the earlier part, marking the speaker's determination to leave the temptations of "die dunkle Frühe" behind and welcome the arrival of daylight. To do so, he must give up his previous emphasis on interior vision and return to a more conventional relation between self and world. The almost theatrical exclamation "Hinweg, mein Geist!" reminds us of Mörike's relation to Goethe. Unlike Goethe's Faust, the speaker of Mörike's poem does not let himself be lulled by the moment's promise of fulfillment. Instead, the speaker of "An einem Wintermorgen" steps back, as it were, from the scene that now unfolds before his eyes as if in a theatre: "Dort, sieh, am Horizont lüpft sich der Vorhang schon!" (There, look, the curtain rises already on the horizon; line 34).

For the modern reader, a central image in the final stanza of "An einem Wintermorgen" is astonishing, almost surrealist. Certainly, the striking use of synaesthetic effects seems to anticipate modernist techniques. Observing the rapidly changing scene, the speaker sees the color-streaked sky with the rising sun as a face formed by a purple lip that seems to start breathing and an eye that flashes forth. Supplanting the speaker's initial hope that night would bring insight and ecstasy, the emergence of day brings a new determination to keep moving forward. The phrase "auf einmal" at the beginning (line 3) and end (line 38) of the poem indicates this correspondence and contrast. With its poetic diction and resonant intonation ("Beginnt im Sprung die Königlichen Flüge!"), the final line identifies an equivalent in nature to the speaker's turn to the light of day and a more rational position. When a friend suggested to Mörike that he should position "An einem Wintermorgen, vor Sonnenaufgang" as the opening piece in his 1838 collection of his poetry, he did so, giving the poem an additional layer of meaning as an announcement of his departure from the Romantic concept of night as an organ for understanding.

These two early poems by Mörike provide the framework necessary for understanding such later poems as "An eine Äolsharfe" (To an Aeolian Harp; 1837), written in free verse with rhythms that recall, in snatches, fragments of ancient Greek odes. For the Romantics, the wind harp had been a metaphor for the poet's ability to capture the voice of nature and transform it into language. Aeolian harps had become enormously popular during the eighteenth century. They consisted of a large rectangular wooden box with gut strings loosely stretched across bridges on the short ends; when wind was allowed to move through the instrument, the strings reacted with a strangely compelling swelling and ebbing sound. For Romantic poets in both England and Germany, the Aeolian harp became a metaphor for both the human soul and poetry itself. Mörike's poem continues these traditions. As the strings of the harp resound in the wind, they produce a "melodische Klage" (melodious plaint) that seems to be inspired by a muse of the air:

> Angelehnt an die Efeuwand
> Dieser alten Terrasse,
> Du, einer luftgebornen Muse
> Geheimnisvolles Saitenspiel,
> Fang an,
> Fange wieder an
> Deine melodische Klage!

(Leaning against the ivy-covered wall of this old terrace, mysterious stringed instrument of an air-born muse [note that Mörike elides the second "e" of the adjective "luftgeborenen"], begin, begin again your melodious lament!)

In tune, as it were, with the harp music, the speaker's heart also becomes an instrument, played on by the same winds that cause the harp to resound. Like the ebb and swell of the mysterious melody, the speaker's emotions also seem to grow and fade away. In contrast to the German Romantics, however, the instrument's secret message is not understood as the voice of nature itself: rather, it is regarded as an equivalent of sorts for the human psyche as it responds to multiple sensory stimuli:

> Ihr kommet, Winde, fern herüber,
> Ach! von des Knaben,
> Der mir so lieb war,
> Frisch grünendem Hügel.
> Und Frühlingsblüten unterweges streifend,
> Übersättigt mit Wohlgerüchen,
> Wie süß bedrängt ihr dies Herz!
> Und säuselt her in die Saiten,
> Angezogen von wohllautender Wehmut,
> Wachsend im Zug meiner Sehnsucht,
> Und hinsterbend wieder.

(Winds, you come over from afar, alas, from the freshly greening mound of the boy who was so dear to me. And brushing spring blossoms on your way, oversated with lovely scents, how sweetly you cramp my heart! And ripple toward me in the strings, attracted by the beautiful sound of melancholy, swelling in the course of my longing, and dying away again.)

The arc of the sentence that opens this section (lines 8–11) must be read as "Ihr kommet, Winde, von dem frisch grünenden Hügel des Knaben, der mir so lieb war." Most scholars understand the "boy" as Mörike's younger brother August, who had died suddenly and under somewhat mysterious circumstances in 1824, in other words thirteen years before the composition of the poem. Yet even without knowing this fact, we can recognize that "An eine Äolsharfe" has to do with loss and mourning: the "Hügel" is a grave mound on which the grass grows freshly green every spring despite the time that has passed since the death of the beloved boy. Mörike gives another clue as well: the epigraph from Horace that precedes the poem proper. Mörike's contemporaries would have been familiar with this text. It is a stanza from Horace's Odes II, 9, a poem that chides its addressee, a certain Valgius, for excessive mourning. Nature's foul seasons, says the poet, do not continue unabated; not even Achilles mourned his friend Antilochus forever, nor did Troilus' family weep unceasingly over his death. Mörike's poem is a response to the reproach that mourning should not go on forever. The complex syntax of lines 8–11, especially the interpolated "Ach!" of line 9, render the speaker's struggle to put into words the feelings that still accompany thoughts of the dead youth. Recalling the waxing and waning line lengths of the opening, this second section continues to imitate the sound of the Aeolian harp with its irregular lines. Like the melodious plaint of the harp, the winds that blow from the grave bear with them both sweetness and melancholy. Saturated – "übersättigt," as the speaker recognizes – with the scent of spring blossoms, the winds act as a reminder of the sweet thoughts he still has for his brother, while also causing his heart to constrict with pain. The paradoxical sounds of the wind harp, with its plaintive melody, seem to be translated here into the speaker's feelings, which the play of the winds renders sweet and distressing at once: "wie süß bedrängt ihr dies Herz!". The poignancy of this experience is rendered by a combination of sensory impressions: touch ("streifend"), smell ("Wohlgerüche"), and sound ("wohllautend"). The verb "säuseln" is difficult to render in English, but it is certainly an auditory effect. Mingling with these sense perceptions are emotions, "Wehmut" und "Sehnsucht," that well up and die away again in the speaker's psyche.

And yet there is a sudden change in this pattern, indicated by the adverbial phrase "auf einmal" at the beginning of the third section:

> Aber auf einmal,
> Wie der Wind heftiger herstößt,
> Ein holder Schrei der Harfe
> Wiederholt, mir zu süßem Erschrecken,

Meiner Seele plötzliche Regung;
Und hier – die volle Rose streut, geschüttelt,
All ihre Blätter vor meine Füße!

(But all at once, as the wind blows more strongly, a lovely cry of the harp
repeats, to my sweet alarm, my soul's sudden response; and here – the
full-blown rose, shaken, strews all its petals at my feet!)

With this sudden gust of wind, the speaker's psyche merges with the harp,
becoming a sound box that resonates with the instrument's "holder Schrei."
The English word "cry" does not fully render the German "Schrei" in this
context, where it might almost as well be considered a shriek. The paradoxical
sound from the harp is picked up in the "süßem Erschrecken" that jolts the
speaker. Sound is of course created by vibrations, and in the final lines of the
poem the full-blown rose also resonates with the sweetly piercing cry as it
strews its petals on the ground. These lines, with their inserted dash after the
second word and the past participle "geschüttelt" interpolated between the
verb and its object, are brilliantly designed. Not only do they capture the jolt
to the speaker's emotions, they also emphasize once again the interaction of
time and place that is a principal driver of the poem.

Modern readers may feel rather troubled by this rose, which seems gratu-
itously introduced at the end of the poem; furthermore, roses do not bloom
in spring, nor is it presented as growing in the landscape. Rather, it enters the
poem quite frankly as a symbol placed, as it were, on the metaphorical grave-
stone that is the poem. A traditional poetic emblem of the relation between life
and death, the rose's final shedding of its petals is a reminder of the fragility
even of poetic memorial.

All of these poems by Mörike do more than simply explore the complex
interaction of the self and the senses: they also trace and comment on the
process of poetic creation itself. This is one of several reasons why these texts
can be seen as preparing the way for modernity. The lyric poetry of Annette
von Droste-Hülshoff, one of Mörike's contemporaries, shares many of the
attributes we have seen in Mörike. I will look in some detail at one of her
poems and sketch more briefly some of the major concerns in another.

The first of our poems by Droste is "Im Grase" (In the Grass; 1844):

Süße Ruh', süßer Taumel im Gras,
Von des Krautes Arome umhaucht,
Tiefe Flut, tief, tief trunkne Flut,
Wenn die Wolk am Azure verraucht,
Wenn aufs müde schwimmende Haupt
Süßes Lachen gaukelt herab,

Liebe Stimme säuselt und träuft
Wie die Lindenblüt' auf ein Grab.

Wenn im Busen die Toten dann,
Jede Leiche sich streckt und regt,
Leise, leise den Odem zieht,
Die geschloßne Wimper bewegt,
Tote Lieb', tote Lust, tote Zeit,
All die Schätze, im Schutt verwühlt,
Sich berühren mit schüchternem Klang
Gleich den Glöckchen, vom Winde umspielt.

Stunden, flücht'ger ihr als der Kuß
Eines Strahls auf den trauernden See,
Als des ziehnden Vogels Lied,
Das mir niederperlt aus der Höh',
Als des schillernden Käfers Blitz
Wenn den Sonnenpfad er durcheilt,
Als der flücht'ge Druck einer Hand,
Die zum letzten Male verweilt.

Dennoch, Himmel, immer mir nur
Dieses eine nur: für das Lied
Jedes freien Vogels im Blau
Eine Seele, die mit ihm zieht,
Nur für jeden kärglichen Strahl
Meinen farbig schillernden Saum,
Jeder warmen Hand meinen Druck
Und für jedes Glück meinen Traum.

(Sweet rest, sweet rapture in the grass, surrounded by the scent of herbs, deep waters, deep, deep drunken waters, when the cloud evaporates in the azure, when sweet laughter flickers down on the tired, drifting head, a beloved voice murmurs and trickles like lime blossom upon a grave.// When the dead, every corpse then begins to stretch and move in my bosom, gently, gently drawing breath, moving closed lashes, dead love, dead desire, dead time, all the treasures buried in the rubble, begin to touch one another with a shy sound like snowdrops played by the wind.// Moments [Droste uses an antiquated meaning of the word "Stunden" here] more fleeting than the kiss of a light ray on the mourning lake, than the song of the departing bird that trickles down to me from on high, than the flash of the iridescent beetle hurrying through the sun's path, than the fleeting pressure of a hand lingering for the last time.// And yet, heavens, just one more thing, just this one thing for me: for the song of every free bird in the blue, a soul that joins it in flight, for every scant ray my iridescent colored hem, for every warm hand my pressure, and for every happiness my dream.)

The poem has a distinctly meditative quality, but unlike the nature poems by Mörike that we have looked at, it does not sound like a dramatic monologue. We do find a strong emphasis on sensory impressions, however. Sight, hearing, smell, and touch (alas, there is no reference to taste) interact to create the poem's texture. Some of these impressions are explicit: the grassy aroma in line 2 (smell), the laughter in line 6 and the birdsong of line 19 (hearing), the iridescent colors of the beetle in line 21 or the sunlight in lines 18 and 22 (sight), the pressure of a hand in lines 23 and 31 (touch). Other impressions are less directly represented: in addition to the fragrance of the grass, the speaker presumably also has a tactile sense of it as she tumbles on it in the poem's opening lines. And in some instances different senses are brought together, as in the case of the ray of light that kisses the surface of the lake in the third stanza. As the poem unfolds, it becomes increasingly unclear what elements of nature are present, as opposed to remembered or imagined. The "süßes Lachen" and "liebe Stimme," for example, are marked as illusions by the verb "gaukelt." Looking back to the opening lines, we now realize that even the scene in the grass is a memory that belongs to the "tiefe Flut" that lies just below full waking consciousness.

Droste builds this poem on a long-standing literary tradition: that of the *locus amoenus* or "pleasant place." Conceived as a trysting-place for lovers, this special setting usually consists of a grassy spot, a gentle breeze, some form of water, and one or more trees. The topos goes back to classical antiquity and is also a feature of medieval poetry (see Chapter 2). Although the *locus amoenus* did often function as an external equivalent for a state of mind, Droste develops this notion in a striking manner. Here, the characteristic elements of the pleasant landscape become a gathering-place for scattered memories. The second stanza makes this evident in an almost spooky way, by presenting the speaker's recollections as dead bodies that gradually come to life, stretching their limbs, drawing breath, and starting to open their eyes. "Tote Lieb', tote Lust, tote Zeit" become treasures buried beneath the rubble of the past. Yet despite the metaphor of dead bodies, opening the memory chamber does not reveal a cabinet of horrors. Instead, the treasures gently chime as they come into contact with one another. Biographically, the memories here are of Droste's younger friend Levin Schücking, who was both a substitute son for her and the object of more than motherly desire. By the time of this poem's composition, their friendship was largely over (in part because he had married a woman closer to his own age), but they still corresponded about their writing. Like the link with the dead brother in Mörike's "An eine Äolsharfe," however, the connection between Schücking and Droste adds poignancy to "Im Grase," but the poem also stands well on its own without this extra information. Again and again, the text refers to death and loss: the linden tree that ripples above a grave, the treasures of the past that lie buried in rubble, the pressure of a hand that lingers for one last time. As in Mörike, the emphasis is on the fleeting nature of these things, but in contrast to Mörike, the speaker of Droste's poem insists on their continued existence and even their intensification in memory. Time is first specifically mentioned in line 13 ("tote Zeit"), but the passage of time is evident in many small details such as the departing bird and the hurrying beetle in stanza 3.

"Im Grase" does not reinforce the transitory nature of things by lightening the meter in the manner of Mörike. Instead, it uses firm rhythms with a preponderance of one-syllable words at crucial junctures and full, regular rhymes (note, however, that not every line rhymes). Resonant words with full vowels occur frequently, and important words are repeated. In addition to the obvious repetitions in the lines "Tiefe Flut, tief, tief trunkne Flut" and "Tote Lieb', tote Lust, tote Zeit," other key terms are also repeated, although with greater separation. "Leise," "flüchtig," "Strahl," "Vogel," "schillernd," "Druck," "nur" – this last in the plea or prayer of stanza 4 – all of these give structure to the constantly shifting scenario. And although the speaker loses herself in the memory of lost times, she nonetheless retains the ability to perceive beauty despite loss and to conceive the hope of the final stanza that is represented by imagination and dream. Like Mörike's nature meditations, this poem too is a text about the creation of poetry. Not accidentally does birdsong figure in the concluding stanza, along with a hope for identification with the bird's flight. The reference to "meinen farbig schillernden Saum" is not simply a domestic metaphor that refers to the hem of a dress: it also evokes something like a magic cloak whose iridescent colors recall the natural garment of the beetle.

The poems of Droste's last years (she died, possibly of pneumonia, in 1848) include some of her most substantial. "Mondesaufgang" (written in 1844 and published in 1845; Moonrise) provides a fine example of her adaptations of Romantic requisites to the new interest in sensory perception. The poem is too long to be quoted in full here, but some of its salient features demonstrate concerns common to both Droste and Mörike. First, a sense of expectation, here encapsulated in the moonlight that the speaker awaits on her balcony; second, an understanding of nature as composed of manifold small but telling details, here exemplified by fireflies and moths; third, a pervasive feeling of loss, in this instance "ein verlornes Leben" (a lost life) and "ein verkümmert

Herz" (a withered heart; the omission of the ending "-es" on "verkümmert"
is merely a poetic device); and finally, a connection between the outer and the
inner world, as when raindrops on the branches illuminated by the rising moon
appear to contain within them the flickering light of a domestic lamp. But as in
the case of the uncannily awakening corpses in "Im Grase," "Mondesaufgang"
also includes terrifying images in the form of mountain peaks that resemble
a circle of dark-robed judges, assembled to receive a malefactor before their
tribunal. Droste does not shy away from this kind of vision, even when, as in
this case, it seems overdrawn. Mörike tends not to develop imagery to such
extremes.

The problem of the self and the senses is taken up again at the turn of the
century by such poets as Hugo von Hofmannsthal and Rainer Maria Rilke.
Hofmannsthal's "Vorfrühling" (Early Spring; 1892) might well be set against
Mörike's "An eine Äolsharfe":

> Es läuft der Frühlingswind
> Durch kahle Alleen,
> Seltsame Dinge sind
> In seinem Wehn.
>
> Er hat sich gewiegt,
> Wo Weinen war,
> Und hat sich geschmiegt
> In zerrüttetes Haar.
>
> Er schüttelte nieder
> Akazienblüten
> Und kühlte die Glieder,
> Die atmend glühten.
>
> Lippen im Lachen
> Hat er berührt,
> Die weichen und wachen
> Fluren durchspürt.
>
> Er glitt durch die Flöte
> Als schluchzender Schrei,
> An dämmernder Röte
> Flog er vorbei.
>
> Er flog mit Schweigen
> Durch flüsternde Zimmer
> Und löschte im Neigen
> Der Ampel Schimmer.

Es läuft der Frühlingswind
Durch kahle Alleen,
Seltsame Dinge sind
In seinem Wehn.

Durch die glatten
Kahlen Alleen
Treibt sein Wehn
Blasse Schatten.

Und den Duft,
Den er gebracht,
Von wo er gekommen
Seit gestern nacht

(The spring wind passes through bare avenues; strange things are in its
movement.// It has cradled itself where there was weeping, and has
nestled itself in disordered hair.// It shook down acacia blossoms, and
cooled glowing, breathing limbs.// It stroked lips that were laughing, it
felt its way through soft and wakeful fields.// It slid through the flute as a
sobbing cry, it flew past emerging dawns.// It flew silently through
whispering rooms and bent down to put out the lamp's glimmer.// The
spring wind passes through bare avenues; strange things are in its
movement.// Through the smooth, bare avenues, it blows pale
shadows.// And the fragrance it brings, from where it came just last
night [note the lack of punctuation here])

The blowing wind has gathered up traces from its journey, "seltsame Dinge"
that seem to be part of its motion. The reader expects these traces to consist
in scents, as is the case in Mörike's poem; yet here, scent is not mentioned
until the final stanza. Most of the elements it has collected are emotions or
expressions of emotion such as weeping and laughter. It has touched human
beings but also passed through natural landscapes and tree-lined avenues. The
fluid quatrains sometimes focus on nature alone, sometimes on human life
alone, but often they mingle the two. The wind is not merely an element
in nature, but it also becomes a vehicle for human feelings: "Es glitt durch
die Flöte/ Als schluchzender Schrei" (stanza 5). By the same token, domestic
settings like the room of stanza 6 are described as "flüsternd" rather than
as containing whispering people in them. Laughter in this poem is similarly
attributed to "Lippen" rather than to individual people.

A striking aspect of the poem is the absence of an explicit "Ich." The closest
hint we have is the final line, "seit gestern nacht," which situates the speaker
in a temporal relation to the wind. The word "gestern," however, is a relative

term that does not tell us anything about a particular experience. We do not know, for example, whether the wind's journey has encompassed more than a single night. In terms of space, too, we cannot estimate where the speaker is located and what parts of the wind's travels he or she has seen, knows about, or imagines. Some kind of consciousness is presumably registering the various sights, sounds, and feelings, but it does not provide a focal point in which these can be collected as a unified picture. There may be a hint in the reference to "blasse Schatten" that appear to be driven along by the wind. Despite the unifying force of the alternating rhyme scheme and the frequent enjambments, the images themselves are disjunct, and seem to be drawn together by the power of accumulation rather than by a single coherent vision. In this regard, the poem is an apt expression of what the critic Hermann Bahr was to call, in an essay of 1904, "Das unrettbare Ich" (the unsalvageable self). With this term, Bahr attempted to summarize the ideas of the psychologist Ernst Mach, who argued in his 1885 book *The Analysis of Sensations* that the self is nothing other than a bundle of impressions registered. Describing Mach's study as a philosophy of impressionism, Bahr's essay had a significant influence on impressionist art and literature.

Rilke's poem "Am Rande der Nacht" (At the Edge of Night; 1902) makes explicit the way in which, according to turn-of-the-century thinking, the self is constituted in sensory impressions:

> Meine Stube und diese Weite,
> wach über nachtendem Land, –
> ist Eines. Ich bin eine Saite,
> über rauschende breite
> Resonanzen gespannt.
>
> Die Dinge sind Geigenleiber,
> von murrendem Dunkel voll;
> drin träumt das Weinen der Weiber,
> drin rührt sich im Schlafe der Groll
> ganzer Geschlechter ...
> Ich soll
> silbern erzittern: dann wird
>
> Alles unter mir leben,
> und was in den Dingen irrt,
> wird nach dem Lichte streben,
> das von meinem tanzenden Tone,
> um welchen der Himmel wellt,
> durch schmale, schmachtende Spalten

in die alten
Abgründe ohne
Ende fällt...

(My room and this expanse, awake over the countryside where night is
falling – that is one thing. I am a string stretched across broad, echoing
resonances.// The things are violin bodies full of muttering darkness; in
them dreams the weeping of women, in them the resentment of whole
generations moves in its sleep... I am to tremble with silvery tones: then
everything beneath me will come to life, and everything that loses its
way in the things will strive toward the light which, from my dancing
tones around which heaven swells, will fall through narrow, languishing
cracks into abysses without end...)

The speaker of this poem sees himself as a string vibrating over a sounding
box ("eine Saite,/ über rauschende breite/ Resonanzen gespannt"). Although
he uses the quintessentially Romantic word "rauschen" to describe the sounds
latent in the sounding box, he does not use the Romantic and post-Romantic
metaphor of the Aeolian harp. Nor does he use the image of wind striking
the string. Things themselves, he claims, are resonance chambers. Within
their darkness, human emotions are contained, just as they are in the wind of
Hofmannsthal's "Vorfrühling." But the "Dinge" of this poem are quite different
from the mobile wind of Hofmannsthal's text. "Dunkel" does not just pertain
to the sounding-box of stringed instruments into which we can peer through
a dark hole, but also to the opacity of objects that cannot speak of their own
accord. The speaker of Rilke's poem feels that he is meant to vibrate along with
these objects, and that if he does so, they will somehow come to life. He sees
his own vibrating psyche in terms of sympathetic resonances. Yet he recognizes
that life, conceived in this way, would be highly precarious, since it would wax
and wane according to the tones with which it resonates. As a metaphor for
the speaker of the poem, the vibrating string suggests that he is dependent on
the world of things: he gives audible expression to them, but does not shape or
structure them. Nor is he a guarantor of their permanence, however faithfully
he renders them in sound, for ultimately the light sought out by whatever is
immanent in things must fall back into "alte Abgründe." The speaker feels
entirely passive, powerless to create in language the lasting qualities that have
traditionally been seen as the achievement of verbal art. The irregular line
lengths, especially in the passage where the speaker imagines the swell and ebb
of musical tones, recalls Mörike's use of varying line lengths in "Im Frühling"
and "An eine Äolsharfe." In contrast to those poems, however, which come to
at least some formal type of resolution, Rilke's "Am Rande der Nacht" simply

trails away. The title of the poem thus refers not only to the opening situation where the speaker looks out from his bedroom onto the nighttime landscape, but also to the position of the receptive poet who wishes to illuminate reality but is incapable of giving it definitive shape. "Am Rande der Nacht" gives voice to the deepest fears of the turn-of-the-century poet for whom the self is nothing more than a collection of fragile sensory impressions.

Chapter 8

Modernism and difficulty

In previous chapters we have learned how to work with poems by focusing on their most puzzling features and asking how they function within the whole. We have also seen that seemingly straightforward poems can often reveal surprising complexity. In this chapter, I will consider several different types of poetic difficulty in an attempt to show some characteristic aspects of modernist texts and the challenges they pose for the reader. To understand poems from any period, we sometimes need to have particular knowledge. In the most straightforward cases, consulting a dictionary or encyclopedia to find out about names, places, or special vocabulary may give us a foothold for further exploration. Sometimes a compact reference work is not sufficient, however. Let us look back at two examples from the nineteenth century, preceding the advent of German modernism in the last decade of that century. A case in point is Mörike's "Gesang Weylas" (Weyla's Song; 1831), with its opening line, "Du bist, Orplid, mein Land!" Most basic accounts of Mörike's life and work reveal that Orplid and Weyla are part of a fantasy developed by Mörike and a friend of his during their schooldays: Orplid is an imaginary island and Weyla its proprietary goddess. Yet this knowledge does not make the poem completely transparent. Here is the text:

> Du bist Orplid, mein Land!
> Das ferne leuchtet;
> Vom Meere dampfet dein besonnter Strand
> Den Nebel, so der Götter Wange feuchtet.
>
> Uralte Wasser steigen
> Verjüngt um deine Hüften, Kind!
> Vor deiner Gottheit beugen
> Sich Könige, die deine Wärter sind.

> (You are Orplid, my country! which gleams far off; your sunny shore
> evaporates the mist from the ocean that moistens the cheeks of the
> gods.// Primeval waters rise rejuvenated around your hips, my child!
> Before your divinity, kings who are your attendants bow.)

From the second stanza, we gather that the goddess Weyla regards Orplid with special affection, addressing the island as her "child." Yet in apparent contradiction to Weyla's protective posture toward the land, Orplid seems to be connected with the divine. Positioned between sky and sea, the island is in constant connection with natural processes of change and transformation: warmth from the sun causes mist to rise upward from its sandy shore, while it is also embraced by the cyclic action of ocean tides. While Weyla speaks in the manner of classical antiquity of "Götter" in the plural, she also sees the unceasing exchange between land and water as conferring a kind of "Gottheit" on the island itself. Worldly rulers – the attendant kings mentioned in the final line of the poem – are constrained to show obeisance to the island's transformative powers. The continual rejuvenation of the waters that have surrounded Orplid since primeval times is a kind of natural mirror of Weyla's own creativity as expressed by her song. Orplid itself becomes a figure for the intrinsic relation between nature and poetry. Later in this chapter, we will look back at this poem in order to identify the changes that have taken place between the private fantasy of "Gesang Weylas" and the hermetic character of modernist poetry.

Another type of obscurity that will appear once again in modernism can be found in Hölderlin's late hymns, written in the early 1800s. Two main sources account for much of the challenge these texts pose: first, Hölderlin's close study of the ancient Greek poet Pindar, and second, his involvement with German Idealist philosophy at a crucial moment in its development. These difficulties are heightened by Hölderlin's own idiosyncratic thought, itself fundamentally resistant to articulation in language. The opening lines of "Mnemosyne" (1803) convey a sense of this problem:

> Reif sind, in Feuer getaucht, gekochet,
> Die Frücht und auf der Erde geprüfet und ein Gesetz ist,
> Daß alles hineingeht, Schlangen gleich,
> Prophetisch, träumend auf
> Den Hügeln des Himmels.

> (Ripe, dipped in fire, cooked are the fruits and tested on the earth and a law exists that everything goes inward, like snakes, prophetic, dreaming on the hills of heaven.)

The syntax of these lines renders them almost untranslatable (note that the verb "are" has been shifted in the English to make the opening phrases somewhat clearer). The subject of the sentence, "Frücht" (the final "e" of the plural has been elided) does not appear until the beginning of the second line.

The initial adjective, "reif," the verb "sind," and the two participial phrases that follow it, "in Feuer getaucht" and "gekochet" (an older form of the past participle), hold the reader in suspension until the subject finally arrives. The underlying syntactic structure imitates a common pattern in ancient Greek, where a predicative adjective is placed first in the sentence: instead of "the horse is strong," Greek says "strong [is] the horse." Hölderlin's friends and former classmates at the seminary he attended in Tübingen would have been fully familiar with this structure; to their ears, "reif sind die Früchte" would have carried an echo of their studies of ancient Greek texts. This imitation of Greek syntax makes the poem sound like a translation from an ancient text; coupled with the reference to an unfamiliar "Gesetz" and a bizarre simile involving snakes, the opening lines of Hölderlin's hymn seem to emerge from an alien culture. It is hard to know where to look for clues that might unravel these baffling lines. Should we look for parallels in texts from Greek antiquity? Do we need to acquaint ourselves with some unspecified chapter in anthropology? The title of the poem points to Greek mythology, Mnemosyne being the mother of the muses and herself the goddess of memory. The deaths of the ancient heroes, Achilles, Ajax and Patroclos, are the subject of the final section of the fifty-one-line poem. From this context, we may assume that the snake image may have something to do with the shedding of skin, a phenomenon used in many cultures as a symbol of death and rebirth. The law mentioned in line 2 is presumably the cyclic nature of life. Yet much remains, even in these opening lines, that calls out for further explication. Deciphering this passage alone would require an extensive arsenal of information drawn from Hölderlin's work as a whole, the texts he had studied by other authors, and the belief systems with which he was familiar. The complex syncretic vision he constructs in this and other late poems cannot be apprehended by readerly intuition alone. Yet at least to a certain degree, the more work the reader has to do, the more attractive the text becomes: the more we participate in the construction of a meaningful whole, the greater our emotional investment in the text. The continuing fascination of Hölderlin's poetry owes much to the challenge it presents.

While Hölderlin is a key figure for modernist poets writing in German, their own poems tend to rely on a somewhat more willful deployment of difficulty. Their delight in unusual words yields more readily to understanding, if only because such words can be looked up in a dictionary or an encyclopedia. Sometimes a rare word highlights ambiguities that pervade the text on the metaphoric level. Yet even an ordinary word can become a puzzle, as we shall see when we examine Hofmannsthal's "Ballade des äußeren Lebens." Another stumbling block presented by poetry in the late nineteenth and early twentieth centuries is its heavy use of allusion to other texts. Only a reader steeped in the cultural context of the time can judge how readily contemporary readers would have been able to identify such allusions. Finally, the modernist period is marked by an interest in esoteric systems of thought such as a set of ideals shared by Stefan George and his circle, or the more personal philosophy Rilke develops in his *Duineser Elegien*, the opening lines of which he believed had come to him by "dictation." In this chapter, we will explore a range of examples from modernist poetry in German and suggest ways in which we can confront the challenges such work presents.

"Die Moderne" was the term German writers themselves used to describe the new forms of art and literature that began to emerge in the 1890s and continued throughout the first three decades of the twentieth century. It was a period of rapid sociological change due to the rise of urbanism and technology; in 1914, the upheaval of World War I exacerbated this sense of disorientation. These outward changes were accompanied by intense literary experimentation. Yet the many different forms of experiment mean that we can hardly speak in terms of a cohesive period. In the European countries, a series of aesthetic movements succeeded one another in rapid succession, with the result that modernism is more properly a set of only loosely related modernist movements. In many respects, "die Moderne" as evidenced in German-language poetry was part of European modernism, but it also had its own inflections. While German-speaking writers picked up impulses from French Symbolism and Italian futurism, the broad sweep of German modernism was initiated by what is known as the *Sprachkrise* (crisis of language) of the late nineteenth century. Language skepticism was not limited to the turn-of-the-century, however: it informs German-language literature over a large sweep of the twentieth century.

The language crisis had two different, but related, roots: first, the works of Nietzsche, and second, the writings of the empiricist philosophers and psychologists, notably Ernst Mach in his *Analyse der Empfindungen* (Analysis of Sensations; 1886). Nietzsche's radical dissociation of language from truth and his insistence on the lack of a transcendental vantage-point that could override ever-changing individual perspectives became key ideas for a younger generation of writers and thinkers deeply steeped in his thought. Mach's views of the self as a bundle of loosely associated particles in a state of constant reorganization without ever settling around a coherent center added a psychological dimension to the skeptical posture Nietzsche had initiated. These counter-intuitive ways of thinking explain both the shock and the fascination with which readers responded to the new texts that appeared at the turn of the century.

Hugo von Hofmannsthal began to explore problems of language in the 1890s: the years 1894 and 1895 are the most fecund period for his lyric poetry. His remarkable "Ballade des äußeren Lebens" (Ballad of External Life; 1895) has come to be a touchstone for the *Sprachkrise*:

> Und Kinder wachsen auf mit tiefen Augen,
> Die von nichts wissen, wachsen auf und sterben,
> Und alle Menschen gehen ihre Wege.
>
> Und süße Früchte werden aus den herben
> Und fallen nachts wie tote Vögel nieder
> Und liegen wenig Tage und verderben.
>
> Und immer weht der Wind, und immer wieder
> Vernehmen wir und reden viele Worte
> Und spüren Lust und Müdigkeit der Glieder.
>
> Und Straßen laufen durch das Gras, und Orte
> Sind da und dort, voll Fackeln, Bäumen, Teichen,
> Und drohende und totenhaft verdorrte . . .
>
> Wozu sind diese aufgebaut? und gleichen
> Einander nie? und sind unzählig viele?
> Was wechselt Lachen, Weinen und Erbleichen?
>
> Was frommt das alles uns und diese Spiele,
> Die wir doch groß und ewig einsam sind
> Und wandernd nimmer suchen irgend Ziele?
>
> Was frommts, dergleichen viel gesehen haben?
> Und dennoch sagt der viel, der "Abend" sagt,
> Ein Wort, daraus Tiefsinn und Trauer rinnt
>
> Wie schwerer Honig aus den hohlen Waben.

(And children grow up with deep eyes that know of nothing, grow up and die, and all people go their own ways.// And sweet fruits emerge from bitter ones, and fall at night like dead birds and lie a few days and turn rotten.// And always the wind blows and again and again we hear and utter many words and feel desire and fatigue in our limbs.// And streets run through the grass and townships are here and there, full of torches, trees, and ponds and threatening ones and deadly dried-up ones . . . // Why have these been built? And don't resemble one another at all? And are countlessly many? Why do laughter, weeping, and turning pale alternate?// Of what use is all this to us and these games, we who are, after all, grown up and eternally solitary and in our wanderings never seek any goal?// What is the use of having seen so many such things?/ And yet, he says much who says "evening," a word from which melancholy and sadness flow// Like heavy honey from the hollow combs.//)

The poem bears the title "ballad," but it has neither a traditional ballad form (rhymed four-line stanzas) nor the narrative impulse of a ballad. Instead, it consists of a strange combination of tight form and loose logic. The form is terza rima (in German, "Terzinen"), an Italian verse structure that consists of tercets that are at once self-contained (by the embracing rhymes in the first and third line of each tercet) and linked with the entire poem (by the rhyme of the middle line, which becomes that of the first and last lines of the succeeding tercet). Whereas the isolated final line normally completes the middle rhyme of the last complete tercet, this is not the case in Hofmannsthal's poem, which rather pointedly leaves the verb "sagt" without a closing rhyme (in technical terminology, it is a "Waise" or orphan; see glossary). Set against this relatively structured form is the loose concatenation of observations and remarks connected by "and." Compounding this contradiction is the mysterious word "Abend" in the third-last line, a suggestive term whose meaning is not made explicit. Its unexpected appearance at this point in the poem and its unexplained relation to the image of honey slowly pouring from the comb leave us in doubt about whether this is a private usage or whether Hofmannsthal's contemporaries would have shared the unspecified associations the text seems to attribute to the word "Abend." The effect is very unsettling. We may feel that we intuit the implications of the word, but we cannot be sure that we have fully plumbed its depths.

The puzzling nature of the poem – but also its appeal – rests on the central paradox of impressions that fail to add up to a single whole and that cannot be understood in terms of ordinary logic. Cause and effect are no longer in commission here. Reality is nothing more than a cluster of dissociated objects. Things both natural and man-made fail to fall into a meaningful pattern, and the speaker, disoriented by their seeming lack of relation, is bewildered by their multiplicity. Though he does recognize some kinds of process in the world – children growing and fruits ripening – he cannot identify the reasons behind these processes. His continued questions about the purpose of "all this" lead to no answers, just as the pathways through the grass lead to no goal. The randomness of nature is paralleled by an equivalent randomness in the human psyche, which seems to be seen from the same detached standpoint as the townships. Intriguingly, the series of three nouns that characterizes the townships, "Fackel, Bäume, Teiche" is echoed by the series of three emotional states, "Lachen, Weinen und Erbleichen," whose rationale remains hidden to him. In each case, the series of nouns is ever so slightly out of kilter.

Despite this extreme dissociation, the speaker is still able to construct two similes: the ripe fruits that fall to the ground like dead birds, and the emotions that seem to flow from the word "Abend" like heavy honey. Similes usually serve to clarify what might not be immediately intelligible, but here they complicate or even undermine what they are supposed to explain. Whereas the comparison with dead birds negates any positive associations attached to ripe fruit, the image of flowing honey countermands the negative connotations of "evening" as an ending, possibly even a kind of death. In this respect, "Ballade des äußeren Lebens" demonstrates an important aspect of modernist poetry, its emphasis on paradox and ambiguity.

Alongside the paradox of a self that continually seems to dissolve in the onslaught of impressions, "Ballade des äußeren Lebens" also exemplifies the paradox of language that, while aiming to describe external reality, can never fully grasp it. We hear and speak "viele Worte," but these words seem random and empty. Yet by means of its paratactical syntax (the many phrases and clauses connected by "and") the speaker steps back from the one metaphor he might have employed in this context: the notion that words are merely empty wind. At the end of the poem, when he makes the claim, "und dennoch sagt der viel, der 'Abend' sagt," he seems to offer a metaphor, but resists spelling out its implications. Associative thinking replaces causality and reason. Seven years later, Hofmannsthal will have his fictive figure, Lord Chandos, ruminate on the problem of language in a letter to his predecessor, Francis Bacon, the British nominalist of the seventeenth century. Titled simply, "Ein Brief," this imaginary letter appeared in 1902 and exerted a powerful influence on German-speaking writers of the time.

Rilke's poetry is particularly marked by these influences, though full artic-ulation of the language crisis emerged somewhat later in his work than it did in Hofmannsthal's. All young poets of the day read Nietzsche, however, and Rilke was no exception. Although he was in fact a deeply religious person, his poetry volume *Das Stundenbuch* (The Book of Hours, 1903) presents God as a projection of the monk who is praying to him: "Was wirst Du tun, Gott, wenn ich sterbe?" (What will you do, God, when I die?). It is an interesting twist on Nietzsche's motif of the "death of God." Rilke's earliest poems are saturated with a sense of the fragility of self and the impossibility of separating the self from the many impressions it absorbs from the world around it. His volume *Mir zur Feier* (To Celebrate Myself; 1897–1899) testifies to this issue. In the first decade of the twentieth century, Rilke took a different approach to the problem. Instead of focusing on the deliquescent self, he now explored the subject–object relation in the context of optical perception. We can observe this most clearly in texts from his *Neue Gedichte* (New Poems; 1907–1908), of which the best known is "Der Panther," first published in 1903:

> Sein Blick ist vom Vorübergehn der Stäbe
> so müd geworden, daß er nichts mehr hält.
> Ihm ist, als ob es tausend Stäbe gäbe
> und hinter tausend Stäben keine Welt.
>
> Der weiche Gang geschmeidig starker Schritte,
> der sich im allerkleinsten Kreise dreht,
> ist wie ein Tanz von Kraft um eine Mitte,
> in der betäubt ein großer Wille steht.
>
> Nur manchmal schiebt der Vorhang der Pupille
> sich lautlos auf –. Dann geht ein Bild hinein,
> geht durch der Glieder angespannte Stille –
> und hört im Herzen auf zu sein.

> (His gaze has grown so weary from the passing bars that he can retain nothing. It seems to him as if there were a thousand bars and behind a thousand bars no world.// The soft tread of silken strong steps, turning in the smallest of circles, is like a dance of power around a center, in which, numb, a great will stands.// Only sometimes does the curtain of the pupil silently rise –. Then an image enters, passes through the tense stillness of the limbs – and in the heart, ceases to exist.//)

The tightly wrought syntax of this poem is quite the opposite of Hofmannsthal's more loosely structured "Ballade des äußeren Lebens." With its alternating rhymes, its multiple alliterations and its strategic use of alliteration, Rilke's poem is centered on the "Tanz von Kraft" performed by the panther. This aspect of the poem remains abstract. Yet the subtitle of the poem, "Im Jardin des Plantes, Paris," indicates a real location for the captive animal; indeed, Rilke frequently visited the zoological garden in Paris to view the large cats, the gazelles, flamingos, parrots, and other exhibits. Although this indication of place in the subtitle suggests that the text will give priority to the real, the body of the poem works hard to complicate any simple conception of reality. In his two volumes of poems, *Neue Gedichte* and *Der Neuen Gedichte anderer Teil* (New Poems and New Poems Part II; 1907 and 1908 respectively), Rilke developed a type of poem about objects that aimed to exclude the emotions of the observer. In practice, however, Rilke's poems about objects are less objective than his own remarks lead one to expect. Sentimental feeling is indeed avoided; but the poems are at least as much concerned with the process of seeing as with the objects themselves. And seeing, as turn-of-the-century psychologists had established, is more problematic than we usually imagine.

This question is raised in the second part of the first stanza, where the speaker tells us how things seem to the panther as he paces in his cage. "Ihm ist, als ob": this focus on the panther's view of the bars as an interminable series that cuts him off from the outside world calls forth our sympathy for the animal's predicament. The bars, which from the panther's point of view seem to be passing by him incessantly, have so mesmerized him that he can no longer retain visual impressions. This is an impressive opening stanza, but how can we know whether the panther does see things in this way? Are we justified in attributing to the panther the kinds of responses that we ourselves might have if we were held in captivity? If this is a poem in which an animal is seen as an object, why does it anthropomorphize the panther by telling us how outside reality "appears" to the animal?

In the second stanza, the perspective shifts to a view from above, allowing us to see the circle formed by the panther's pacing. Through assonance and alliteration, the lithe yet powerful gait of the panther is rendered as an aesthetic event. Lines 6 and 7, themselves the center of the poem, describe the circle and its own center. Yet again, this description fails to remain completely objective: instead, the final lines of the stanza introduce a simile that attempts to represent the circle shaped by the panther's steps. In addition to its aesthetic implications, there is also a scientific aspect to this simile: "wie ein Tanz von Kraft um eine Mitte" suggests something like electromagnetism. At this point, the bodily presence of the panther recedes behind the abstraction of the powerful yet numbed will that seems to exist independently of the animal (the text does not say "sein großer Wille" but "*ein* großer Wille"). In this image, there is more than a trace of Nietzschean vitalism in the sense of a tight organic functioning that generates its own energy and power.

The final stanza of the poem rescinds all possibility that the viewer could enter into a relation with the animal. The panther's eyelid is now described as a "Vorhang" or curtain that opens as if mechanically and the image of the outside world enters the pupil of the eye as if by its own propulsion. Instead of passing directly to the panther's brain, it goes through his tensely muscular limbs to the animal's heart. There, the speaker tells us, it ceases to exist ("[es] hört im Herzen auf zu sein"). These lines are the most puzzling of the entire poem. It is no longer clear at all that the animal can "see" in the sense in which human beings usually understand that process. This new perspective on the animal's visual perception puts into question the opening stanza, which had invited us to empathize with the panther by imagining his gaze as if it might be our own. The poem as a whole, like most of the poems in the two volumes of Rilke's *Neue Gedichte*, in fact highlights problems intrinsic to the subject–object relationship. How can we truly know what we are seeing, and to what extent might our vision be contaminated, as it were, by imaginative projections that are linked more closely to ourselves than to the object?

Indeed, looking back at "Der Panther," we can see that the large creature is initially described in terms that might almost as well apply to a world-weary turn-of-the-century flâneur. Yet after the first stanza, the poem makes a decisive move away from decadence and toward modernism. We see this most clearly in its mystifying last line. What does it mean that the image of the outside world ceases to exist in the panther's heart? Readers who understand this to mean that inner and outer worlds come together have very little evidence with which to bolster that claim; one could equally argue the opposite. Aided by the finality of rhyme, the poem seems to conclude on a definitive note, but at the same time its last line offers a puzzle that cannot readily be solved. Furthermore, the constant movement between the concrete and the abstract, the physical presence of the panther and imaginative constructions the speaker places on it, makes it difficult to determine where the emphasis of the poem lies. The text suggests at first that we can imagine what the panther sees and thinks, but then it seems to take back that idea. What actually happens inside the panther is something we fundamentally cannot know. Instead of the realism suggested by the subtitle, the poem is in fact a Symbolist text whose central object – the panther – resists any clear decoding. Indeed, language, however brilliantly deployed in the depiction of the panther's movements, seems quite inadequate as a vehicle for understanding the animal's interior (if it has one).

In 1914, Rainer Maria Rilke wrote a strikingly modernist poem on the problem of language:

> Ausgesetzt auf den Bergen des Herzens. Siehe, wie klein dort,
> siehe: die letzte Ortschaft der Worte, und höher,
> aber wie klein auch, noch ein letztes
> Gehöft von Gefühl. Erkennst du's?
> Ausgesetzt auf den Bergen des Herzens. Steingrund
> unter den Händen. Hier blüht wohl
> einiges auf; aus stummem Absturz
> blüht ein unwissendes Kraut singend hervor.
> Aber der Wissende? Ach, der zu wissen begann
> und schweigt nun, ausgesetzt auf den Bergen des Herzens.
> Da geht wohl, heilen Bewußtseins,
> manches umher, manches gesicherte Bergtier,
> wechselt und weilt. Und der große geborgene Vogel

kreist um der Gipfel reine Verweigerung. – Aber
ungeborgen, hier auf den Bergen des Herzens...

(Exposed on the heart's mountains. Look, how small there, look: the last
village of words, and higher, but how small, too, one last farmstead of
feeling. Do you see it? Exposed on the heart's mountains. Stony ground
under one's hands. Here no doubt blossom a few things; from the mute
cliff an unknowing plant emerges and blooms, singing. But the knowing
one? Oh, he who began to know and is silent now, exposed on the
heart's mountains. There wander no doubt, their consciousness intact,
many a thing, many secure mountain animal moves and stays. And the
great sheltered bird circles around the pure refusal of the peaks. –But
unsheltered, here on the heart's mountains...)

Dispensing with rhyme, the poem uses irregular rhythms and line lengths.
Yet submerged in the free verse form are occasional allusions to classical elegiac
meters: the frequent dactyls and the mid-line caesuras are like fragmentary
reminiscences of earlier forms. The first line is in fact a straight classical
hexameter (see appendix on metrics):

Āusgĕ|sētzt ăuf dĕn| Bērgĕn dĕs| Hērzĕns.| Sīĕhĕ wĭe| klēin dŏrt

If we insert markings to indicate naturally stressed syllables, we will see that
almost all of them coincide with the "long" syllables of the classical meter.
There is only one exception, the word "áusgesètzt," which takes a secondary
stress in its final syllable, making the pattern from antiquity less mechanical.
The skill with which Rilke creates this meter is apparent. Yet the scheme rapidly
breaks down, as it also does in his *Duineser Elegien*, which he had already begun
when he composed this poem. Like many other texts from this period that he
chose not to publish, "Ausgesetzt auf den Bergen des Herzens" is a spin-off
from the larger project of the *Elegies*.

"Ausgesetzt" is constructed as a set of complex paradoxes. Its opening
metaphor, repeated twice in the course of the poem, highlights the insubstantial
nature of what would normally be substantial: the Alpine setting. Words that
denote objects – "Berge," "Ortschaft," "Gehöft," "Kraut," "Bergtier," "Vogel" –
are juxtaposed with strangely indeterminate expressions formed from neuter
adjectival nouns: "einiges," "manches." Against this paradoxically determinate
and indeterminate scenery, a cerebral strand is formed by the abstract noun
"Bewußtsein" and the simpler words referring to knowing and not knowing.
Plants, which have no consciousness, are set off against human beings, who
know, or perhaps only begin to know. A certain playfulness motivates the
development of the poem's central metaphor, "die Berge des Herzens," but it

is countermanded by the desperate gesture of the speaker, whose knowledge seems insufficient in the face of his exposure on the metaphorical mountain peaks which refuse him all shelter. The speaker seems to be in two places at once: observing the scene from below, along with someone else who is observing it with him and climbing bit by bit up the inhospitable mountainside. While he asks his companion to look up at the vanishingly small objects on the mountain, he is also profoundly alone, exposed without hope of human help. Climbing higher and higher, he passes village and farmstead, finally reaching places above the timber line where only a tenacious plant can grow and a few resilient animals make their way. The great bird that circles the peaks is at ease in the thin air, but the speaker feels endangered.

At the heart of these paradoxes is the fundamental problem of language. While it serves to express thoughts and feelings, it is not completely adequate to this task. As the speaker moves beyond the bounds of conventional language, he is obliged to work harder, and he does so by resorting to almost extravagant turns of phrase; but these do not suffice either. In the end, pressing language so hard only reveals its fundamental brittleness. In this respect, the poem shares some of the same concerns as Hofmannsthal's "Ein Brief." In contrast to the fictive Lord Chandos, however, the speaker of Rilke's poem does not speak fluently of the dilemma of language: instead, articulation increasingly breaks down, notably in line 9 with its elliptical question and the almost stammering exclamation that follows: "Aber der Wissende? Ach, der zu wissen begann/ und schweigt nun, ausgesetzt auf den Bergen des Herzens." The final, subjectless phrases of the poem, set off from the rest of the poem by a dash and ending with dots of suspension, suggest that language may be in its final throes: "– Aber ungeborgen, hier auf den Bergen des Herzens . . . " The poem, itself a reflection on the possibility of poetry, puts language in the paradoxical situation of simultaneously expressing and withholding meaning.

This effect is not surprising. The phrase "Bergen des Herzens" seems almost like a variant of Hölderlin's "Hügeln den Himmels" in the poem "Mnemosyne." Indeed, Rilke had immersed himself in Hölderlin's poetry ever since he was first introduced to it in 1910. Rilke's use of indeterminate abstractions such as "einiges" and "manches" recalls similar formulations in Hölderlin's hymns, as do the interpolated questions that remain unanswered and the emphasis on the problematic nature of knowledge and consciousness. What makes Rilke's "Ausgesetzt auf den Bergen des Herzens" a modernist text rather than a mere imitation of Hölderlin's difficult late style? Like "Mnemosyne," Rilke's "Ausgesetzt" despairs about the possibility of knowledge and insight in a period when the world no longer appears coherent. Whereas the speaker of "Mnemosyne" seeks guidance from remnants and recollections of a time when the world still seemed whole, the speaker of "Ausgesetzt auf den Bergen des Herzens" is already moving forward in an apocalyptic landscape, trying to cling to remnants of coherence even as they become sparser and slighter. Instead of the resonance that Hölderlin's poem acquires from multiple memories of classical antiquity, Rilke's poem carries a single, bold metaphor through to its most extreme expression, the incomplete sentence with which it ends.

Georg Trakl is another modernist whose poetry owes much to Hölderlin's late hymns. His use of color has much in common with Expressionist art; yet his idiosyncratic imagery appears akin to a private language. Viewed from a biographical perspective, the strangeness of Trakl's poetry may have to do with his unstable personality, his use of drugs, and a possible incestuous relationship with his sister. When his works first appeared in a historical-critical edition that tracked the genesis of his poems across several versions, readers were astounded to discover that, in revising his work, he often crossed out one word and replaced it by its opposite or by a word from a very different semantic field. Was Trakl insane? Or was this a calculated gimmick? How could one evaluate this kind of poetry? Rapidly, two camps opened up in the scholarly field, one claiming that Trakl's word choice was inconsistent and could thus not yield any clear interpretations, the other arguing that Trakl's notion of semantic and associative connections was a creative rethinking of normative usage. Still, close work on key words and word clusters can shed light on the apparent contradictions in his texts.

Let us look at a short poem, "Gesang einer gefangenen Amsel" (Song of a Captive Blackbird; 1915), which Trakl dedicated to his mentor Ludwig von Ficker:

> Dunkler Odem im grünen Gezweig.
> Blaue Blümchen umschweben das Antlitz
> Des Einsamen, den goldnen Schritt
> Ersterbend unter dem Ölbaum.
> Aufflattert mit trunknem Flügel die Nacht.
> So leise blutet Demut,
> Tau, der langsam tropft vom blühenden Dorn.
> Strahlender Arme Erbarmen
> Umfängt ein brechendes Herz.

> (Dark breath in green branches. Little blue flowers hover around the face of the solitary man, his golden tread dying away under the olive tree. Night flutters up on drunken wing. Humility bleeds so quietly, dew, which drips slowly from the blossoming thorn. The pity of radiant arms embraces a breaking heart.)

Our attention goes immediately to the use of colors: "grün," "blau," "golden" (green, blue, golden), along with a set of other words related to darkness and light: "dunkel," "Nacht," "strahlend." To these we might also add the word "blutet," which introduces the color red. We also find hints of Christian religion, most obviously in the word "Dorn," but also in the reference to the "Ölbaum." Looking more closely at the color words, we discover that, while "grün" is used in a relatively familiar way ("green branches" stands in for branches with green leaves), "golden" modifies a noun that we don't normally think of as having color: the gait of a person walking. "Blau" is a somewhat special case, since although there are certainly such real-life things as blue flowers, a reader familiar with German poetic tradition would immediately think of the motif of the "blaue Blume" in Novalis's novel *Heinrich von Ofterdingen* (Henry of Ofterdingen; 1802), where it functions as a symbol of poetry. Looking back at the first three lines of "Gesang einer gefangenen Amsel," we can observe a movement from referential meaning (green branches) through symbolic meaning (blue flowers) to something much more difficult to classify (golden tread). It is as if the poem begins by taking us, associatively, through a brief history of poetry. The "goldener Schritt" might be a synaesthetic image in which one sense impression mingles indistinguishably with another: the tread of the solitary man is something audible (as suggested in line 4, where it "dies away"), but it is linked with a color adjective that makes it almost something visible. This synaesthetic effect is characteristic of Symbolist poetry in the period around 1900. Looking back at line 1, we now see that there, too, one sense impression is combined with another: "Dunkler Odem [Odem = Atem] im grünen Gezweig." Obviously, we can't see this breath, but it is described as dark, and it is inserted into an otherwise visual description. Not only because it is dark, but also because we do not know where it comes from, the breath seems threatening. Still, the little blue blossoms that surround the solitary man's face and the reference to his "golden" tread contrast with the sinister effect of the mysterious breath.

Line 5 consists of a single sentence, located at the very center of the poem: "Aufflattert mit trunknem Flügel die Nacht." Its placement suggests its pivotal function. It also calls attention to itself because of its divergence from normal word order: the usual syntax would be "die Nacht flattert . . . auf." The sudden emergence of night makes one think of a bat or a night bird that disturbs the otherwise silent scene. The phrase "mit trunknem Flügel," with its singular noun and the lack of a definite or indefinite article, is highly poetic. Here again, we notice that the adjective is one not usually coupled with the noun: people or animals may be drunk, but not wings. In fact, the unusual image cites a phrase from Mallarmé's sonnet "Le vierge, le vivace et le bel aujourd'hui" (The virginal, living, and lovely today; 1885), a poem famous for its difficulty. The central figure in Mallarmé's poem is a swan that has become trapped in an ice-covered lake. Trakl's blackbird, caught in the thorns, is a variant and perhaps even a reversal of Mallarmé's trapped swan. In different ways, both birds stand for poetry itself, especially in its past forms. In Mallarmé's poem, the speaker imagines what it might be like if the ever-fresh present ("aujourd'hui") were to rupture the icy surface of the lake with "un coup d'aile ivre" (a flap of [its] drunken wing), thus freeing at least the head and neck of the trapped swan, if not also its frozen plumage. In Trakl's poem, the captive blackbird seems to sing while it bleeds on the blossoming thorn bushes.

The last four lines of Trakl's "Gesang einer gefangenen Amsel" seem extremely abstract, largely because the two nouns "Demut" and "Erbarmen" function almost like allegorical figures that one might find on monuments. What remains of the natural setting, the "Tau" and the "Dorn" are drawn into this abstract realm of sorrow, suffering, and noble emotion. The appositional relation of "Tau" to "Demut" complicates any easy allegorical decoding. We would like to say that "Tau" represents tears; but it is also intimately linked with humility. As the poem nears its conclusion, it attains a high degree of ambiguity. What are the "strahlende Arme" of the penultimate line? We want to think of them as either human or angelic, but they are not. They are the arms of pity, sketchily, but not fully personified. Whose heart is breaking at the end of the poem? Is it that of the solitary man or that of the captive blackbird? Have the two merged in some unexplained and possibly unfathomable way?

The motif of intoxication (the drunken wing of night) in the middle of the poem harks back to a long tradition of poetic creativity. In the early twentieth century, many readers would have thought of Nietzsche's concept of the "Dionysian," an ecstatic force named after Dionysos, the ancient Greek god of wine. Foregrounding this element, Trakl's poem seems to defy rational understanding, unfolding a kind of thought most closely related to intoxication or madness. Yet, in a manner characteristic of modernist poetry, it also presents itself as carefully constructed. The relation of "Schritt" to "Ersterbend" (lines 3 and 4) is chiastically reconfigured in that of "blutet" (line 6) to "blühend" (line 7). In each case, living and dying are linked: steps die away, and bleeding gives way to blossoming; alliteration is at work in each of the two pairs. The two present participles "ersterbend" (line 4) and "blühend" (a participial adjective; line 7) are also chiastically linked. The verb "aufflattert" at the beginning of line 5 is matched by "umfängt" at the beginning of line 9, but that also harks back to "umschweben" in line 2. Taking the cue from the word "Dorn," we can understand these parallels and reversals as part of a redemptive scheme addressed by the speaker of the poem.

The blackbird is one of Trakl's favorite motifs, and it seems to represent both poetry and lament. Even without knowing this, however, we can see why a captive blackbird might be sorrowful. The green branches of the opening line refer to nature in its natural state, which the bird can no longer fully experience. In that state, the bird is at one with nature, and thus it sees nightfall as the arrival of another large bird. Such a reading, however, cannot be carried through the entire poem: it simply does not do enough to explain the various images. Increasingly, the poem insists on its more symbolic reading: one in which the blackbird stands in for the poet in the modern, alienated world, where the traditional notion of the "breath" of inspiration has become a "dark breath." But even that reading does not fully pan out. With the motif of the thorn, Christian imagery also enters the text, so that "breath" now also stands for God's animation of human beings, and Christian qualities such as humility and pity emerge as powerful responses. At the end of the poem, pity reaches out with radiant arms, but the last word of the poem is "ein brechendes Herz." Whatever we know about the redemptive power of Christ, we are still left with human sorrow. The most important feature of this poem is its polyvalence, its ability to work within several different sets of conceptual frameworks at once. That may make it "obscure," but that obscurity is also part of its theme. This vision of the world and of man's place in it is so complex that it can only be articulated by sliding metaphors that cross the boundaries between conventional semantic fields. Unlocking this type of text depends on several factors: identifying the ways in which language functions within the poem ("cracking the code," as it were, of the speaker's associative imagination); situating the poem in its period, especially with respect to important precursor traditions such as French Symbolism; and being willing to entertain a conflicting set of belief systems. The difficulty this poem presents for its readers arises primarily from its attempt to pull into its ambit a variety of seemingly contradictory elements.

The blackbird poem provides an excellent foundation for Trakl's last poem, written in response to his experiences as a medical officer (he was a trained pharmacist by profession) in World War I. In 1914, when he volunteered in the German army, he was sent straight to Grodek (in Galicia; now in Ukraine). There, in the course of battle, he confronted nightmarish carnage, compounded by a lack of medications and medical supplies for the wounded. He became so disturbed that he committed suicide by taking an overdose of cocaine. His poem "Grodek" captures the disturbing nature of his war experience:

> Am Abend tönen die herbstlichen Wälder
> Von tödlichen Waffen, die goldnen Ebenen
> Und blauen Seen, darüber die Sonne

Düstrer hinrollt; umfängt die Nacht
Sterbende Krieger, die wilde Klage
Ihrer zerbrochenen Münder.
Doch stille sammelt im Weidengrund
Rotes Gewölk, darin ein zürnender Gott wohnt
Das vergoßne Blut sich, mondne Kühle;
Alle Straßen münden in schwarze Verwesung.
Unter goldnem Gezweig der Nacht und Sternen
Es schwankt der Schwester Schatten durch den schweigenden
                                                    Hain,
Zu grüßen die Geister der Helden, die blutenden Häupter;
Und leise tönen im Rohr die dunklen Flöten des Herbstes.
O stolzere Trauer! ihr ehernen Altäre
Die heiße Flamme des Geistes nährt heute ein gewaltiger
                                                    Schmerz,
Die ungebornen Enkel.

(In the evening the autumnal woods resound with deadly weapons, the
golden plains and the blue lakes over which the sun rolls more darkly;
night embraces dying warriors, the wild lament of their broken mouths.
But silently in the grazing field red cloud gathers in which an angry god
dwells, shed blood, moonlike coolness; all roads converge in black decay.
Under golden branches of the night and stars the sister's shadow sways
through the silent copse, to greet the spirits of the heroes, the bleeding
heads; And quietly in the reeds resound the dark flutes of autumn. O
prouder sorrow! You bronze altars [no punctuation here except the line
break] the hot flame of spirit is nourished today by a powerful pain, the
unborn grandchildren.)

This battlefield description cannot be explained by the horrors of war alone;
rather, it bears the particular stamp of modernist poetry in the Symbolist
tradition. We find here some of the same colors as in "Song of a Captive
Blackbird": gold, blue, red, black. Along with these colors, light and darkness
form a potent element of the poem's structure. Tree branches occur again,
though here in a metaphor that attempts to capture the network of the stars
against the night sky. Some paradoxical expressions also appear, but now
they are clearly motivated by the military conflict that has turned an otherwise autumnal scene of fields, meadows, and lakes into an apocalyptic vision.
Smoke from gunfire occludes the sun so that its disk "rolls more darkly" just
above the horizon. As evening progresses, the meadows fill with red cloud
and the blood of dead and dying soldiers; yet at the same time, the moon is
beginning to cast its cool light upon the scene, and the stars have arisen in the

night sky. The juxtaposition of the natural landscape and the gruesome scene of carnage intensifies the horror and also the poignancy of the description. The placement of the verb "umfängt" before its subject in line 4 heightens the contrast between the disappearance of the sun, a natural, everyday occurrence, and the monstrous slaughter of the warriors.

Onto this Expressionist scene steps the mysterious "sister" of line 12. In German, "Schwester" means both sister and nurse ("Krankenschwester"). In Trakl's previous poetry, this figure has already been elevated to mythic status as a spirit who appears in times of crisis. Referring to earlier poems does not, however, eliminate the puzzling nature of this figure. Note that the sister herself does not appear, but rather her shadow or shade ("Schatten"). Her step is not firm: she staggers through the trees as if stunned or intoxicated – we do not know which. The copse is a traditional motif that suggests a sacred grove dedicated to a divinity; often such a copse contains a temple where adepts may worship. The bronze altars, albeit metaphorical and not actual, emerge from this idea of the small wood dedicated to worship.

Now several connections and contrasts become apparent. First, the co-presence of two different views of the divine: the angry, raging god of line 10 (akin to, but not identical with, the Old Testament God) is set against the idea of the sacred wood drawn from classical antiquity with its polytheistic beliefs. Second, the "golden branches of night and stars" are homologous, as it were, with the trees of the sacred grove. Third, the sister comes to greet the spirits of the heroes, just as night has received them in line 4. Yet she does not glorify war: rather, she exemplifies humane empathy. And finally, the "dunkeln Flöten des Herbstes" resound quietly, as the "herbstlichen Wälder" had resounded more terrifyingly with the firing of weapons at the beginning of the poem.

But the poem is still not finished. Its astonishing conclusion consists of an almost classical apostrophe to sorrow and the bronze altars of remembrance. Curiously, two different syntactical strategies are used for addressing sorrow, on the one hand, and the bronze altars, on the other. Why does the speaker not use the "O" form in both instances? Why does he use the comparative form, "stolzere Trauer" rather than the more usual "stolze Trauer"? Further, how can the pain of unborn grandchildren nourish "die heiße Flamme des Geistes"? And what is the relationship between "ihr ehernen Altäre" and "die heiße Flamme des Geistes"? Oddly, there is no punctuation between the two phrases. A strange slippage partially undercuts the noble sentiments and classical reminiscences. The comparative adjective "stolzer" provides an important clue to the poem's final lines. In lieu of the cliché "proud sorrow" that is often pressed into service in ceremonies for fallen soldiers, the speaker of this poem invokes a "prouder sorrow" that rises above this conventional phraseology: it is a sorrow born of humane empathy for the loss of lives. In the woods outside Grodek, there is no temple with an eternal flame burning in memory of the dead soldiers; "Geist" – and of course the poem itself – stand in for the absent monument. "Geist" is the opposite of body, and it stands here for high ideals that threaten to be occluded by the ideology of war. This poem is not a war memorial in verbal form, but an anti-war memorial. Through its concluding gesture, "Grodek" reconfigures Horace's concept of the poem as a "monument more lasting than bronze." This monument is created not by poetry as such, but by poetry that unmasks the violence of modern warfare and replaces it by a new empathy of spirit. In this respect, "Grodek" takes its place in an international modernism that mediates between antiquity and the twentieth century, seeking new forms of expression to represent new conceptions of the role of intellect. To make sense of the poem, we need to bring to bear not only Symbolist synaesthesia and Expressionist use of strong color, but also the classical tradition of poetry in honor of fallen soldiers.

In English literature, the work of Ezra Pound and T. S. Eliot represents most strikingly the modernist conjunction of feeling and intellect. In German poetry, Gottfried Benn is their closest counterpart. His poem "Der Sänger" (The Singer; 1925) articulates the struggle between a classical ideal and the modern world. Here are the first two stanzas:

> Keime, Begriffsgenesen,
> Broadways, Azimuth,
> Turf- und Nebelwesen
> mischt der Sänger im Blut,
> immer in Gestaltung,
> immer dem Worte zu
> nach Vergessen der Spaltung
> zwischen ich und du.
>
> neurogene Leier,
> fahle Hyperämien,
> Blutdrucksschleier
> mittels Coffein,
> keiner kann ermessen
> dies: dem einen zu,
> ewig dem Vergessen
> zwischen ich und du.

> (Embryos, genesis of concepts, broadways, azimuth, turf racing and fog creatures are mixed in the blood by the singer, always in formation, always seeking the word toward forgetfulness of the split between I and

you.// Neurogenic lyre, pale hyperemias, blood pressure veils by means of caffeine, no one can take the measure of this: toward the one thing, always toward forgetting between I and you.)

Part of the "difficulty" provoked by these stanzas derives from vocabulary not common to everyday language. Employing a bold mixture of words from different fields – biology, medicine, navigation, myth, poetry, sport, the city –, the poem invokes the earliest origins of life before the rise of consciousness. With the split between subject and object, new ways of thought emerge such as the witty connection between "Turfwesen" (the horse racing business) and "Nebelwesen" (creatures of the fog). In an earlier poem, "Gesänge" (Cantos, 1913), the speaker had expressed a longing to return to our "Ururahnen" (most ancient of ancestors) and become "ein Klümpchen Schleim in einem warmen Moor" (a clump of slime in a warm swamp). One of the key ideas in Benn's writing prior to 1945 is the concept of a regression that might counter the modern tendency to excessive cerebration; only once this regression has been performed and the modern self dissolved will a new shaping of reality be possible. In "Der Sänger," the speaker points to a welter of technical specialties, each with its own terminology, that blocks access to the desired sense of wholeness. Although the poet is still designated by the Homeric term "singer," he struggles to navigate (the word "azimuth" is significant here) the path back to the primal condition. Modern and ancient ideas jostle in his bloodstream, but they fail to settle into a coherent vision. Today's poetry, as the second stanza cynically explains, arises from either neurosis or too much caffeine. In the early twentieth century, the word "caffeine" must have sounded more like a technical term than it does today, and the medical terminology that opens the same stanza reinforces that effect. At the same time, Benn's use of the scientific name for the operative element in coffee introduces an ironic element into the poem: other texts by Benn mention a stronger drug, cocaine, for example "Kokain" (Cocaine, 1917) and "O Nacht" (O Night; also 1917). In fact he, like some other doctors of the time, eventually became addicted to cocaine. For the purpose of understanding the poem, however, the crucial point does not so much lie in Benn's personal experience, but with his suggestion that a range of drugs from caffeine to cocaine has come to substitute for the Dionysian cult of wine associated with the creation of poetry.

The third and final stanza of "Der Sänger" moves explicitly to a contrast between the traditional and the modern poet:

> einstmals sang der Sänger
> über die Lerchen lieb
> heute ist er Zersprenger

mittels Gehirnprinzip,
stündlich webt er im Ganzen
drängend zum Traum des Gedichts
seine schweren Substanzen
selten und langsam ins Nichts.

(While the singer sang of lovely larks, today he is an exploder by means
of mental processes, hour by hour he weaves the whole moving toward
the dream of the poem his heavy substances rarely and slowly into
nothing.)

In a 1956 revision, Benn removed the songbirds in favor of a reference to
the dualism of subject and object. The "Gehirnprinzip" (literally, principle of
mind), in contrast to the relatively feeble states of intoxication brought about
by neurasthenia or caffeine, is a force powerful enough to shatter everything.
In this way, a new beginning takes place, one that can weave the substantial
into something insubstantial on the way to realizing the "Traum des Gedichts"
(dream of poetry).

What makes this poem modernist is not just its use of modern terminology
or difficult concepts: it is the sheer audacity with which it reconfigures the
notion of poetic creativity. While retaining the ancient notion of weaving that
underlies the very word "text," the poet also breaks up familiar structures
and reshapes them into something purely cerebral. The underlying notion of
productive nihilism was part of the Nietzschean heritage. If we look back at
Mörike's "Gesang Weylas," we can identify several changes that have taken place
between the 1830s and the 1920s. In Mörike's poem the power of creativity is
attributed to nature and its attendant gods, including Weyla herself: Weyla's
song is only possible because of the lung-like relationship between the imagined
island and its natural context. The poem functions by means of connections
between sky, water, and land that blend these individual elements into a single
whole. In Benn's "Der Sänger" poetry is the result of a tension between mental
processes embedded in specialized concepts and an only dimly expressible
longing to return to a more unified, but also more primitive approach to the
world that precedes rational thought. In the case of "Gesang Weylas," the
haunting names of the singer and her island transport the reader into a poetic
realm where the notion of creative wholeness is still intact. In the case of "Der
Sänger," the bard can only look back with nostalgia at this ideal, knowing
that the analytical nature of modern thought prevents its restoration. It helps
to know the meaning of words like "azimuth" and "hyperemia," but such
knowledge cannot overcome the fragmentation and alienation that are the
very point of Benn's poem. As readers, we can only accept what Benn, like

many other modernist poets, regards as the modern condition: we can make sense of the poem, but we cannot eradicate its radical disjunctions.

The idea that language was less a unifier than a divider continued in Benn's poetry well into the 1940s. His poem, "Ein Wort" (1941; A Word) testifies to the persistence of this issue:

> Ein Wort, ein Satz –: aus Chiffern steigen
> erkanntes Leben, jäher Sinn,
> die Sonne steht, die Sphären schweigen
> und alles ballt sich zu ihm hin.
>
> Ein Wort –, ein Glanz, ein Flug, ein Feuer,
> ein Flammenwurf, ein Sternenstrich –,
> und wieder Dunkel, ungeheuer,
> im leeren Raum um Welt und Ich.
>
> (A word, a sentence –: from ciphers rises recognized life, sudden meaning, the sun stands still, the spheres are silent and everything condenses toward it [i.e. the word or sentence].// A word –, a flash, a flight, a fire, a flame thrown, a streak of a star –, and then darkness again, monstrous, in the empty space around World and Self.)

The poem, itself as condensed as the "word" it celebrates, seems at first enigmatic; yet the term "Chiffer" (cipher) suggests that it may perhaps be possible to decode it. The first stanza, which at least includes some finite sentences, indicates that a single word or phrase may bring unexpected insight. Indeed, its revelations may be so stunning that the sun stands still and the cosmic harmony falls silent. The word, which in itself condenses profound meaning, also attracts other words that condense themselves around it. The second stanza sketches the epiphanic nature of the word through a list of possible metaphors, all of them connected with sudden light. But such flashes, the poem concludes, are only moments in a larger context where darkness reigns and world and self are isolated in empty space.

"Ein Wort" articulates an old theme in poetry, one that gained prominence during the Romantic period: the notion of a privileged moment that brings insight in an otherwise dark world. Such moments are what Hölderlin called "der ewige Augenblick." In light of this tradition, Benn's "word" is synonymous with poetry. Appropriately for a text about the epiphanic power of poetry, the form Benn chooses is a short one, and his style telegrammatic. Dashes punctuate the text at three points, suggesting, as it were, the gap the poetic word must jump if light is to flash forth. Cosmic imagery – the sun, the "spheres," and the stars – indicate the reach of the word as it transcends self and world, if only for an instant. The notion of the harmony of the spheres is an old one that has been superseded by modern astronomy, yet the poem still has recourse to this mode of thought, as it also does to the Biblical phrase "die Sonne steht," a reference to Joshua 10: 12–13, when God makes the sun stand still in order to help the Israelites in their fight against the city of Gibeon. The allusion – with the past tense of the Biblical passage changed into the present tense – implies that through the power of the poetic word something akin to a miracle can still occur today. The poem ends, however, on a more pessimistic note, reaffirming a fundamental separation of self and world.

In the early years after World War II, Benn's poetry became more formal, more aesthetically oriented, and more insistent on its autonomy from other concerns. His highly cerebral and finely chiseled forms continued to combine allusions to other poetry with scientific and technical terms in a controlled version of modernism. A new generation of poets was particularly attracted to his programmatic essay "Probleme der Lyrik" (Problems of the Lyric; 1951), deriving in part from ideas of Ezra Pound, which rapidly acquired canonical status. For many poets, this text, with its rejection of adjectives and similes, became a guide to the composition of modern poetry.

A more significant coda to the story of modernism and difficulty can be found in poetic responses to the Holocaust, the topic of our next chapter. Nelly Sachs's personal belief system, inspired by the Jewish mysticism that she read intensely during her exile from Nazi Germany, poses problems of understanding for the uninitiated reader. Paul Celan's development of an ultimate polysemic language replete with allusions to other texts, technical terms from geology and other sciences, and private references that are now gradually being deciphered by specialists, represents one of the most formidable challenges that have emerged in the wake of modernist poetic practices. In particular, Celan's radical extension and reshaping of these practices testifies to the long reach of modernist poetry into the third quarter of the twentieth century.

Chapter 9

Poetry after Auschwitz

When Theodor W. Adorno first wrote of poetry "after Auschwitz," he can hardly have imagined that this concept would unleash a long-running debate. In his 1949 essay "Kulturkritik und Gesellschaft" (Cultural Criticism and Society), on the dialectical relation between enlightenment and barbarism, Adorno argued that we had reached a final stage:

> Kulturkritik findet sich der letzten Stufe der Dialektik von Kultur und Barbarei gegenüber: nach Auschwitz ein Gedicht zu schreiben ist barbarisch, und das frißt auch die Erkenntnis an, die ausspricht, warum es unmöglich ward, heute Gedichte zu schreiben.
>
> (Cultural criticism finds itself confronting the last stage in the dialectic of culture and barbarity: to write poetry after Auschwitz is barbaric, and that corrodes even the recognition that articulates why it has become impossible to write poems today.)

Only much later did Adorno elaborate on this statement, first in his "Rede über Lyrik und Gesellschaft" (On Lyric Poetry and Society; 1957) and then in his essay "Engagement" (Commitment; 1962). The impossibility of writing poetry after Auschwitz, he explained, has to do with the very nature of lyric poetry itself. For Adorno, the lyric is a genre remote from the world of reality: it is poetry that posits "den Traum einer Welt ... , in der es anders wäre" (the dream of a world in which things would be otherwise). After the Eichmann trial of 1961 and the Frankfurt Auschwitz trials of 1963–1965, which brought specific details about the Nazi death camps to public consciousness, Adorno shifted ground somewhat, recognizing that poetry could play a role in expressing human suffering. Still, he refused to modify his statement of 1949: poetry is in a paradoxical situation, and if it engages with Auschwitz, it takes on a complex and difficult task.

This chapter will look primarily at texts by three of the earliest poets to write consciously in the wake of the Nazi crimes; the main focus will be on a crucial period from the late 1950s to the early 1960s. The first is Nelly Sachs, a Jewish poet who, with her elderly mother, escaped Nazi Germany and went into exile in Sweden. For a time, she was regarded as the primary spokesperson for the victims of Auschwitz. The second, ultimately to become the most prominent, is Paul Celan (a pseudonym that is a near-anagram of his real name, Antschel), the son of Jewish-Romanians who perished in an internment camp in Transnistria; he himself survived a forced-labor camp in Romania. Celan corresponded with Nelly Sachs and met her briefly in 1960. The third is Ingeborg Bachmann, an Austrian writer of non-Jewish heritage who felt permanently marked by the Nazi occupation of Austria which she had experienced as a young girl. As an adult, she opposed the presence of former Nazis in influential positions in post-war Austria. Bachmann admired the work of Nelly Sachs and dedicated one of her poems to her. She had a passionate affair with Celan, first between 1947 and the early 1950s and then again briefly in 1957. All three poets won distinguished literary prizes, and Nelly Sachs received the Nobel Prize for Literature in 1966. In their poetry, their public statements, and their correspondence, they engage in a complex conversation about the appropriateness of aesthetic form, the problem of love poetry, and the question of language after Auschwitz.

The canonical poem for "poetry after Auschwitz" is Celan's "Todesfuge" (Death Fugue). Written in 1944, the poem derives in part from Celan's own labor-camp experience, in part from what he had learned about the death camps; it also picks up images from a poem by Immanuel Weissglas. A first version of the poem was published in a Romanian translation under the title "Tangoul Mortii" (Death Tango; 1947), but Celan changed the title to "Todesfuge" for its German publication in 1948. The opening metaphor, "schwarze Milch der Frühe" (black milk of morning), recalls similar paradoxical images in Georg Trakl, as well as the influence of Romanian surrealism. But the most compelling feature of "Todesfuge" is its artful interweaving of opposing elements: the German and the Jewish, fair hair and dark hair, music and death, beauty and violence. The statement, "der Tod ist ein Meister aus Deutschland" (death is a master from Germany) bursts into the counterpoint of the poem with sinister effect. At the end of the poem, two figures are contrasted: the quintessential German women, Margarete (from Goethe's *Faust*) and Sulamith (from the Biblical Song of Songs).

When a famous critic asked Celan about the image of the "Grab in der Luft," the poet replied: "in *this* poem, it is neither a borrowing nor a metaphor." He was talking about the smoke from the crematoria that rose above the concentration camps. Despite the poem's basis in reality, Celan became increasingly distrustful of the way "Todesfuge" was becoming a fetish in postwar Germany. Although it was not the cause of Adorno's objections to "poetry after Auschwitz" (Adorno had not read the poem when he coined the phrase),

Celan himself began to think that he had not been right to cast his material in a musical form that might seem to aestheticize the reality of the death camps. In response to Adorno's dictum, he began to develop a different style of writing that he called "grey" poetry. This was a spare, terse style that avoided overt emotion and beautiful effects.

In "Meridian," his Büchner Prize acceptance speech of 1961, Paul Celan reminded his audience of Büchner's character Lenz, who sets out for a walk on January 20. Celan proposes something quite radical for his time:

> Vielleicht darf man sagen, daß jedem Gedicht sein "20. Jänner" eingeschrieben bleibt? Vielleicht ist das Neue an den Gedichten, die heute geschrieben werden, gerade dies: daß hier am deutlichsten versucht wird, solcher Daten eingedenk zu werden?
>
> (Perhaps one may say that every poem has its "20th of January" inscribed into it? Perhaps what is new about the poems that are being written today is precisely this: that they attempt most clearly to remain mindful of such dates?)

With this proposal that poems take their starting-points with specific dates, Celan breaks with Adorno's definition of "lyric expression." Once a date – and with it historical reality – is connected with a poem, it loses the untrammeled or pure quality often associated with the lyric. The "20th of January" is not simply a metaphor for the historicity of poetry, however: it is also the date of the Wannsee Conference in 1942, when what the Nazis called the "Final Solution" – the extermination of all Jews – was first proposed.

One poem by Celan addresses the question of its "date" in the title: "Tübingen, Jänner" (1963; the South German form of "January" echoes the usage in Büchner's novella). A related poem mentions a place in its title, though not a date: "Zürich, Zum Storchen" (Zurich, at the Stork Hotel; 1960).

> Vom Zuviel war die Rede, vom
> Zuwenig. Von Du
> und Aber-Du, von
> der Trübung durch Helles, von
> Jüdischem, von
> deinem Gott.
>
> Da-
> von.
> Am Tag einer Himmelfahrt, das
> Münster stand drüben, es kam
> mit einigem Gold übers Wasser.

Von deinem Gott war die Rede, ich sprach
gegen ihn, ich
ließ das Herz, das ich hatte,
hoffen:
auf
sein höchstes, umröcheltes, sein
haderndes Wort –

Dein Aug sah mir zu, sah hinweg,
dein Mund
sprach sich dem Aug zu, ich hörte:

Wir
wissen ja nicht, weißt du,
wir
wissen ja nicht,
was
gilt.

(Our talk was about too much, about too little. About you and the
transcendent You, about clouding by things light, about things Jewish,
about your God.// About that. On the day of an ascension, the cathedral
was over there, it came across the water with some glimmers of gold.//
Our talk was about your God, I spoke against him, I allowed the heart
that I had to hope: for his highest, his most deathrattled, his railing
word – // Your eye looked at me, looked away, your mouth addressed the
eye, I heard:// We – just don't know, you know, – we – we – just don't
know – what – counts.)

The poem tells of a conversation between Celan and Nelly Sachs (to whom
the poem is dedicated). Traveling from Sweden to receive the Annette von
Droste-Hülshoff Prize for poetry in Konstanz, Sachs was anxious about
entering Germany for the first time since her exile. When Celan offered to
meet her in Zurich, she felt that he might offer her comfort and support
before she traveled on. They spent three days together in Zurich: 25–27 May,
1960. Celan wrote "Zürich, Zum Storchen" at the end of the month, after
his return to Paris. Apart from the description of the cathedral at the water's
edge, there is little about this poem that is "lyrical" in the conventional sense
of the word. Even the descriptive passage is somewhat odd: it speaks of the
"Tag einer Himmelfahrt" (note that in German, "Himmelfahrt" means both
Ascension, "Christi Himmelfahrt," and Assumption, "Mariä Himmelfahrt").
We know from biographical materials that it was Ascension Day, 26 May, 1960.
Not only in this usage, but also in the rest of this passage, there is a peculiar

lack of specificity, a casualness or even carelessness about the description. The cathedral appears "mit einigem Gold" (literally: with some gold), and the movement of its image across the water is denoted by the simple verbs "stand" and "kam." It is as if the speaker were shifting the classic tourist scene away from center stage, rejecting any attempt to convey the magic of the place. The simple diction contrasts strikingly with the abstract opening lines of the poem and their evocation of deep philosophical questions. The word "davon," separated oddly across two lines by a hyphen, marks the shift from the difficult language of the opening and indicates, with a somewhat denigrating gesture, a return to the world of reality. Yet the building is a house of worship, not a worldly edifice, and thus the poem suggests that it would not be wrong to broach religious topics. Similarly, although the cathedral stands firmly on the ground, the speaker mentions only its reflection in the water, seemingly moving toward the observers on the other side of the river. The vignette is not presented as a poetic unity, but as a picture that can only be put together with some hesitation (notice the line break between "das" and "Münster").

The viewers do not pay much attention to this place, but instead continue their discussion about religion. The poem's speaker argues against his friend: he has lost all hope of communication with God. He argues that God's "highest word" could only be uttered in a death rattle. At this point, it becomes clear that there are actually two defining dates behind this poem: first, May 26, 1960, when Celan and Sachs viewed the Zurich cathedral from across the river, and second, January 20, 1942, the Wannsee Conference that set the Holocaust in motion. Celan's inability to believe in a just God derives from the latter "20th of January."

The last two sections of the poem are marked by increasing hesitation. The speaker and his friend, though not entirely disembodied, subsist only in the form of eye and mouth. Communication occurs at cross-purposes, and we do not hear how the speaker responds to his friend's comment on the unfathomable nature of God.

At the level of the words in the text, the comment that "wir wissen ja nicht" (we just don't know) appears like a gracious way out of an awkward disagreement about the existence of God. But Nelly Sachs's experience with religious belief was complicated. While her assimilated family belonged to the Jewish community in Berlin, they had never been practicing Jews. When the Nazi racial laws made it impossible for her to stay in Germany safely, Sachs's non-Jewish friends helped to organize her departure for Sweden. On the very day when Nelly received an order to report for deportation, she and her mother received their Swedish visas, and they were able to take the very last passenger flight that left for Stockholm, in May 1940. There Nelly Sachs began to explore her Jewish heritage for the first time and to establish a new sense of Jewish identity. In 1950, after her mother's death, she began to read deeply in the *Kabbalah*, a Jewish-mystic commentary on the Hebrew Bible. In particular, she read a chapter from the *Zohar* or "Book of Splendor" (a major document of Jewish mysticism written in thirteenth-century Spain) in Gershom Scholem's translation. Inspired by Jewish mysticism without slavishly following it, Sachs began to gain a measure of hope. She was especially attracted by the concept of the *shekina*, the presence of God in the world (this was the reading she preferred; other readings see the *shekina* as the feminine aspect of God). Scholem explained that the exile of the *shekina*, its banishment from God, could be understood as both the exile of Israel and the alienation of the soul from the divine. God, in Jewish mysticism, could choose either to reveal himself or to withdraw from human awareness. Thus from Nelly Sachs's perspective, the final statement of "Zürich, Zum Storchen" may also have been an expression of mystical belief. In this context, the image of the cathedral moving across the water "mit einigem Gold" might be read as a kind of revelation in which, on Ascension Day, a Christian house of worship sends forth glimmers of gold to two Jewish poets, one a mystic and the other a man who has lost belief.

Whereas Nelly Sachs's early poetry, *In den Wohnungen des Todes* (In the Houses of Death; 1947) and *Sternverdunkelung* (Eclipse of the Stars; 1949), directly addresses the murder of Jews during the Holocaust, her later volumes increasingly focus on the relation between human beings and the divine. An illuminating contrast with Celan's "Zürich, Zum Storchen" is provided by a key poem in Sachs's *Flucht und Verwandlung* (Flight and Transformation; 1959), published just one year before her meeting with Celan in Zurich:

> In der Flucht
> welch großer Empfang
> unterwegs–
>
> Eingehüllt
> in der Winde Tuch
> Füße im Gebet des Sandes
> der niemals Amen sagen kann
> denn er muß
> von der Flosse in den Flügel
> und weiter–
>
> Der kranke Schmetterling
> weiß bald wieder vom Meer –

Dieser Stein
mit der Inschrift der Fliege
hat sich mir in die Hand gegeben–

An Stelle von Heimat
halte ich die Verwandlungen der Welt –

(While fleeing, what a grand reception along the way – // Wrapped in
the cloth of the wind feet in the prayer of the sand that can never say
Amen for it must go from the fin to the wing and beyond – //The sick
butterfly soon knows once again about the ocean – this stone with the
inscription of the fly has given itself into my hand – //Instead of home, I
hold the transformations of the world –)

"In der Flucht" alludes to several types of exile at once: the author's exile
from Germany, Israel's exile in the desert, and the soul's exile from God. The
world is conceived as a struggle between flight and rest, dynamic and static
forces. To take flight is to escape from the heaviness of earthly existence and
to become part of the most transitory elements of nature, yet it is also a way
of grasping the hidden structures that lie behind the surface of reality. Every
image in the poem can be read on multiple levels. "Wrapped in the cloth of the
wind" includes elements of protection and exposure. Apparent oppositions are
part of a transformational process that can be seen in the larger movement of
evolution ("from the fin to the wing") as well as in individual phenomena such
as the butterfly who emerges to adulthood through metamorphosis and the
prehistoric fly whose outline remains on a fossil. The butterfly is a traditional
symbol of transformation: one might think of Goethe's well-known poem
"Selige Sehnsucht" (Blessed Longing; 1819), in which the butterfly perishes
in a candle-flame and is yet somehow transfigured. Sachs's butterfly image
derives not from observation of nature, but from Jewish mysticism, where it
functions as an image for the soul. Sachs only barely avoids sentimentality
here. Yet there are also more subtle touches: wind is a natural force, but also
an allusion to God's creation of man and to the inspiration that gives birth
to poetic utterance. The "inscription" of the fly in the stone reworks the
traditional concept of nature as a book. The entire poem is held together by
the contrast between exile and home, where exile is at once a state of loss and a
transcendence of gravity. Suggesting that the exiled soul can ultimately move
beyond pain by accepting the "transformations of the world," this poem hints
at a kind of hope not expressed in the comments Celan attributes to Sachs in
"Zürich, Zum Storchen." The book of *Zohar* had shown Nelly Sachs how to
overcome human alienation from God while also confirming the transforming
power of poetry.

The *Zohar* plays an increasingly central role in Nelly Sachs's conception of the creative task. In her subsequent volume, *Fahrt ins Staublose* (Journey Beyond the Earthly; 1961), she traces the journey the poet must make from the earthly realm to a state of transcendence. One short poem from this collection illustrates her shift to abstraction in this phase:

> Du
> in der Nacht
> mit dem Verlernen der Welt Beschäftigte
> von weit weit her
> dein Finger die Eisgrotte bemalte
> mit der singenden Landkarte eines verborgenen Meeres
> das sammelte in der Muschel deines Ohres die Noten
> Brücken-Bausteine
> von Hier nach Dort
> diese haargenaue Aufgabe
> deren Lösung
> den Sterbenden aufgegeben wird.
>
> (You, occupied in the night with unlearning the world from far far off
> your finger painted the ice grotto with the singing map of a hidden sea
> that gathered the music into the shell of your ear bridge-building-stones
> from Here to There this precise problem whose solution is assigned to
> the dying.)

Words like "singend" and "Noten" indicate that the subject of this poem is lyric poetry itself. Poetry sets itself the task ("Aufgabe" means both task and problem; the word "Lösung" in line 11 confirms the presence of both meanings) of building a bridge from the earthly to the transcendent. It also sets a task for the reader, enacted in this poem by syntactical problems created by the lack of punctuation. The unusual placement of verbs in lines 5 and 7 complicate the puzzle. At the same time, however, the poem presents itself an assemblage, a conglomeration of images that does not hold together logically. How can one reassemble the pieces with painstaking accuracy ("haargenau") when there are so many rifts and contradictions in the material? Even the person addressed, the "Du" of the opening line, remains obscure. Is it an intimate friend, is it the reader, or is it a form of self-address on the part of the speaker? Finally, if the problem is assigned to the dying, how can the "Du" possibly hope to accomplish it? We are left with the suggestion that writing poetry is not only a way of "unlearning the world," but also a kind of dying.

The poem is carefully constructed. Meaning, space, time, and relationships of all kinds partake in a fundamental and insoluble ambiguity. The poem hints at a journey into a sphere beyond the earthly, one that we cannot fully accomplish in life, but that we can anticipate through the medium of poetry with its special combination of loosely and tightly bound structures. "Du/ in der Nacht" makes an important statement about the function of the lyric, presenting it not as a flight from reality, but as a journey into insight.

Flight is the theme of an important sequence of poems "Lieder auf der Flucht" (Poems in Flight) in Ingeborg Bachmann's last volume of poetry, *Anrufung des Großen Bären* (Invocation of the Great Bear [Ursa Major]; 1956). The phrase "auf der Flucht" means "while fleeing," of course: it means an attempt to escape from something or someone threatening. Yet Bachmann refrains from delineating too clearly what this threat may be. The individual poems, fourteen in all, seem relatively simple, and in the main they employ familiar lyric forms. Opening with a motto from Petrarch, the sequence contains allusions to traditional poetry as well as echoes of the postwar Gottfried Benn. Here is the sixth in the sequence, an untitled poem that explores the question whether love poetry can be written after Auschwitz:

> Unterrichtet in der Liebe
> durch zehntausend Bücher,
> belehrt durch die Weitergabe
> wenig veränderbarer Gesten
> und törichter Schwüre –
>
> eingeweiht in die Liebe
> aber erst hier –
>
> als die Lava herabfuhr
> und ihr Hauch uns traf
> am Fuß des Berges,
> als zuletzt der erschöpfte Krater
> den Schlüssel preisgab
> für diese verschlossenen Körper –
>
> Wir traten ein in verwunschene Räume
> und leuchteten das Dunkel aus
> mit den Fingerspitzen.

(Instructed in love by ten thousand books, made learned by the passing down of scarcely alterable gestures and foolish vows – // initiated into love but here, for the first time – // when the lava poured down and its breath met us at the foot of the mountain, when finally the exhausted crater revealed the key to these enclosed bodies – // We entered the accursed spaces and shed light on the darkness with our fingertips.)

Bachman was living in Naples when she wrote this poem: the volcanic images were part of her experience there. Her companion at the time was the composer Hans Werner Henze, for whom she wrote ballet libretti; it precedes by a year the beginning of her affair with Paul Celan. This poem is the only one in the sequence "Lieder auf der Flucht" that uses the "we" form. The motif of the volcano looks back to Goethe, whose account of his 1787 visit to Vesuvius is a *locus classicus* (canonical text) for the description of an active volcano. Goethe reports that from time to time, the volcano erupts, but in quieter moments, tourists can go up to the crater and take a look inside. Then they must quickly scramble back down to avoid being caught in the next eruption. In Bachmann's poem, the word "Hauch" – the hot breath of the volcano that sweeps over the visitors at the foot of the mountain – alludes to the breath of God during the creation of Adam and Eve or the breath of the muse in the moment of poetic inspiration. Since this is also a poem about love, it is also about the lovers' passion. By the same token, the phrase "verschlossene Körper" suggests not only victims who have have remained buried in the crater of the volcano, but also the lovers' bodies, which had for a time been closed to each other. The contrast between "unterrichtet in der Liebe" and "eingeweiht in die Liebe" suggests the difference between book-learning and personal experience, and thus harks back to Goethe's *Römische Elegien* (see Chapter 5). But it diverges from Goethe's sequence by implying that the new knowledge is akin to being initiated into a mystery cult.

Yet Bachmann's lovers are not initiated into a new mode of worship. Rather, the volcano image becomes a metaphor for the catastrophe of the Holocaust. The last three lines of the poem allude to the hermetic nature of poetry after Auschwitz. The phrase "verwunschene Räume" (the verb "verwünschen" means to cast an evil spell) suggests the topography of the concentration camps and the evil spell that they have cast over German history. To enter such claustrophobic places is hardly what lovers would desire. The darkness of these spaces is not only a result of evil, but also a justification for the obscure nature of the poetry they engender. In what way can the lovers' fingertips illuminate the darkness of these spaces? Literally, this would only be possible if they were radioactive. Maybe they are, in some metaphorical sense.

Behind the poem lies an important question: what does it mean to live after Auschwitz? Or after Hiroshima? Does not the knowledge of such horrendous events diminish in some significant way the emotions of love or the experience of epiphany? In Bachmann's poem, the lovers' relationship acquires its most intense form against the backdrop of catastrophe. The poem asks whether we can still subscribe to the traditional claim that poetry sparks a moment of illumination in which life suddenly makes sense.

"Lieder auf der Flucht" forms the final sequence of the last book of poems – the last poems altogether – that Ingeborg Bachmann published in her lifetime. We now know that she did continue to write some poetry, but chose not to publish it. Although she had received prizes for her poetry, she had been writing narrative prose all along, and it was to prose that she devoted herself after 1956. During the Auschwitz trials of 1963–1965 she began to read extensively about law and medicine during the Third Reich. Her series of novels and narrative fragments published posthumously under the title she herself used for the project, *Todesarten* (Modes of Death; 1995), explored these topics, expanding them to include the suffering of women in a society dominated by men.

During the brief reprise of her love affair with Celan in 1957, the latter wrote substantial parts of his poetry volume *Sprachgitter* (Speech-Grille; 1959). In addition to exploring issues of language, communication, and silence, these poems also deal with the question of love after Auschwitz. For many years, it was thought that original manuscripts of a large number of texts by Celan were lost (though copies of them were housed in a German archive). In 2001, the missing originals were found in a closed section of Ingeborg Bachmann's papers in the Austrian National Library. Among them were twenty-one poems from *Sprachgitter*. One of these is Celan's reworking of the Tristan and Isolde story, "Matière de Bretagne," upon which we have already touched in Chapter 2. The manuscript of another poem in this group, "Weiß und Leicht" (White and Light) bears the inscription, "Für Dich, Ingeborg, für Dich – " (For you, Ingeborg, for you –). The title poem of the volume, "Sprachgitter," is not one of the handwritten versions he gave to Bachmann, but it is certainly a love poem:

Augenrund zwischen den Stäben.

Flimmertier Lid
rudert nach oben,
gibt einen Blick frei.

Iris, Schwimmerin, traumlos und trüb:
der Himmel, herzgrau, muß nah sein.

Schräg, in der eisernen Tülle,
der blakende Span.
Am Lichtsinn
errätst du die Seele.

(Wär ich wie du. Wärst du wie ich.
Standen wir nicht
Unter *einem* Passat?
Wir sind Fremde.)

Die Fliesen. Darauf,
dicht beieinander, die beiden
herzgraue Lachen:
zwei
Mundvoll Schweigen.

(Eye-round between the bars.// Eyelid, fluttering creature rows its way upward lets a glance escape.//Iris, swimmer, dreamless and cloudy: the sky, heartgrey, must be near.// On an angle, in the iron candleholder, the smoking wood chip. From the direction of the light you can guess at the soul.// (If only I were like you. If only you were like me. Didn't we stand under a *single* tradewind? We are strangers.)// The tiles. On them, close together, the two heartgrey pools: two mouthfuls of silence.)

Composed of a series of short sentences or phrases without clear connection to one another, the poem does not give up its secrets easily. The title, "Sprachgitter," means a window through which nuns in closed orders communicate with visitors from the outside. While the grille is designed to make communication possible, it also interferes with direct exchange, in part because the speakers cannot see each other's full expressions. "Sprachgitter" is the first of a series of nouns in the poem that suggest the presence of real objects without making them clearly visible. The speaker seems to be pointing things out, but it is hard to make them add up to a coherent scene. A curious section in parentheses breaks up the sequence of nouns and noun phrases without indicating its bearing on the accretion of phenomena. It is as if the poem were written in a private shorthand. In short, "Sprachgitter" presents a classic case of the hermetic poem.

One way to deal with this sort of text is to gather its various elements into groups. In the first three sections of the poem, we find three words connected with the eye: "Augenrund," "Lid" (= Augenlid), and "Iris" (eyeball, eyelid, and the iris of the eye). "Licht," in the fourth section, can only be perceived by the eye. The neologism "herzgrau" occurs twice in the poem, which gives it a certain prominence. Where there is a heart, there may also be a soul, and indeed, we find the word "Seele" at the end of the fourth section. Water is present both explicitly, in the two "herzgraue Lachen" ("Lachen" means "pools" here, and has nothing to do with laughter), and implicitly at the beginning of the poem where we find something rowing and something else swimming. In the parenthetical section, a tradewind ("Passat") is mentioned, a phenomenon one finds only on the ocean. Finally, the title of the poem, with its evocation of speech, is countered by the final word "Schweigen."

Having established these word clusters, we can shift the focus to the most difficult words and phrases – what I have termed in earlier chapters the "puzzles" of the poem. One of these is "Flimmertier Lid" in the second line. In my prose translation above, I rendered this as "eyelid, flutter creature," but this is only an approximate translation. More accurately, the eyelid together with the eyelashes is envisaged as a single-cell creature covered by vibratile filaments. A reader of German poetry in 1959 would have immediately made the connection to a famous description by Gottfried Benn of the poetic process: seeking an image for the poet's groping attempt to find words for what is initially inchoate, Benn used the term "Flimmerhaare" (vibratile hairs). The term is by no means limited to organisms of the type that Benn liked to imagine inhabiting the primeval slime. Yet the evocation, via Benn, of such primitive organisms helps us begin to understand how the eye metaphor functions in "Sprachgitter." To the speaker of the poem, the eyelid resembles a small animal moving in a liquid medium by means of vibratile organs. The eyeball of the opening line appears behind "bars" that turn out to be the eyelashes, fluttering like the hairs of the primitive unicellular being. Celan develops a brilliant, if somewhat hidden, cross-linguistic pun here: a technical word for vibratile hairs or "Flimmerhaare" is cilia; and the French word for eyelash is "cil." The eyelid and moving lashes look like a creature using its vibratile organs to make its way up through the viscous surface of the eye. While the eyelid is rowing, the iris of the eye is swimming. This is certainly a far-fetched way to describe someone waking up and starting to open their eyes. But the whole point of the poem is to draw connections between waking up from sleep and finding the right words for a poem. In female mammals, cilia also exist in the fallopian tubes and serve to move the ovum to the uterus. Another kind of vibratile motion is exemplified by the oscillation of the flagellum, which gives sperm its motility. The seemingly arcane imagery of vibratile hairs thus enables a dual reference to the mechanisms of eyesight and of procreation. If we add to this ambiguity the fact that vibratile motion is also a form of sound – even though it might subsist below the hearing threshold and even the threshold for mechanical measurement of sound frequencies – we find ourselves in the realm of creativity in several senses. In Celan's "Sprachgitter," the evolution of complex animals from unicellular creatures, the conception of a child through copulation, and the creation of poetry (audible words or song) come together in a complex and daring metaphor.

There is another, less arcane element at work here as well. A familiar tradition in German literature is the idea of the eye as a window to the soul: an example is Gottfried Keller's poem "Abendlied" (1872), which opens by apostrophizing the speaker's eyes: "Augen, meine lieben Fensterlein" (eyes, my dear little windows) and urging them to stay receptive to the outside world for as long as possible. One day, however, the eyelids will close, death will come, and the soul will find rest. In the last moments before death, however, there will be a small glimmer in each eye: "Noch zwei Fünklein sieht sie glimmend stehn,/ Wie zwei Sternlein innerlich zu sehn" (the soul still sees two small sparks glowing, like two stars seen internally) – and then the little lights waver and go out. The poet concludes by urging his eyes to drink in as much as they can while there is still time: "Trinkt, o Augen, was die Wimper halt,/ Von dem goldnen Überfluß der Welt!" (Drink in, O eyes, whatever the eyelash can hold of the world's golden excess!).

One way to read Celan's "Sprachgitter" might be as a rewriting of Keller's "Abendlied." Indeed, the sparks of light in the eyes that glimmer, waver, and then go out in Keller's poem are picked up in the fourth section of Celan's "Sprachgitter." Here there is a "smoking wood chip" in an iron holder (the word "Tülle" here means the socket of a candle holder, the part into which the candle is inserted); and, in an analogy to Keller's connection between the eye and the soul, we learn that one can discern the soul by observing the direction of the light. The light in the pupil of the eye is dim, like a piece of tinder that has almost burned out. In contrast to Keller, Celan denies the notion that there is any "golden excess" in the outside world. In "Sprachgitter," everything is grey and gloomy. The sky (or heaven) does not provide hope, but is a grey backdrop reflected by the iris. At the end of the poem, the two pools – or are they the two eyes (pools of tears, one might even venture to say) – are just as grey as the sky.

In the parenthetical section – an aside, as it were – the speaker considers the relation between the two lovers in terms of identity and difference. Feeling that they have sailed together, driven by the same tradewind, they wish to claim identity. But "wir sind Fremde." As he recognizes in the final section of the poem, they are at once together and apart, like a pair of eyes in the face. In the end, the two pools of water are identified with "zwei/ Mundvoll Schweigen." The pervasiveness of grey, the sorrows shared but not identical, and finally the speech grille that facilitates but also impedes communication, are marks of Celan's struggle with the problem of poetry after Auschwitz. The motif of "greyness" links the poem with Celan's turn away from the more aesthetic verse he had in his early phase. "Sprachgitter" is an excellent example of his spare but deeply moving "grey style."

If "Sprachgitter" is essentially a love poem that also revolves around the problem of language after Auschwitz, "Tübingen, Jänner" (1963) is a poem about language that situates Celan himself within the tradition of hermetic poetry. Like "Zürich, Zum Storchen," it is a poem that refers to a specific place. The word "Jänner" (south German dialect for January) picks up the motif of the "the 20th of January" that Celan had discussed in his prize speech, "Meridian." Unlike the Zurich poem, which refers to a meeting with a living poet, Nelly Sachs, "Tübingen, Jänner" looks back to Hölderlin and his final mental illness, when he was cared for in a tower on the Elbe. Hölderlin believed that he was living in a time too late for poetry, a time when one could only ask, despairingly, what use there was for poetry "in dürftiger Zeit" (in a needy time). When Hölderlin succumbed to his psychological affliction, he had trouble speaking coherently, but ingeniously invented a special word, "Pallaksch," that meant both yes and no. Celan's poem argues that if a man like Hölderlin, with his sense for the prophetic, were to come into the world today, he could do nothing other than to babble. Poetry after Auschwitz, according to "Tübingen, Jänner," is poetry deprived of its ability to make clear statements, poetry that can only stutter.

This chapter has dwelt mainly on the early phases of the debate over poetry after Auschwitz, when the question was most acute. As lyric poetry became more overtly political in the wake of the Student Revolution of 1968, it took a more pointed, skeptical, and ironic stance. Refraining from the hermeticism of the earlier phase, this poetry articulated in more straightforward language the admonition that we should "never forget." Peter Rühmkorf's "Bleib erschütterbar und widersteh" (Remain Shockable and Resist; 1979) is characteristic of the warning tone of poetry in this phase.

Let us look now at two poems that exemplify later stages in the lyric reflection on Auschwitz. Ulla Hahn's ingenious poem "Nach Jahr und Tag" (After Many a Year; 1983) reminds us that even the most innocent of activities take place against a barely conscious recognition of the Nazi crimes. The title indicates the extent to which Auschwitz still functions – after many a year – as a crucial *terminus post quem*, the date after which everything appears different. Each section of the poem needs to be read on two levels: that of contemporary life, and that of life in the extermination camps:

> Ein Waggon fährt vorbei
> Er hat Kohle geladen
>
> Männer links Frauen rechts
> Zu den Kabinen im Freibad
>
> Schuhe liegen auf einem Haufen
> Im Sommerschlußverkauf
>
> Haare warden geschnitten
> Zu einer neuen Frisur

Menschen gehen ins Bad
Zum Baden

Ein Feuer brennt
Es wärmt

Rauch steigt auf
Eine Kerze verlischt.

(A railroad car passes by it is loaded with coal// Men to the left, women
to the right go into the changing rooms at the swimming pool// Shoes
lie in a heap in the end-of-summer sales// Hair is cut in a new way//
People go into the pool to swim// A fire is burning it warms us// Smoke
rises a candle goes out.//

These double-edged lines function as reminders that, even though we see
ourselves as firmly anchored in the present, another historical reality – the
memory of Auschwitz – continues to subtend the world of today.

In contrast to Hahn's poem, Durs Grünbein's "Gedicht über Dresden" (Poem
about Desden; 1991) turns its attention away from Auschwitz and toward the
Allies' bombing of Dresden during World War II. Replete with allusions to
Dresden's past, Grünbein's poem calls for historical and cultural knowledge
on the part of the reader and needs to be carefully deciphered:

> Scheintote Stadt, Barockwrack an der Elbe,
>   Schwimmend in brauner Lauge, spät fixiert
>   Taucht sie aus Rotz und Wasser auf, ein Suchbild
>   Ein Puzzle, königlich, mit dem der Krieg
>   Die Schrecken der Zerstörungswelt entschärfte.
>   . . . was diesen Brücken keinen Abbruch tat,
>   Der Silhouette nicht, den schmalen Türmen
>
> Chiaveris Schwan und dem Balkon Europas, –
>   Sandstein, der alles weichmacht was hier aufwächst.
>   Das beste Depressivum ist der genius loci
>   An einem Ort, gemästet mit Erinnerungen,
>   Schwammfäule, schön getönt als Nostalgie
>   Narkotisch wie die psychotropen Jamben,
>   Die anglo-amerikanische Version von nevermore,
>
> Auch Dresden ist ein Werk des Malerlehrlings
>   Mit dem in Wien verstümperten Talent
>   Der halb Europa seinen Stilbruch aufzwang.
>   In diesem Fall ergab sich wie von selbst
>   Die Technik flächendeckender Radierung

Durch fremde Bomber, Meister ihres Fachs
In einer Nacht mit schwarzem Schnee im Februar.

Getreu den Plänen seines Kunstfreunds Speer
(»Die Zukunft, Albert!«) bleibt von Bausubstanzen
Nach tausend Jahren noch, groß im Verfall
Die Schönheit der Ruinen, ihr Ruinenwert,
So praktisch kommt Romantik in der Hand
Von Ingenieuren. Ein Gesamtkunstwerk
Singt unter Trümmern noch in höchsten Tönen.

Im Futur II wird alles still geworden sein.

(Seemingly dead city, Baroque wreck on the Elbe swimming in brown liquid, belatedly developed. It surfaces out of the snot and water, a puzzle with hidden images. A puzzle, kingly, with which the war neutralized the horrors of the world of destruction. Which did not diminish these bridges nor the silhouette, the narrow towers// Chiaveri's swan and the balcony of Europe, – sandstone that softens everything that grows here, the best depressor is the genius loci in a place fattened by memories, wet mold, beautifully tinted as nostalgia narcotic like the psychotropic iambs, the Anglo-American version of "nevermore,"// Dresden is also a work of the painter's apprentice whose talent, stunted in Vienna, forced his style-break upon half of Europe. In this instance the technology of carpet sculpting by foreign bomber planes, masters of their subject in a single February night with black snow.// True to the plans of his artistic friend Speer ('The future, Albert!') what still remains of building substance after a thousand years, great in decline the beauty of ruins, their ruin value. Romanticism turns out to be practical in the hands of engineers. A total work of art still sings in highest tones among the rubble.// In the future perfect everything will have fallen silent.)

Using what the poem's speaker calls "die anglo-amerikanische Version von nevermore," in other words iambic pentameter, the poem evokes the city on the Elbe as a "Barockwrack" swimming in an unpleasant brown liquid and threatened by wet rot. Patterns on the surface of the contaminated water make it look like a picture-puzzle, perhaps in much the same way as Grünbein's poem presents itself as a poem-puzzle that seems to invite us to think about what pictures we might see in the neat form of its lines, sloping regularly inward like overgrown ode strophes, while at the same time overloaded with an irregular accretion of images. The gaps in the city's architecture caused by the Allies' wartime carpet-bombing join with the slow erosion of its sandstone buildings to create a sense of decay and decline that allude to a favorite motif of the Baroque period, *vanitas*. The Italian Gaetano Chiaveri was a master architect and builder who designed and directed the construction of the Catholic Church of the Royal Court of Saxony between 1738 and 1749. The word "Schwan" alludes both to one of the shapes favored by the Dresden manufacturers of Meißen porcelain and to the way Chiaveri's church seems to float on the water like a swan. The "balcony of Europe" refers to one of the sights of Dresden, garden terraces designed by Count Brühl in *c.* 1740 and imitated by the stair-step shape of the poem's stanzas. The original Baroque city situated on the river Elbe created effects that led to its designation as the "Florence on the Elbe." Yet, as Grünbein notes, there is also a certain beauty to the damaged city that makes it more akin to the fake ruins of which the Romantics were so fond. The term "Ruinenwert" was coined by Albert Speer, who was for a time Hitler's chief architect. Speer's theory was that a good building should be thought of as one that, at some point in the future, would make an impressive ruin. In this city, it is easy to fall prey to nostalgia. Using metaphors derived from photography, the poem likens the city on the brown river to a sepia image developed belatedly ("spät fixiert") and tinted like an old photo colored by hand ("schön getönt als Nostalgie"). But the poem also reminds us that the city's present form, though directly caused by Allied bombers, is indirectly also "ein Werk des Malerlehrlings . . . der halb Europa seinen Stilbruch aufzwang" – in other words Hitler, who had originally hoped to be an artist. Using a term of rhetoric, "Stilbruch" (a stylistic incongruity or sudden change in style), the poem introduces the verbal arts in addition to the visual arts. It does not take long for music to enter the scene, as the speaker goes on to suggest, ironically, that through the actions of "total war" Dresden has become a kind of Wagnerian "Gesamtkunstwerk" (total work of art) that continues to sing in the tones of high art. It is as if the ruined architecture were vibrating to an inaudible tuning fork. In a final twist, the poem concludes by looking to a future when even this song will finally fall silent: "Im Futur II wird alles still geworden sein." The speaker understands his present position not just as "after" Nazism and World War II, but also as "before" a possible final cataclysm that we may yet bring upon ourselves.

Looking back over this series of poems, it is clear how profoundly their authors understand "Auschwitz" as a radical base line from which everything has to be rethought. What began as a brief example in Adorno's essay on the dialectic of enlightenment and barbarism became a stimulus for continual reappraisal of the contemporary world over a period of more than fifty years. Although the engagement with Adorno was stronger in the early decades of this period, the notion of Auschwitz as the initiating event for late twentieth- and early twenty-first-century poetry has not completely disappeared. Indeed, an entire series of writers, including Hans Magnus Enzensberger, Hilde Domin, and Günter Grass, essentially agreed with Peter Szondi's observation, "Nach Auschwitz ist kein Gedicht mehr möglich, es sei denn auf Grund von Auschwitz" (No poem is possible after Auschwitz unless it be one written because of Auschwitz).

Chapter 10

Political poetry

German scholars often comment that the term "politische Lyrik" seems to be something of an oxymoron. Yet in classical antiquity and the Middle Ages, there was no perceived tension between the two elements of which the term is composed. For many centuries, song and metrical language were the acknowledged forms of high literature. With the advent of Romanticism, however, the term "lyric" began to acquire a special meaning. In addition to an emphasis on the musical aspect of poetry, the Romantics thought of certain types of poetry as particularly adapted for subjective expression. "Lyric" poetry increasingly came to refer to texts that captured subjective responses to external stimuli and conjured up a fleeting moment of fulfillment. This type of poem – we might think of Eichendorff's "Mondnacht" (Moonlit Night; 1835) – is scarcely compatible with politics in the ordinary sense of the term. The distinction between the apparent spontaneity of lyric expression and the type of reasoning that subtends political thought is what gives rise to the idea that "politische Lyrik" is a paradox.

Under certain circumstances, however, seemingly apolitical poetry can perform a political function. This is the case, for example, with the nature poetry that expressed a coded opposition to Nazism during the Third Reich, or with the formalist experimentation that acted as a critique of the German Democratic Republic. Even the poetry of the "New Subjectivity" that followed the overtly political poetry of the early 1970s takes a political position through its ubiquitous nostalgia for a more politically active period.

In this chapter, we shall focus on poetry that is itself conscious of the paradoxical character of texts that present political issues in aesthetic forms. This choice should not be understood as implying that national anthems, party rally songs, or straightforward political verse satire is not interesting and worthy of careful study. Nonetheless, poems that speak to the complex relation between ideology and aesthetics can give us insights that allow us to think more sharply about the nature of political poetry. Although positioned at the end of this book, the chapter is not meant to imply that political poetry is the dominant form of recent German poetry. Instead, many forms of poetry continue to coexist, written in almost all of the registers we have explored in earlier chapters.

If German Romanticism was the high point in the exploration of the subjective lyric, its immediate aftermath laid the foundation of modern skepticism about the possibility of lyric poetry in its purest forms. Heinrich Heine was the key figure in the reflection on and response to Romanticism, and his political poems became a touchstone for subsequent thought about what "politische Lyrik" might be.

Heine's voluntary exile in France had given him a broader and more complex view of Germany's situation in the 1830s than he might otherwise have had. Disappointment with the failure of his countrymen to bring about a revolution akin to the overthrow of the French *ancien régime*, he decided to leave for France. Arriving in Paris in spring 1831, he did not see the dark side of the French Revolution until the bloody uprising of June 1832, which left him profoundly disillusioned about the possibility of realizing the social ideals that had motivated the initial French Revolution of 1789. At the same time, the ambivalent feelings this experience brought forth were also grist to the mill of this master of irony, allusion, and nuance. In a number of prose works, notably his *Börne-Denkschrift* (Börne Memorial; 1839; a testimony to the life of his fellow radical Ludwig Börne) and his important essay on German culture, *Die Romantische Schule*, Heine reflects on the complex nature of patriotism. Finally, after twelve years in Paris, he goes back to Germany to visit his ageing mother. Upon his return to Paris, he embarks on a long poem titled *Deutschland: Ein Wintermärchen*. Ingeniously combining a simple form – four-line rhyming stanzas – with the presentation of characters and incidents at once moving and comic, realistic and fantastic, he conveys the many-sided nature of his relation both to his native land and the land to which he has "exiled" himself. It is easy to see how a long poem might do justice to the complexity of his simultaneous adherence to and critique of patriotism. In his volume *Neue Gedichte* (New Poems; 1844) he attempts to achieve similar effects in shorter forms. Two of these poems have been much anthologized and often cited. The shorter of the two runs as follows:

> Ich hatte einst ein schönes Vaterland.
> Der Eichenbaum
> Wuchs dort so hoch, die Veilchen nickten sanft.
> Es war ein Traum.

Das küßte mich auf deutsch, und sprach auf deutsch
(Man glaubt es kaum
Wie gut es klang) das Wort: ich liebe dich!
Es war ein Traum.

(Once I had a beautiful fatherland. The oak tree grew so tall there, the
violets nodded gently. It was a dream.// It kissed me in German and
spoke in German – it's hard to believe how good it sounded – the words:
"I love you!" It was a dream.)

Here Heine makes new use of a device he had employed in *Das Buch der
Lieder*: the whimsical evocation of plants and flowers to add a lightly ironic
dimension to what the reader understands to be, in actuality, an exploration of
human emotions. In this poem, the transition from a familiar icon of German
nature, the oak tree, to an almost anthropomorphized flower, the nodding
violet, is delicately achieved. It is of course a cliché to say that violets nod their
heads; but here the downward cast of the violets suggests that Germany's natural
beauty is characterized by charming modesty. Lest the shift from realistic
description to fantastic anthropomorphism seem overdone, the speaker deftly
plays down this effect in his parenthetical comment, "Man glaubt es kaum/
wie gut es klang." Deeply imbued with the German Romantic ethos and at the
same time critical of it, Heine knew well the Romantic notion that the sounds
of nature speak to us and that the poet is the one designated by virtue of his
special gifts to translate that speech into human language. Here, the metaphor
is carried one stage further when the speaker suggests that the natural landscape
of his homeland actually speaks to him "auf deutsch." The repetition of this
phrase suggests at once the deeply emotional character of the experience and
its somewhat ludicrous quality if seen from a more rational perspective. The
final line of the poem, by picking up the words "Es war ein Traum" that had
ended the first set of four lines, does not so much confirm this statement
as invest its key term, "dream," with a different meaning: what had at first
seemed the fulfillment of long-held desire is revealed as nothing other than
an illusion. Yet this deflation of the dream does not simply pull the rug out
from under the speaker's desire to return to the German language and the
German homeland. The poem keeps the two mutually contradictory desires
in tension: the speaker's recognition that he cannot really go home again does
not completely obliterate his desire to do so.

This subtle understanding of what it means to return to one's native land
after a long absence is spelled out at greater length in Heine's famous poem
"Nachtgedanken" (Night Thoughts; 1843), also written after his visit to his
mother in that year. In it, we can trace the deep division in his psyche between

sentimental resignation and continuing political optimism for the future of Germany:

> Denk ich an Deutschland in der Nacht,
> Dann bin ich um den Schlaf gebracht,
> Ich kann nicht mehr die Augen schließen,
> Und meine heißen Tränen fließen.
>
> Die Jahre kommen und vergehn!
> Seit ich die Mutter nicht gesehn,
> Zwölf Jahre sind schon hingegangen;
> Es wächst mein Sehnen und Verlangen.
>
> Mein Sehnen und Verlangen wächst.
> Die alte Frau hat mich behext,
> Ich denke immer an die alte,
> Die alte Frau, die Gott erhalte!
>
> Die alte Frau hat mich so lieb,
> Und in den Briefen, die sie schrieb,
> Seh ich, wie ihre Hand gezittert,
> Wie tief das Mutterherz erschüttert.
>
> Die Mutter liegt mir stets im Sinn.
> Zwölf lange Jahre flossen hin,
> Zwölf lange Jahre sind verflossen,
> Seit ich sie nicht ans Herz geschlossen.
>
> Deutschland hat ewigen Bestand,
> Es ist ein kerngesundes Land;
> Mit seinen Eichen, seinen Linden,
> Werd ich es immer wiederfinden.
>
> Nach Deutschland lechzt' ich nicht so sehr,
> Wenn nicht die Mutter dorten wär;
> Das Vaterland wird nie verderben,
> Jedoch die alte Frau kann sterben.
>
> Seit ich das Land verlassen hab,
> So viele sanken dort ins Grab,
> Die ich geliebt – wenn ich sie zähle,
> So will verbluten meine Seele.
>
> Und zählen muß ich – Mit der Zahl
> Schwillt immer höher meine Qual,
> Mir ist, als wälzten sich die Leichen
> Auf meine Brust – Gottlob! sie weichen!

Gottlob! durch meine Fenster bricht
Französisch heitres Tageslicht;
Es kommt mein Weib, schön wie der Morgen,
Und lächelt fort die deutschen Sorgen.

(If I think of Germany at night, I don't get any sleep, I can't close my
eyes any more. And hot tears flow.// The years come and go. Since I last
saw my mother, twelve years have passed already; my longing and desire
are growing.// My longing and desire are growing. The old woman has
put a spell on me, I keep on thinking of her, may God protect the old
woman.// The old woman is so fond of me, and in the letters she has
written, I can see how her hand trembles, and how deeply her motherly
heart is shattered.// My mind keeps dwelling on my mother, twelve long
years have passed, twelve long years have vanished away, since I clasped
her to my heart.// Germany will exist forever, the state's as fit as a fiddle;
with its oak trees, with its lindens, I'll always find it again.// I wouldn't
have such an appetite for Germany if my mother weren't there, The
fatherland will never go to rack and ruin, yet the old woman could die.//
Since I left the land, many have gone to their graves, people I loved – and
when I count them up, it's as if my heart would bleed to death.// And
count them I must – and with that number my agony wells up more and
more, it's as if the corpses were tossing and turning on my breast –
Thank God, now they vanish! // Thank God! In my window dawns
serene French daylight; my wife comes in, lovely as the morning, and
laughs away my German cares.//)

In placing this poem at the end of his volume *Neue Gedichte*, Heine gave it
a prominent position; it has become one of his best-known poems. It moves
through a range of emotions: despair about what has become of his native
land, sentimental longing in the speaker's desire to see his mother once more,
and the ironic tone of the mocking reference to Germany as a "kerngesundes
Land." The notion of an eternal Germany, exemplified by its powerful oak
and linden trees, cannot be taken without a grain of salt. However long-lived,
even these trees do not live forever. Indeed, the line "Deutschland hat ewigen
Bestand" strains metrically against the pattern established by the four-stressed
iambic lines at the beginning of the preceding stanzas. How are we to scan this
line? Normal speech would require "Déutschland hat éwigen Bestánd," but
this introduces a dactyl into the line and reduces the stresses to three. Readings
that attempt to wrest four stresses out of the line, such as "Déutschland hát
éwigen Bestánd," "Déutschland hat éwigén Bestánd," or "Déutschlànd hat
éwigen Bestánd," are not fully persuasive. Heine is a master of subtle metrical
instability within a seemingly regular strophic scheme, and whenever such

metrical disturbances occur, it is always worth asking whether they add to the meaning. In this instance, the metrical uncertainty of the line undermines the apparent certainty of the statement the line expresses. Yet the third line of the stanza returns to the regular metrical scheme: "Es íst ein kérngesúndes Lánd." By this point, however, we recognize the speaker's irony.

By the time we get to stanzas eight and nine, we even begin to suspect that the deaths that have taken place in Germany during the speaker's absence are not all simply the result of old age and its accompanying illnesses. Why does the speaker imagine that the corpses are tossing about on his breast ("Mir ist, als wälzten sich die Leichen/ Auf meine Brust")? Though not literally to blame for these deaths, he feels the weight of guilt because he has escaped to a place where life is less burdensome. In the end, however, even this quite natural sense of guilt is cast as a characteristically German mode of thought ("deutsche Sorgen") that contrasts with the enlightened good sense of France ("französisch heitres Tageslicht"). The "night thoughts" of the poem's title are dispelled by the light breaking through the window at dawn and the carefree attitude of the speaker's French wife. And yet, this reversal takes place too suddenly and too easily to be completely convincing.

These two poems about Germany illustrate Heine's gift for presenting difficult feelings in all their complexity and for demonstrating that matters of politics are not only part of the world of thought but also of feeling.

In the twentieth century, Heine continues to be a model for political poets, but Bertolt Brecht soon joins him in that role. For poetry after the end of World War II, Brecht's work becomes a yardstick for later writers. At its best, his poems stress the contradictory nature of the human situation. "Schlechte Zeit für Lyrik" (Bad Times for Poetry; 1939), his most frequently anthologized piece, articulates the dilemma of a poet torn between traditional aesthetics and the mandates of his time:

> Ich weiß doch: nur der Glückliche
> Ist beliebt. Seine Stimme
> Hört man gern. Sein Gesicht ist schön.
>
> Der verkrüppelte Baum im Hof
> Zeigt auf den schlechten Boden, aber
> Die Vorübergehenden schimpfen ihn einen Krüppel
> Doch mit Recht.
>
> Die grünen Boote und die lustigen Segel des Sundes
> Sehe ich nicht. Von allem
> Sehe ich nur der Fischer rissiges Garnnetz.
> Warum rede ich nur davon

Daß die vierzigjährige Häuslerin gekrümmt geht?
Die Brüste der Mädchen
sind warm wie ehedem.

In meinem Lied ein Reim
Käme mir fast vor wie Übermut.

In mir streiten sich
Die Begeisterung über den blühenden Apfelbaum
Und das Entsetzen über die Reden des Anstreichers.
Aber nur das zweite
Drängt mich zum Schreibtisch.

(I know: only the fortunate person is loved. We like to hear his voice. His
face is handsome.// The crippled tree in the courtyard bears witness to
the poor ground, but the passersby call it a cripple and rightly so.// I do
not see the green boats and the cheerful sails in the sound. Above all I
see only the fishermen's torn nets. Why do I only speak// Of the fact that
the forty-year-old cottager's wife walks with a stoop? The girls' breasts
are warm as before.// A rhyme in my poem would seem to me like
excessive exuberance.// Within me struggle exhilaration over the
blossoming apple tree and horror at the speeches of the dauber
[= Hitler]. But only the latter forces me to my desk.)

When Brecht wrote this poem, he was in Denmark, where he had already
spent six years in exile from Hitler's Germany. Unlike those writers who were
in the good graces of the Nazi authorities and whose works were thus allowed
to be published, Brecht knows that his voice cannot be heard in the very
country where his protest against Nazi policies and actions could perhaps
make the greatest difference: Germany itself. The speaker of the poem is well
aware of the many things around him that might otherwise have moved him
to write: the lovely scene of boats in the narrows ("Sund" means an ocean
inlet), the breasts of young women, the blossoming apple tree. Against these
visible objects, he sets social concerns, embodied in the stooped forty-year-
old woman and the torn nets of fishermen. When he finally mentions Hitler's
speeches in the last section of the poem, we realize that the problems of poverty
in Denmark have called to his mind the even greater damage emanating from
the German dictator. By using the word "der Anstreicher," Brecht alludes to
Hitler's artistic ambitions: in his youth, Hitler had twice applied unsuccessfully
to the Academy of Art in Vienna. His talent was mediocre at best, and many
of his paintings were copies of motifs from postcards. Although I have translated Brecht's scornful term for this thoroughly trivial painter as "dauber,"
the word "Anstreicher" actually means house-painter. The speaker of Brecht's
poem ignores the fishing boat scene – itself a conventional motif in amateur

painting – and, while still aware of the young women's "warm breasts," rejects the erotic as an appropriate topic for his poem. Through a series of contrasts between aesthetic beauty and social poverty, he acknowledges his struggle to turn away from conventional poetic or artistic topics to warn of the danger of Hitler and his regime. By articulating the tension between timeless aesthetics and contemporary political urgency, Brecht disarms those readers who might be put off by a single-mindedly ideological poem. In this way, the title, "Schlechte Zeit für Lyrik," ultimately suggests its opposite: that difficult times might in fact be the most productive moments for subtle poetry.

When writers reconnected with poetic tradition after the end of World War II, they often included reflections about the status and function of poetry in their texts. Günter Eich's "Inventur" (Inventory; 1947) has come to be an iconic text for the period, included in most anthologies and regarded as the prime exemplar of the "Stunde Null" (zero hour), a perceived caesura immediately following the end of World War II. Composed during Eich's internment as an American prisoner of war in 1945/46, "Inventur" is less a manifesto for a new start in postwar poetry than a reflection on the poetic avenues that still remain for an author confined to a prison camp. The poem's combination of simplicity and flexibility is what allows it to function as an iconic text for the postwar period. As its title indicates, the poem is an inventory, or stocktaking, of what the speaker still possesses: cap, coat, shaving kit, plate, mug, canned food, bread bag, socks, handkerchief, a length of tent fabric, a sheet of cardboard on which to lie at night, and some string. In addition to this relatively mundane equipment, the prisoner also names some less predictable objects: a nail, a propelling pencil refill, and a notebook. He uses all three of these things for writing: the nail to inscribe his name on the tin plate and mug, and the pencil lead to write verses in the notebook. The plain language he uses to list his belongings would seem to belie his interest in poetry were it not for a subtle touch in the penultimate stanza:

> Die Bleistiftmine
> Lieb ich am meisten,
> Tags schreibt sie mir Verse,
> Die nachts ich erdacht.

> (I love the propelling pencil refill most, in the daytime it writes verses for me that I thought up during the night.)

The contrastive structure of lines 3 and 4 of this stanza alludes to the balance of night and day in Goethe's most famous Roman elegy (see Chapter 5). In Eich's poem, however, there is no sleeping woman on whose back the poet can tap out his meter: instead, all that separates him from the naked ground is a makeshift sheet of cardboard. The poem itself, with its unrhymed two-stressed lines, seems almost artless. Yet the speaker also suggests that concrete objects are not all that remains: his bread bag also conceals "einiges, was ich/ niemand verrate" (some things I won't reveal to anyone). Whatever these private items may be, they are too special even to be named in the poem. In that respect, they have something in common with his desire to write verse, another crucial part of his innermost self.

Almost two decades later, Hans Magnus Enzensberger published a poem that clearly builds on Eich's well-known text. The title, "Küchenzettel" (Bill of Fare; 1964) suggests that this, too, will be a kind of list; despite its title, it is less a menu than a visual stock-taking:

> an einem müßigen nachmittag, heute
> seh ich in meinem haus
> durch die offene küchentür
> eine milchkanne   ein zwiebelbrett
> einen katzenteller
> auf dem tisch liegt ein telegramm.
> ich habe es nicht gelesen.
>
> in einem museum zu amsterdam
> sah ich auf einem alten bild
> durch die küchentür
> eine milchkanne   einen brotkorb
> einen katzenteller.
> auf dem tisch lag ein brief.
> ich habe ihn nicht gelesen.
>
> in einem sommerhaus an der moskwa
> sah ich vor wenigen wochen
> durch die offene küchentür
> einen brotkorb   ein zwiebelbrett
> einen katzenteller.
> auf dem tisch lag die zeitung.
> ich habe sie nicht gelesen.
>
> durch die offene küchentür
> seh ich vergossene milch
> dreißigjährige kriege
> tränen auf zwiebelbrettern
> anti-raketen-raketen
> brotkörbe
> klassenkämpfe.

links unten ganz in der ecke
seh ich einen katzenteller.

(On a lazy afternoon, today in my house I see through the open kitchen
door a milk can, an onion chopping board, a cat dish, on the table lies a
telegram. I haven't read it.// In a museum in Amsterdam I saw in an old
picture through the kitchen door a milk can, a bread basket, a cat dish.
On the table lay a letter. I haven't read it.// In a summer house on the
Moskwa [river] a few weeks ago I saw through the open kitchen door a
bread basket, an onion chopping board, a cat dish. On the table lay the
newspaper. I didn't read it.// Through the open kitchen door I see spilled
milk, Thirty Years' Wars, tears on onion chopping boards, anti-rocket
rockets, bread baskets, class struggles.// Right in the lower left-hand
corner I see a cat dish.)

Though couched in apparently simple language, this poem reverses Eich's
emphasis on writing as the primary strategy for survival. In response to Eich,
Enzensberger contrasts the intimacy of domestic scenes with the international
political situation. He constructs his poem by a series of repetitions and oppositions. Three kitchen scenes form the backbone of the poem: the speaker in his
own house, a genre painting from an earlier period that he remembers from a
visit to Amsterdam, and a scene in a summer house in Russia. The verb "sehen"
refers both to actual vision in the present and to pictorial representation. Yet
these two seem to be strangely conflated at the end of the poem, when the
view through the open kitchen door suddenly appears itself as a painting with
a "lower left-hand corner." Three textual documents also punctuate the poem:
the telegram on the kitchen table in the present day; the letter on the table in
the Dutch painting; and the newspaper in the Russian summer house that the
speaker saw just a few weeks ago. He has not read any of these texts, even though
the telegram implies some sort of urgency. The letter in the Dutch painting is
not addressed to the speaker, and we do not know whether it lies open or bears
writing clear enough for its viewer to decipher. Finally, we have no information
about the summer house on the Moskwa and in what sense the speaker may
have visited it or perhaps just seen a photograph of it somewhere. If the latter,
then perhaps the present tense of line 23 ("seh ich vergossene Milch") does not
refer to the scene in the speaker's own kitchen, but to the scene in the photo.
In any event, the verb "sehen" now encompasses more than concrete objects:
the spilled milk becomes metaphorical, a reference to centuries of opportunities with nothing to show for them; the tears are not so much caused by
onion chopping as by reflections on these missed opportunities; and the bread
baskets doubtless refer to the agriculturally productive areas of the world. By

introducing the term "Klassenkämpfe," the speaker reveals his Marxist affiliations. But what of the cat dish that remains a constant throughout the poem? The textual insistence on this object makes it more than just a requisite of the domestic scene: perhaps it is an emblem of our care for creatures dependent on us, a sign of a humane concern that persists despite the more hostile emotions we also experience.

Hans Magnus Enzensberger, already a distinguished figure in the 1950s and 1960s, continued to be leading voice during the entire last quarter of the twentieth century. His poems "Bildzeitung" (1957; the title is the original name of the German tabloid newspaper now known as *Bild*) and "Ins Lesebuch für die Oberstufe" (For the Advanced High School Reader; also 1957) can be found in many anthologies. As Germany pulled itself out of the early postwar years, political poetry reemerged, often returning to models made familiar by Heine and Brecht (although Benn's 1951 essay "Probleme der Lyrik" continued to influence a more aesthetic strain). Wolf Biermann, a poet and singer who began writing in the GDR but was eventually denied citizenship and forced to move to West Germany, was one of Brecht's most important successors. Erich Fried, another poet in the Brechtian tradition, engaged with the aesthetic tradition by revealing its political shortcomings. His volume *Zweifel an der Sprache* (Doubts about Language; 1974) takes up the issue of the *Sprachkrise* from a perspective that takes into account the problematic position of poetry in a more politically aware cultural context. Here is a programmatic passage from the over ten-page title poem of this collection:

> Wer zweifelt an einer Sprache
> die sagen kann
> "Ich habe Hunger"
> oder "Ich habe Angst
> vor dem Altwerden"
> oder "Ich will noch nicht sterben"?
> Oder *wer* zweifelt an den Worten
> "Militärputsch in Chile"
> und an den Worten "Verhaftete werden gefoltert"
> und an den Worten "Erschossene werden verladen
> auf Hubschrauber und in den Stillen Ozean geworfen"?

> (Who has doubt about a language that can say "I'm hungry" or "I'm afraid of growing old" or "I don't want to die yet"? Or *who* has doubts about the words "military coup in Chile" and the words "prisoners will be tortured" and the words "those who have been killed will be loaded onto helicopters and dropped into the Pacific Ocean"?)

While this passage identifies the motivation behind the poem, it is not entirely typical of "Zweifel an der Sprache." The success of the poem lies in the brilliance with which it manipulates language itself:

> Wenn der Zweifel zur Sprache kommt
> kommt auch die Sprache zum Zweifel
> und die vom Zweifel berauscht waren
> lernen die nüchterne Sprache
> und die von der Sprache berauscht waren
> lernen den nüchternen Zweifel
> und die Sprecher werden endlich zu Zweiflern
> und die Zweifler werden endlich zu Sprechern
> Und zweifellos verdienen die Zweifler aller Art
> soviel Glauben
> wie die Gläubigen aller Art
> Zweifel verdienen

> (When doubt comes to language, language also comes to doubt and those who were intoxicated by doubt learn sober language and those who were intoxicated by language learn sober doubt and the speakers finally become doubters and the doubters finally become speakers and no doubt the doubters of all kinds deserve as much belief as the believers of all kinds deserve doubt)

In this and similar passages, Fried's poem reveals its relationship to experimental "language poetry" – indeed, Fried notes that he wrote the text as a contribution to a conference on the topic "Zweifel an der Sprache" that was also attended by devotees of concrete poetry (poems composed so that they created recognizable shapes on the page). Fried was not himself a concrete poet; this poem addresses, rather, the fundamental problem of the language crisis: the paradox that doubt about language can only be expressed in language itself. Yet his approach to this paradox is radically different from that of Hofmannsthal (see Chapter 8). Fried is not looking for hidden truths that cannot be expressed in language: his aim is not to conjure up a mystical realm such as that invoked by the word "Abend" in Hofmannsthal's "Ballade des äußeren Lebens," but instead to show the shortcomings of everyday language when it comes to social and political issues such as hunger, poverty, and war. In the first section quoted above, he attacks the use of the passive voice to report crimes against humanity as in the sentences "Verhaftete werden gefoltert" or "Erschossene werden verladen/ auf Hubschrauber und in den Stillen Ozean geworfen." Who is responsible for these actions? The passive voice ("werden" in German) sidesteps this question entirely. By drawing attention to this usage, Fried urges the reader to be more alert to language and its potential abuses.

The *Neue Subjektivität* (New Subjectivity) movement of the late 1970s appeared at first glance to be a reaction against the political poetry that immediately preceded it. Most of the poets who participated in this movement were born during the last years of World War II; they had been active in the anti-Vietnam demonstrations of the turn into the 1970s and the student revolution that called for a less "authoritarian" style of education. Now they were already looking back with nostalgia at the time when mass protest had led to a bizarre kind of elation. Enzensberger's extrapolation of broad political ramifications from apparently domestic scenes no longer appeared as easy. The poets of the New Subjectivity depict life at home as filled with endless minor activities such as opening cans of ravioli, running Saturday afternoon baths, or poring over old photo albums. Seemingly mundane, the poetry of this group was nonetheless still fueled by a political undercurrent: not only did the poets describe the small comforts of every day, they also criticized the apparent complacency with which they seemed to have taken up a petty-bourgeois lifestyle. On the one hand, their work was nourished by a Brechtian aesthetic, especially in its emphasis on the inevitable entanglement of feeling and action; but on the other hand, they also took issue with his contention that the main impulse for poetry should be political events of a major type ("die Reden des Anstreichers," as Brecht had put it in "Schlechte Zeit für Lyrik"). By depicting a superficial self-contentment that appeared to have settled in following the political movements of the early 1970s, these poets also drew attention to the problematic absence of a political spur to action.

In the title of his poetry anthology *Und ich bewege mich doch: Gedichte vor und nach 1968* (And Yet I Move: Poetry before and after 1968; 1977), Jürgen Theobaldy alludes to Galileo's cry after his condemnation for heresy: "und sie bewegt sich doch!" (and yet it [the earth] moves). In one of his own poems in this anthology, Theobaldy uses the image of cold tea that has turned bitter as a metaphor for the time after the collapse of the student movement of 1968. Ruminating about the fact that most revolutions begin in spring or summer, he notes in his "Gedicht aus der Kälte" (Poem from the Cold; 1974) that the student revolt began in May:

> und obwohl sie nicht gelungen ist
> war es eine Zeitlang schön warm
> Zieh dich gut an. Ich kippe den Tee aus
> das Beste kommt erst später
> aber es kommt.

(And although it [the student revolution] didn't succeed, the weather
was nice and warm for a while. Wrap yourself up well. I'll throw the tea
out the best doesn't come until later but it does come.)

Cold tea has a very different sense in Helga Novak's "Lied vom alten Tee"
(Song of Cold Tea; 1975), which Theobaldy positions in the anthology immediately after his "Gedicht aus der Kälte." In Novak's poem, the political impli-
cation of inactivity is more pointed than in Theobaldy's work:

seht die braune Kanne mit dem Satz
die Tülle ist verstopft und riecht
warum trank er den Tee nicht
als er noch heiß war

seht den Schimmelhut wie weißer Samt
der in der Kanne schwimmt und glänzt
warum trank er den Tee nicht
und ist davongeeilt

seht die innen feuchte beschlagene Dose
die Blätter gequollen duften nicht mehr
wann haben sie ihn geholt
warum ist er fort

hört das Knistern unter den Schuhen
verschütteter Tee auf dem Fußboden
kamen sie wie üblich um fünf
und hat er gezittert.

(look at the brown teapot with the dregs the spout is stopped up and
smells why didn't he drink the tea while it was still hot// look at the cap
of mold like white velvet floating in the pot shining why didn't he drink
the tea why did he dash off// look at the damp, cloudy inside of the
caddy the swollen leaves have lost their scent when did they come to get
him why is he gone// listen to the crackling sound beneath our shoes tea
leaves strewn on the floor and did he tremble.)

Novak uses small domestic details to point up the sinister undercurrent to
life in the GDR. The cold tea is a clue to be interpreted against the backdrop
of political intimidation. Little by little, the speaker draws attention to the
dregs in the teapot, topped by a shiny white skin of mold, the slight fogging
inside the open tea caddy, and finally the scattering of tea leaves on the floor
(the crackling sound underfoot suggests not liquid tea, but dried tea leaves
that have accidentally fallen on the floor). From the evidence of the mold and
the swollen tea leaves in the caddy, the speaker constructs a time line for the

event that she at first does not wish to contemplate. Description alternates with questions that mark her increasing realization that the tea drinker must have been forcibly taken away. The omission of question marks suggests that the speaker already has some idea about what the answers might be. By the fourth section of the poem, the speaker confronts the situation outright: "wann haben sie ihn geholt." The final lines, "kamen sie wie üblich um fünf/ und hat er gezittert" brings two disparate matters together: the cruel timing of the event and the feelings of its victim.

Sarah Kirsch's "Ende Mai" (The End of May; 1976) is a seeming nature or love poem that has political implications because of the division of Germany into two separate nations:

> In ganz Europa ist jetzt das Gras da; überall
> Grünen die Linden, manchenorts Nuß und Wacholder. Winde
> Jagen viel Wolken fetzenweis über die Klingen
> Der Faltengebirge. Durch erfundene Drähte
> Über und unter der Erde geben die Menschen sich Nachricht.
>
> Du schick die leichteste
> Aller Tauben windförmig sie bringt
> Ungeöffnete tagschnelle Briefe. Schatten
> Unter den Augen; mein wüster Herzschlag.
>
> Unfroh seh ich des Laubs grüne Farbe, verneine
> Bäume, Blumen und niedere Pflanzen: ich will
> Die Blätter abflattern sehen und bald. Wenn mein Leib
> Meine nicht berechenbare Seele sich aus den Stäben
> Der Längen- und Breitengrade endlich befreit hat.
>
> (All over Europe the grass has emerged; everywhere the linden trees turn green, and in some places nut trees and juniper. Winds blow many clouds in tatters over the blades of the fold mountains. Through invented wires above and beneath the earth people send one another messages.// You, send the lightest of all doves in the shape of wind it brings unopened day-quick letters. Shadows under the eyes; my wild heartbeat.// Unhappy I see the green color of the leaves, deny/ trees, flowers, and lower plant forms: I want to see the leaves flutter upward and soon. When my body has finally freed my unpredictable soul from the bars of latitudes and longitudes.)

At the time when she wrote "Ende Mai," Sarah Kirsch was living in East Berlin while her lover, Christoph Meckel, himself a writer, was living in West Berlin. The poem sets their separation by the Wall against the backdrop of nature, which pays no heed to artificial barriers. For the natural world, "ganz

Europa" remains undivided. As spring arrives, it turns the continent into multiple shades of green represented by grass, lindens, nut trees, and juniper. By naming specific plant forms, the speaker recognizes that individual variety is as much part of nature as the oneness of the color green. The winds blowing across the "Faltengebirge" (fold mountains, a geological term that presumably refers here to the Harz range), create another natural counterpoint to the theme of separation. Whereas the division between the two Germanies ran vertically, the Harz mountains traverse the center of Germany horizontally. Fold mountains are formed by movement of tectonic plates beneath the surface of the earth, creating an upward thrust shaped like a fold of cloth. In the case of the Harz mountains, this folding began in the Palaeozoic period; the geological complexity of the range results from multiple folding events. Despite subsequent erosion, the Harz mountains (technically a fault-block range) still rise very high. More importantly, they have a significant place in German myth and literature. The "Walpurgisnacht" or witches' Sabbath in Goethe's *Faust* takes place on the highest point of the Harz mountains, the Brocken.

However much of this long history may be present in the "Faltengebirge" of Kirsch's "Ende Mai," we certainly cannot ignore that the mountain range is associated in the poem with danger. Winds "hunt" clouds across the mountaintops, tearing them into shreds. The high ridges are described as knife blades or swords ("Klingen"). The shredding force of the winds contrasts with the telephone and telegraph wires that enable messages to be sent regardless of the obstacles posed by geographic or political boundaries. These wires are "erfunden" – human inventions rather than natural formations.

The opening scene is a highly complex antithesis to the traditional lovers' meeting place with its grass, trees, and gentle breeze. Yet something of the earlier topos reemerges in the metaphoric transformation of the vicious winds into "die leichteste/ Aller Tauben." In the middle section of the poem, the lovers' communication takes the form of imaginary letters. These letters, "tagschnell," seem to move by thought waves alone: they do not need to be opened to be received and understood. "Taube" means both dove and pigeon, and so we can imagine these birds as carrier or homing pigeons that allow the lovers to communicate across borders. The dark shadows under the speaker's eyes and her "wild heartbeat," evoked in two verbless phrases, are somehow associated with the birds and the rapid communication they represent. In the ethereal realm suggested in this part of the poem, however, there is no need to specify the details of the connection. The poem itself is lifting off.

Once the speaker has attained this poetic realm, actual nature is no longer necessary. Indeed, the green color of "trees, bushes, and lower plant forms" ceases to give the speaker pleasure. When she expresses a wish for autumn to come quickly, it is because she is no longer reliant on the cycles of nature to achieve ecstasy through the imagination. The final lines of the poem look to a time when geography, with its longitudinal and latitudinal lines, will no longer hold the speaker captive. Longitudes and latitudes are a grid imposed on the earth by human beings: they are a conceptual system that has no concrete reality. Implicitly, the prison bars of these lines are connected with the artificial dividing line between the two Germanies. While the poem ends with the word "befreit," this freedom is something that, at the time of the poem, can only be imagined, a freedom that will come "endlich," but is not here yet.

Formally, "Ende Mai" deploys Sarah Kirsch's characteristic use of very lightly punctuated sentences, syntax that stops just short of "running on," and frequent use of enjambments. "Du schick die leichteste/ Aller Tauben windförmig sie bringt/Ungeöffnete tagschnelle Briefe" is an example of these techniques that have come to be known as the "Sarah Sound." Yet despite the apparently free form of the verse here, there are several recollections of classical meters. Line 5 is a traditional classical hexameter; and the final phrase of the poem, "endlich befreit hat," echoes the metrical pattern of the final feet of the hexameter line. (For more on these forms, see the appendix on meter, as well as Chapter 5). Thus, even in the most strictly formal aspects of the poem, the complex intercalation of the natural and the artificial, unity and division, human feelings and political constraints, makes itself felt.

After the fall of the Berlin Wall in 1989, there were public expectations that literature would capture the heady excitement of the event itself. Durs Grünbein, a poet who had moved from East to West Berlin well before 1989, seemed to be the designated author. He responded to the changed situation with ambivalence and disillusion in a series of poems written in 1989 under the title *Sieben Telegramme* (Seven Telegrams) that appeared in Grünbein's volume *Schädelbasislektion* (Lesson from the Base of the Skull; 1991). Here is the first poem in the series:

> Komm zu dir Gedicht. Berlins Mauer ist offen jetzt.
> Wehleid des Wartens, Langeweile in Hegels Schmalland
> Vorbei wie das stählerne Schweigen . . . Heil Stalin.
> Letzter Monstranzen Glanz, hinter Panzern verschanzt.
> Langsam kommen die Uhren auf Touren, jede geht anders.
> Pech für die Kopffüßler, im Brackwasser abgesackt.
> Revolutionsschrott *en masse*, die Massen genasführt
> Im Trott von bankrotten Rotten, was bleibt ein Gebet:
> Heiliger Kim Il Sung, Phönix Pjönjangs, bitt für uns.

(Come to your senses, poem. Berlin's Wall is now open. The woes of
waiting, languor in Hegel's narrow land gone like the steely
silence . . . Hail Stalin. The shine of the last monstrances, piled up
behind tanks. Slowly the clocks come up to speed, each keeps a different
time from the others. Too bad for the cuttlefish, sunken in the brackish
water. Scrap metal *en masse* from the revolution, the masses led by their
noses in the daily round of bankrupt mobs, what remains [is] a prayer:
Saint Kim Sung Il, Pyongyang's phoenix, pray for us.)

Instead of eagerly awaiting its chance to rejoice over the fall of the Wall, the
poem needs to be urged back to consciousness. In a series of alliterations that
recall the earliest Germanic verses, the speaker conjures up the stasis that had
accompanied the many years of waiting for a solution to the divided Berlin. The
image of monstrances piled behind armored vehicles and the later reference to
scrap metal left from the revolution suggests that poetry itself may be a mere
relic that has lost is value in the new political situation. The phrase "was bleibt"
is an allusion to Hölderlin's poem "Andenken" (1803), which concludes with
the words: "was bleibet aber, stiften die Dichter" (what remains, however, is
founded by poets). In Grünbein's poem, what remains is nothing so certain.
Rather, it is only a cynical prayer to the leader of North Korea, a land that, in
contrast to East Germany, still remains a communist country.

Gerhard Falkner uses postmodern techniques to suggest the remoteness
of the German poetic tradition from the present day in his poem "Droben
Wohnen" (Living Up There; 2008). The oddly positioned slashes indicate brief
pauses in performance of the poem:

Die Nächte werden immer kleiner. Immer teurer.
Wie Mittage schon fast / auf ihren nadelspitzen Höhepunkten steckend –
nur schwarz und unerhört und kalt
Kein Orpheus. Kein Orakel. Kein Orplid.
Höchstens Rilkes Fünfte. Und das Gras /
das funkelnd um die Häuser zieht.
Ich will, flussaufwärts, deinen nackten Adern folgen
bis meine Augen ihre Quellen finden.
Und apropos Quelle.
Ich wohne zwar gleich um die Ecke / doch ich bin
ein Andersdenkender.
In meinen Räumen gibt es keine
tragende Wand. Die Träume sind
auf sich gestellt und
das Papier, auf dem sie sich erfüllen
das hat keinen Rand.

Uns zwingt allein die Schrift
uns endlich zu entscheiden:
VIP Lounge oder Kolchose? /
Entweder das entweder oder das oder!
Aber, soll das heißen, wir haben keine andere Wahl?
Was ist denn dann mit wandern gehen. Auswärts essen.
Droben wohnen. Ruhig sein?

(The nights become smaller and smaller. More and more costly. Almost
like middays perched on their needle-sharp tips – only black and
unheard of and cold No Orpheus. No oracle. No Orplid [the fantasy
land imagined by Mörike]. At most Rilke's Fifth. And the grass that,
twinkling, surrounds the houses. I wish to follow your naked veins
upriver until my eyes find their sources. And à propos sources. I live
right around the corner but I think differently. In my rooms there are no
load-bearing walls. Dreams are stacked up on one another and the
paper, on which they fulfill themselves had no edges. Only writing forces
us to decide at long last: VIP lounge or collective farm? Either the either
or the or! But, does that mean we have no other choice? What's wrong
with going hiking. Eating out. Living up there. Being calm?)

The poem's title, "Droben wohnen," alludes to Hofmannsthal's "Manche
freilich" (Some, of course; 1895/96), a poem structured around class difference.
There, those who labor in the bowels of a large ship from premodern times,
often chained to one another while they work the heavy oars, are contrasted
with the masters who spend their time above deck in the free air beneath the
open sky:

Manche freilich müssen drunten sterben,
Wo die schweren Ruder der Schiffe streifen,
Andre wohnen bei dem Steuer droben,
Kennen Vogelflug und die Länder der Sterne

(Some, of course, must die down below, where the heavy oars of ships
brush past, others live up near the helm, know the flight of birds and the
lands of the stars)

Despite their separation, the lower and the upper levels form a multiply interconnected whole. The concluding stanza of Hofmannsthal's poem makes clear
that his own part in this larger complex goes beyond the aestheticist posture
with which he had often been associated. In this respect, "Manche freilich" is
somewhat unusual for Hofmannsthal's lyric poetry of the mid 1890s.

In addition to this allusion to Hofmannsthal, Falkner also refers to two
other poets: Rilke, whose *Fünfte Elegie*, a poetic meditation on the creative
arts, is mentioned as if it were his Fifth Symphony; and Mörike, whose poem

"Gesang Weylas" apostrophizes an imaginary land named Orplid that was a focus of Mörike's youthful poetic fantasies. The Orphic and oracular traditions are also evoked in the early part of Falkner's poem. Toward the end of "Droben wohnen," the speaker engages with the traditional idea that writing has a significant moral impact. The decision he gives as his example is an updated version of Hofmannsthal's distinction between those above decks and those below: the VIP lounge and the collective farm. In this way, Falkner uses intertextual allusion to make us think more closely about the function and possibilities of poetry. Yet his text also expresses frustration with binary divisions: "Entweder das entweder oder das oder!" (Either the either or the or!). Disrupting normal syntactic and logical structure in this manner is one of Falkner's trademark techniques, one that works brilliantly in oral performance. Here, by pulling apart the conjunctions "either" and "or," Falkner asks us to question the notion that alternatives always come in twos. The question that follows, "soll das heißen, wir haben keine andere Wahl," suggests simultaneously that we are not subject to determinism and that we may have more than two alternatives to choose from. Additional choices might be everyday activities like going hiking or eating out – or aesthetic activities like enjoying poetry: "droben wohnen."

I would like to conclude by exploring a text from another contemporary poet, Marion Poschmann (b. 1969), who uses very different techniques to produce a poem that keeps its political implications low-key. Titled "Kleines Rasenstück" (Small Patch of Turf; 2004), her text alludes to Dürer's well-known watercolor *Das große Rasenstück* (The Large [Patch of] Turf; 1503). Dürer's painting, which represents a piece of swampy ground with several different grasses, herbs, and wildflowers, appears at first glance natural and unconstructed. Yet the painting is in fact carefully composed: the vegetation is depicted with the detail and accuracy of a botanical study, and the high point of the painting – the tip of one of the grasses – is placed off-center in accord with the principle of the golden section. In addition to watercolor, Dürer uses graphic techniques, including pen and ink, to sharpen the contours of the plants. The perspective is low to the ground, making the vegetation seem taller. The painting exemplifies the paradoxical nature of realistic representation.

Marion Poschmann's poem creates a counter-image to this celebrated painting, as her title, "Kleines Rasenstück," indicates:

> 100g Gras, wie Licht, das sich bewegte,
> Licht, das knitterte, schnelle Lebensläufe
> ohne Höhepunkte, Schwarzweißaufnahmen:
> nickende Blitze.

Gras spritzte auf, fiel über Gras, von Winden
hingekritzelt, von Winden ausgedehnt nach
Zentimetern, Gras, dieser strenge Glanz, zu
Halmen gefaltet,

Gras überwog uns schon – wuchs Gras darüber,
hob sich, senkte sich, wimmelnd, flimmernd, Gras, so
haltlos wurzelnd über dem hellen Abgrund
unserer Hirne.

(100g of grass, like light, moving, light, crumpling, rapid lives without
highlights, black and white snapshots, nodding flashes.// Grass sprayed
up, fell over grass, scribbled by winds, stretched by winds by centimeters,
grass, this stern shining, folded into blades, // Grass already weighed us
down – grass covered things up, rose, sank, swarming, shimmering,
grass, so unsteadily taking root above the bright abyss of our brains.)

Although the poem appears to describe a natural scene, several elements
suggest that it also has other concerns: "100g Gras" and "wuchs Gras darüber."
The first of these suggests that grass has become a commodity, something one
can purchase by the gram; the second alludes to an idiomatic phrase, "Gras
darüber wachsen lassen," meaning to let something be forgotten or fall into
oblivion. Taken together, we might understand "grass" not only as turf, but
also as marijuana. That would also help explain the final lines of the poem, "so/
haltlos wurzelnd über dem hellen Abgrund/ unserer Hirne." What appears to
be an aesthetic encounter with nature becomes a metaphor for the emptiness
of modern life. Yet the drug can only temporarily obliterate this emptiness; in
fact, it may even exacerbate the "Abgrund unserer Hirne."

It would be incorrect, however, to reduce the poem merely to a commentary
on drug use today. It is also an ekphrastic text that consciously alludes to
Dürer's "Großes Rasenstück"; yet the vegetation here is more unruly than in
Dürer's painting. The word "hingekritzelt" suggests Dürer's use of pen and ink
in the painting, but it refers equally to the scribbling of the poet hastily taking
down impressions of a somewhat different grassy scene. This sketch-like aspect
of the poem is reinforced by the words and phrases that tumble out, seemingly
helter-skelter. In contrast to Dürer's turf patch, which he clearly dug up and
took home to study, the grass in Poschmann's poem is in constant motion,
springing up and falling over, caught by the wind, rising, sinking, and even
"swarming" as if it were a multitude of tiny creatures. The movement is not
of the grass alone, but also of the light reflected from it. The double mention
of "Licht" in the first strophe is intensified in the word "Blitze" and picked
up later by "Glanz" and "flimmernd." In line 2, light is said to crumple. The

black-and-white snapshots, witnesses to earlier times, are of course a product of light leaving traces on film. The word "Blitze" in this context suggests sudden flashes, whether of lightning or from a flash device in photography. The immediacy of the moment is paramount in these lines.

At the same time, however, the poem is artfully composed. It is in fact a Sapphic ode. The short final lines of each strophe and their metrical scheme – a dactyl followed by a trochee – are an identifying feature of this form (see appendix on metrics). Poschmann handles the form with great skill and only one violation of the metrical scheme (in line 3). Her poem even includes a feature first introduced by Klopstock: the "wandering dactyl," a dactyl that occurs in the first foot of the first line, the second foot of the second line, and the third foot in the third line of the strophe. The wandering dactyl is well suited to the movement of the grass in Poschmann's poem. By using this form, Poschmann links back to the great ode tradition initiated in German by Klopstock's experiments in the late eighteenth century.

"Kleines Rasenstück" thus situates itself with reference to two canonical reference points, Dürer and Klopstock, and explores a concern common to both of them, the relation of art to nature. Poschmann's poem develops the paradoxical character of this relationship in a more overt manner. Her text also engages with the Romantics' belief that an encounter with nature can give rise to moments of illumination. The opening reference to "100g Gras" calls this belief into question, and yet evocations of light are present throughout the text. The speaker, almost invisible until the last line of the poem, is in fact highly aware of the ambivalent posture with which we regard the possibility of poetic insight today. The verb "uberwiegen" in the first line of stanza 3 ("Gras überwog uns schon") is ambiguous: although I have translated it as "grass weighs us down," it could also mean "grass outweighs us." Taken together with the phrase "Gras wuchs darüber," it might suggest grass growing on a grave; but the idiom "Gras darüber wachsen lassen" means to let something lapse into oblivion. In the context of this poem the idiomatic phrase evokes not only a mundane desire to avoid difficult realities, but also perhaps a tendency to forget large and troubling events such as the Holocaust or the GDR's oppression of its own people. "Kleines Rasenstück" does not write large its social and political concerns, but they are clearly there beneath a surface in which even grass can take only tenuous hold.

1. The poem in its context

The more you know about the historical and cultural period in which the poem was written, the more easily you will be able to formulate meaningful questions about it. A literary history will help you discover with what period or movement the writer is usually associated. A brief account of that period or movement will inform you about general features that you may also find in the poem you are studying. It is sometimes more difficult to find out the date when the poem was written or first published. Many anthologies are organized by author in the sequence of birth date, but this arrangement often obscures significant overlaps, especially when a poet has had a long career divided into different phases. One multi-volume poetry anthology, *Deutsche Lyrik: Von den Anfängen bis zur Gegenwart in zehn Bänden*, ed. Walter Killy (Munich: Deutscher Taschenbuch Verlag, 2001), arranges poems in order of publication dates, but this is a rarity. Hanspeter Brode's anthology *Deutsche Lyrik* (Frankfurt a.M.: Suhrkamp, 1990) does give the dates of poems beneath each text. These dates do not take complexities of versions into account, but they are very helpful points of orientation. A series of small books in German published during the 1980s, *Gedichte und Interpretationen* (Stuttgart: Reclam, 1982–1984), gives more detailed information about publication dates and versions, together with short, well-informed readings of the selected poems. An additional volume on the Middle Ages appeared under the same main title but without a volume number, in 1993. Scholarly editions of collected works exist in the case of most canonical German poets, and these are the most reliable places to find specific dates and, in many instances, texts of earlier or later versions. In the case of more recent poets, you may need to look at individual volumes of their poetry as it has appeared.

Some poems, especially in the Classic and Romantic periods, first appeared as inset lyrics in novels. Chapter 6 of this book takes up this issue, showing how the poems often look quite different in the context of their novels from the way they appear as independent texts. If you discover that a poem has been published both separately and in a longer text, this fact is almost certainly worth exploring, though obviously you will not always have the time to read a complete novel before you prepare for a class or draft a writing assignment about a poem. Sometimes it makes sense to file away this information for a later opportunity when you might have time to delve more deeply.

Once you have a sense of how the poem fits into its context, a number of questions arise automatically. To what extent is the poem characteristic of its period or movement? In what ways does it diverge from them? Does it confirm the beliefs of its time or present a critique of them? Is there any possibility that the poem relates, directly or indirectly, to an important historical or cultural event?

In this phase of your exploration, make sure to think about such issues as the rational and the irrational, self and nature, the public and the private self, time and memory. The chapters in this book will give you additional ideas about larger themes such as religion, death, or politics.

2. Cracking the poetic code

Poets tend to develop a language of their own. For this reason, the ideal approach would be to read more than one poem by the author of the text you are examining. Time constraints do not always permit this, however; still, there is no need to despair.

How do you dig down into the deeper levels of a poem? Usually, it works better to focus on the words or phrases in the poem that are not entirely clear to you. Circle the spots where the poem becomes obscure, and see if you can fit these difficult passages into a larger pattern. You may find, for example, that the passages that cause the most trouble fall into a single conceptual category or cluster around a set of related themes or issues.

Use at least a medium-sized dictionary to look up all the words, even those you feel sure you know. Often a poet uses or plays upon a secondary or specialized meaning of a word. Some words even have a different meaning in the plural than in the singular. Do not jump to the conclusion that a word is a neologism because you cannot find it in your dictionary. It may make sense to consult a larger or more specialized dictionary. In the case of Paul Celan, who uses many technical words from geology, botany, and related sciences, it is best to consult the notes in the edition by Barbara Wiedemann, *Paul Celan. Die Gedichte: Kommentierte Gesamtausgabe* (Frankfurt a.M.: Suhrkamp, 2003). It will save you from many a pitfall.

Pay attention to the syntax of the poem – the way words are arranged into meaningful grammatical structures. Note where a text diverges from normal syntax and ask yourself why it might do so. A common poetic strategy is to treat separable verbs as if they were not separable: this gives special emphasis to the prefix. An example, drawn from Chapter 1, is Theodor Storm's line "Mit Schlummerduft anhauchen mich die Pflanzen."

Genitive constructions are frequently used in German to form metaphors. The genitive is placed before the noun and the definite article that would normally precede the noun is dropped. An example is the allegorical phrase "der Glieder Kahn" (the boat of the limbs, i.e. the physical human body; "der Glieder" is genitive plural) in Gryphius's sonnet "Der Abend" (Chapter 4). The words "des Mondes freundlicher Zauberhauch" in Goethe's "Im Herbst 1775" is more inventive in its attribution of magical breath to the moon (see Chapter 5).

3. Poetic forms

Obviously, you need to be able to identify a sonnet, an elegy, an ode, or a ballad. In the German tradition, some of these forms are distinctively different from their counterparts in English or other Western languages. In German, the term ode ("die Ode") refers to a poem with a specific metrical structure derived from ancient Greek and Latin poetry; it is not simply an address to an object like Keats' "On a Grecian Urn." The metrics appendix includes three major ode strophes, those that occur most frequently in German poetry. Similarly, an elegy is not merely a poem of mourning, like Gray's "Elegy in a Country Churchyard." Again, meter is a fundamental component in the German tradition: elegies are composed of hexameters and pentameters derived from classical antiquity (these meters are not those we are accustomed to in English; see the metrics appendix for details). Rilke's *Duineser Elegien* is not written in regular elegiac meters, but contains numerous allusions to them and from time to time, an entire line that follows the classical model. The ballad tradition, by contrast, is closely intertwined with the English folk ballad tradition. With regard to the sonnet, German poetry uses some of the forms we know from English verse, although the Shakespearean sonnet, with its final couplet, is less common in German.

Another important poetic subgenre is the "Rollengedicht" (role poem), an equivalent of the English dramatic monologue or mask lyric. This is a poem whose speaker is identified as a specific character: an example is Hofmannsthal's poem "Der Kaiser von China spricht." In other cases, such as Mörike's "An einem Wintermorgen, vor Sonnenaufgang," discussed in Chapter 7, a nameless speaker is depicted in a specific place at a specific time, meditating in monologue form on his perceptions and emotions.

Even when a poem seems clearly to register an actual experience, we should avoid identifying the speaker with the author. In the act of writing, an author invariably becomes, at least in some sense, another person. In this book, I use the term "speaker" to refer to the persona who speaks in the first person. In German, the term used is often "das lyrische Ich" (or simply "das Ich").

The second person pronoun "du" is often difficult to identify in a poem. Does it refer to the speaker's friend or lover, is the speaker addressing himself (a frequent use of "du" in German poetry), or is the "du" an address to the reader? Sometimes more than one of these co-exist in a poem.

4. Standpoint of the speaker

Are there any references to the time and place where the speaker is located? From what vantage-point does he or she view the world? Does the poem maintain a single point of view, or does the angle of vision shift in the course of the poem? If it does, what seems to be the reason for this shift?

In the case of poems where there is more than one speaker such as Goethe's "Erlkönig," ask yourself what purpose this serves. Sometimes both speakers are figures within the imagined situation of the poem, as in Mörike's "Gesang zu zweien in der Nacht" or Eichendorff's "Waldgespräch." In Uhland's "Das Schloß am Meere," the two speakers' experiences are separated by a temporal distance. You need to ask why the poet chooses to present the situation from a dual standpoint.

5. Diction and syntax

The vocabulary used in a poem may be elevated and highly poetic or informal and closer to everyday speech. Dictionaries will indicate when a word is antiquated or mostly used in a special context. Does the language recall the usage of other texts such as the Bible – or folk songs, ballads, or popular songs from our own day?

Are there any words with double meanings? Does the poet's word choice allow for irony or other kinds of ambiguities? Are there phrases where you identify a difference between the surface meaning and a possible "deeper" meaning?

If the speaker seems to be chatting casually without strong emphasis on meter or rhythm, the style is called "parlando." This is a common manner in twentieth- and twenty-first-century German poetry. This is the style of Hans Magnus Enzensberger's "Küchenzettel," discussed in Chapter 10. Parlando poetry is often deceptively simple, but it can also be a good place for hiding irony. Line breaks sometimes alert us to alternate meanings of words and phrases: sometimes a second meaning of a word comes into play when you read the lines without hesitating at the break.

6. Imagery

Any word can become an image. Note metaphors and similes – anything in the poem that can be understood in a way that is not merely literal. Why might a poet prefer to use similes rather than metaphors or vice versa?

As you work through the text, arrange the images in categories, grouping them thematically or even stylistically. Sometimes a poem will abound in references to color, or nature descriptions, or expressions of emotion. Some poems may contain several paradoxical phrases: these are not images, of course, but they also contribute to the overall structure of the poem and may work in tandem with the network of imagery.

7. Meter

Like English verse, German verse depends on stress. In general, German words are stressed on the first syllable. Some long words, especially compound nouns, may also bear a secondary stress at a later point in the word.

As with other formal features, it is usually more meaningful to focus on spots where the poem diverges from its basic metrical pattern or where the scansion becomes ambiguous. In the case of meters derived from classical antiquity, it is crucial to scan both for the scheme set by the classical model and the stresses that one would expect in modern German. Marking the poem with "double scansion" (see metrics appendix) can reveal emphases that go beyond stress as such and reveal emphases that bear upon the meaning of the text.

Be aware that certain metrical terms differ from similar terms in English. "Blankvers" refers only to unrhymed iambic pentameter; other unrhymed lines are called "freie Rhythmen." The words "Hexameter" and "Pentameter" refer to classical meters: both have six stresses, but the first has six feet and the second five feet (see metrics appendix). In German Baroque poetry, six-stressed lines are termed "Alexandriner."

8. Gaps or omissions

If the poem tells a story, are there any parts of it that are not explicitly filled in? An example is the missing element in the narrative sequence in Uhland's "Das Schloß am Meere," where we never find out what happened to the princess who no longer accompanies her parents at the end of the ballad. Another example might be Brecht's poem "Erinnerung an Marie A.," where the initial "A" points less to a missing last name than to the poem's allusions to the Virgin Mary ("Maria").

Are there any spots where the reader needs to "read between the lines" or draw inferences that aren't fully spelled out? Sometimes a poem that is otherwise regular in line length includes only the first part of one line. What is the significance of the missing part? In other regular forms, a poet may omit an expected line, leaving an "orphan" rhyme word; or there may be an additional, seemingly superfluous line. Ask yourself why the poet may have introduced these formal irregularities. Do they reinforce any of the other observations you have made about the poem?

Writing up your close reading

A close reading is a tool, not a theory: try to embed it in a larger framework that gives the fine details of your analysis an overarching meaning. There is no single "right way" to do a close reading, but there are four keys to success:

1. Make sure that you have identified a viable approach to the poem and that you have mapped out a viable argument that responds to an overarching question about the poem.
2. An argument is not a description: you should think of it as something akin to one side of a debate. The side you should be arguing against, as it were, is that of someone who only notices what is obvious. Think of your argument as a statement taking the form "whereas one might think at first glance that . . . , I will show that the poem is more complex than that."
3. Include as many ingredients of the poem – words, images, formal features like rhyme and meter – as possible in your analysis. The more details you can take into account, the better. Use as much as you can from your preliminary exploration of the text.
4. Dwell more on the poem's divergences from expectations than on aspects of the poem that are more obvious. Look back at Chapter 1 of this book to find examples of how to do this.

Group the observations you made in your preliminary exploration of the poem into several categories. These might be clusters of imagery, significant themes, or problems connected with the form of the poem. They might have to do with the situation and response of the speaker. They might also be features that reveal how the poem is characteristic of a period or movement. As you write up your analysis under these headings, bear in mind how your different categories relate to one another. A poem is a complex network of language, and you need to show that you have a good sense of how this network is constructed in the poem. Writing up your close reading in terms of meaningful categories into which the text can be organized is usually a more fruitful, and certainly a more interesting, method than simply going through the poem line by line. Once you have written up these observations about fine details, you may find that the entire poem has become richer and possibly even contradictory. Summarize your findings briefly, taking account of this new perspective.

In a brief conclusion, which need not be more than a sentence or so (especially if you are writing the close reading in an exam), clinch the overall argument of your reading. In what way has your reading revealed new complexities in the poem or uncovered hidden meanings? By answering this question, you will be able to show your reader how you have discovered a richer text beneath the surface of the poem.

German metrics

Feet

In German verse, a *foot* (*Fuß*, m.) is a unit consisting of one stressed syllable (*Hebung*, f.) and one or more unstressed syllables (*Senkungen*). German adaptations of meters from classical antiquity use a different system in which a stressed syllable stands in for what was originally a "long" syllable in Greek and Latin (explained further below).

Types of feet

Note: x stands for an unstressed syllable, / for a stressed syllable

iamb (*Iambus*, m., pl. *Iamben*): x /
dactyl (*Daktylus*, m., pl. *Daktylen*): / x x
spondee (*Spondeus*, m., pl. *Spondeen*): / /
trochee (*Trochäus*, m., pl. *Trochäen*): / x
anapest (*Anapäst*, m., pl. *Anapäste*): x x /

These are the types of feet you will encounter most frequently; other types of feet exist as well, but they are less commonly used. The term "schwebende Betonung" (floating stress) is sometimes used to designate a primary stress followed by a secondary stress – or the reverse; it is rare, however, that there is true uncertainty about which syllable bears the primary and which the secondary stress.

Other useful terms

Upbeat (*Auftakt*, m., pl. *Auftakte*): unstressed syllable at the beginning of a line that does not belong to the first foot.
  Caesura (*Zäsur*, f., pl. *Zäsuren*): a break or pause within a single line.

Note: the German for a line of poetry is *Vers*, m., pl. *Verse*; a stanza is a *Strophe*, f., pl. *Strophen*.

Principal meters used in German verse

A. Stress-based meters

1. Knittelvers (no English term for this verse form) A four-stressed line with any number of unstressed syllables distributed among the stressed ones.

Example:
Héiße Magíster, héiße Dóktor gár (Goethe, *Faust*)

2. Alexandrine (*Alexandriner*) A six-stressed iambic line with a caesura in the middle (sometimes the caesura shifts to fall a little earlier or a little later).

Example:
Die Tűrme stéhn in Glút, ‖ die Kírch ist úmgekéhret (Gryphius, "Tränen des Vaterlandes")

3. "Blankvers" This is *not* what we call blank verse in English; rather it is what we call iambic pentameter. The form was introduced in German in imitation of Shakespeare. Contrast this form with free verse (*freie Rythmen*), unrhymed lines of irregular length.

Example:
Der Tág bricht án, und Márs regíert die Stúnde (Schiller, *Wallensteins Tod*)

4. Trimeter An iambic line with six stresses, divided into three groups by two caesuras.

Example:
Noch únverrűckt, ‖ o schőne Lámpe, ‖ schműckest dú (Mörike, "Auf eine Lampe")

B. Meters from Classical Antiquity

In ancient Greek and Latin, scansion was based on the length of syllables rather than their stress. "Long" syllables either had a long vowel, e.g. "ā" as opposed to "ă," or the vowel was followed by two consonants. As in music, where two half notes take the same time as one whole note, two short syllables took the same time as one long syllable. In some feet, substitution of two short syllables for a long syllable was permitted, but not in all. The rules were complex, but you do not need to know them for the purpose of scanning German verse in classical meters.

In modifying the classical scheme for the German language, poets usually substituted a stressed syllable for a long syllable and an unstressed syllable for a short syllable. In referring to the German versions of classical meters, it is customary to speak of "long" and "short" syllables, even though length is not actually at issue. Adapting classical meters to German was not easy. In particular, there was a lively controversy over the first foot of the hexameter line. Some poets insisted that it consist of two "long" syllables as in antiquity; others permitted a "long" followed by a "short" syllable.

When scanning classical meters in German, it is a good practice also to include stress marks, writing them in above the long (-) and short (˘) signs ("double scansion"). Note that these signs do not change the pronunciation of the vowels; they continue to be pronounced as normal in German. Feet are separated by vertical lines (|). A caesura is marked with a double bar line (‖).

Here are the principal classical meters used by German writers:

1. Hexameter (*Hexameter*, m.)   In distinction to English usage, the term "hexameter" when used with respect to German verse *does not* refer to any line with six stresses. It refers only to the classical version as adapted to German. In the classical hexameter, the fifth foot must always be a dactyl. In the German version, the first foot may be either a spondee or a trochee.

Example:
Frōh ĕm|pfīnd ĭch mĭch| nūn āūf| klāssĭschĕm| Bōdĕn bĕ|gēīstĕrt (Goethe, "Römische Elegien")

Foot 3 has a very nice spondee: "nūn āūf"; dactyls occur in feet 2, 4, and 5. Only the dactyl in foot 5 is required.

Now let us look at where the stresses would occur in this line:
Fróh empfínd ich mich nún aùf klássischem Bóden begéistert

Note: the spondee (- -) in foot 3 now becomes a primary stress followed by a secondary stress. All the other stressed syllables do coincide with "long" syllables: that is the ideal, and when it happens, as in this line, it is a sign that the poet is skilled at handling this meter.

2. Pentameter (*Pentameter*, m.)   In distinction to English usage, the term "pentameter" when used with respect to German verse *never* designates a line with five stresses. Rather, the pentameter line has five feet, divided into two sets of two and a half feet. The line is broken by a caesura (‖).

Example:

Vōr- ŭnd| Mītwēlt| sprīcht‖ laūtĕr ŭnd| rēīzĕndĕr| mīr (Goethe, "Römische Elegien")

> *Note*: the second half of the line must consist of two dactyls followed by a single long syllable.

Now let us look at where the stresses fall in this line:

> Vór- und Mítwèlt sprícht ‖ laúter und reízender mír.

Again, a spondee in the classical meter has become a primary stress followed by a secondary stress. Once again, Goethe has skillfully managed to make the stresses correspond to the classical "long" syllables. If you put these stresses over the top of the "long" and "short" marks, you will have a good example of double scansion.

3. Elegiac couplet or distich (*Distichon*, n., pl. *Distichen*)   This consists of a classical hexameter followed by a classical pentameter.

Example:

> Īm Hĕ|xāmĕtĕr| steīgt dēs| Sprīngquēlls| sīlbĕrnĕ| Saūlĕ,
> Īm Pēn|tāmĕtĕr| draūf ‖ fāllt sĭe mĕ|lōdĭsch hĕ|rāb.
>
> (Schiller)

Note: In the hexameter line, foot 5 is a dactyl as required. Foot 1 uses the optional alternative German version of the classical meter, substituting a trochee (/ x) for what in Greek and Latin was a spondee (- -). In the pentameter line, the second half consists, as required, of two dactyls followed by a single syllable.

4. Ode meters   The term ode (German: "die Ode") does *not* need to be addressed to anyone or anything. In German classical usage, an ode is a poem that uses one of the following meters derived from classical antiquity. Klopstock used many of these meters but also invented variations of his own; his poem "Die frühen Gräber" uses an ode strophe of his own creation. Hölderlin also uses these meters, mostly the second and third of those listed below. The metrical pattern encompasses a whole stanza in each case. Do not expect all of the "long" and "short" syllables to coincide with natural stresses. Nonetheless, you can learn the "feel" of these metrical patterns; the final line of each stanza is a good way to recognize which ode form you have in front of you.

(a) Sapphic (*sapphisch*)

> Blūmĕ | dū stēhst | vērpflănzĕt | wō dŭ | blühĕst,
> Wērt ĭn | dīesĕr Bĕ|schāttŭng | nīcht zŭ | wāchsĕn,
> Wērt schnĕll | wēgzŭ|blühĕn, dĕr | Blūmĕn | Ēdĕns
> Bēssrĕ Gĕ|spīelĭn!

> (Klopstock, "Die tote Clarissa")

(b) Alcaic (*alkaisch*)

> Ĕ|chō dĕs | Hīmmĕls! ‖ hēīlĭgĕs | Hērz! wăr|ūm
> Wă|rūm vĕr|stūmmst dŭ ‖ ūntĕr dĕn | Lēbĕn|dēn
> Schlăfst, | frēĭes! | vōn dĕn | Gőttĕr|lōsĕn
> Ēwĭg hĭ|nāb ĭn dĭe | Nācht vĕr|wēīsĕn?

> (Hölderlin, "Ermunterung")

(c) Asclepiadeic (*asklepiadeisch*)

> Dōch, wĭe | īmmĕr dăs | Jāhr ‖ kālt ŭnd gĕ|sānglŏs | īst
> Zūr bĕ|schīedĕnĕn | Zeīt, ‖ ābĕr aŭs | weīßĕm | Fēld
> Grünĕ | Hālmĕ dŏch | sprōssĕn,
> Ōft eĭn | eīnsămĕr | Vōgĕl | sīngt

> (Hölderlin, "Die Liebe")

Glossary

Note: The list below focuses on terms used in this book and is not meant to be exhaustive. In each instance, the English term (if one exists) is given first; the German term, with its gender in parentheses, is given second.

Alexandrine/ Alexandriner (m): A six-stressed line consisting of alternating unstressed and stressed syllables (iambs), commonly used during the **Baroque** period. When resurrected in later periods, the Alexandrine usually alludes to Baroque traditions.

Alliteration/ Alliteration (f.): Repetition of the same initial sound in stressed syllables. Use of the same consonant in unstressed syllables can contribute to the effect; but make sure that you have found alliteration in at least two stressed syllables before commenting on the technique. In the early Germanic Middle Ages (seventh–ninth centuries), verse was not rhymed; instead, lines were linked by alliteration (in German: *Stabreim* (m.)).

Apostrophe: Address to a person or object. Some theorists of apostrophe are more interested in the absent addressee, but the person or object may also be present to the speaker of the poem.

Assonance/ Assonanz (f): Repetition of vowels, mostly in stressed syllables. The German Romantics were particularly devoted to assonance.

Aufgesang/ Abgesang (m): Terms used mainly with reference to medieval poetry and hymns from the Reformation. The *Aufgesang* is the first part of the poem or section of a poem; it usually consists of two **Stollen** or stanzas sung to the same melody and having the same rhyme scheme. The *Abgesang*, originally sung to a different melody, is the second part of an individual section of the poem. No equivalents for these terms exist in English, although the forms can still be seen in English hymns derived from Luther and his contemporaries.

Auftakt (m.): An unstressed syllable that precedes the first foot of a line; it is equivalent to an upbeat in music.

Ballad/ Ballade (f): A narrative poem that tends to focus on the climactic part of the action. Derived from folk traditions, the ballad usually takes the form of four- or eight-line stanzas with either alternating rhymes or rhymed couplets. A ballad often has a narrator, but it also frequently includes dialogue. Many ballads include refrains.

Baroque/ Barock (m): A German literary period running roughly from 1600 to the 1720s. Characterized formally by ornate flourishes and hyperbolic formulations, poetry from this period is frequently preoccupied with death, devastation, and struggles over religion. There is also a strain of gallant love poetry.

Blankvers (m): This German term refers *only* to unrhymed iambic pentameter, not to other forms of unrhymed verse. Shakespeare was the model for this type of verse in German. See appendix on metrics.

Caesura/ Zäsur (f): In verse forms adapted from Greek and Latin models, certain lines require a pause, sometimes in the middle, but sometimes at other places in the line. Although the pause may be marked by punctuation, it does not need to be; it may simply be located between meaningful groups of words. See appendix on metrics.

Conceit: An extravagant metaphor or turn of phrase, often intellectual in character.

Concrete poetry/ konkrete Lyrik (f): This is the twentieth-century term for poems written in the shape of objects. Baroque poets were also fond of composing poems in recognizable shapes.

Contrafacture/ Kontrafaktur (f): A poem composed in such a way that it can be sung to a familiar melody or in the metrical and stanzaic form of a well-known poem.

Courtly love poetry/ Minnesang (m): A special form of love poetry practiced at court during the high Middle Ages (late twelfth and thirteenth centuries). See Chapter 2 for more on this type of poetry.

Dactyl/ Daktylus (m): One long (or stressed) syllable followed by two short (or unstressed) syllables. For more on length vs stress in German verse, see appendix on metrics.

Dawn song/ tagelied (n): A poem set just before the break of day, when illicit lovers had to part. For more on this form, see Chapter 2.

Decadence/ Dekadenz (f): A term derived from the French word *décadence* to describe certain aspects of poetry around 1900. As a period designation, it is value-neutral. It refers to a type of aestheticism that flourished around the turn of the century, one that placed special value on created as opposed to natural beauty, was sensitive to the workings of external impressions on the nerves, and emphasized rare or precious words rather than ordinary language.

Distich/ Distichon (n): A two-line form based on models from classical antiquity and consisting of a classical hexameter followed by a classical pentameter. Like all verse derived from Greek or Latin models, the distich is unrhymed. For more on this form, see the appendix on metrics.

Dramatic monologue/ Rollengedicht (m): A poem in which the speaker is a distinct character.

Ekphrasis/ Ekphrasis (f.) or Bildgedicht (n.): Derived from the Greek word for "description," ekphrasis (alternative English spelling "ecphrasis") refers to verbal descriptions of works of visual art. The form often foregrounds the ancient rivalry between poetry and painting. In addition to paintings, sculpture or other art objects such as vases or lamps can be the objects of ekphrastic poetry.

Elegy/ Elegie (f.): In German, the term *Elegie* refers to a poem written in classical distichs (see "elegiac couplet" in the appendix on metrics). In classical antiquity, this form was associated primarily with poetry on mourning or love. The word retains its connection with elegiac meters in some twentieth-century German poetry, but gradually it is used more loosely to designate poetry of mourning. It is always wise to check whether remnants of elegiac meters remain in any German poem titled "Elegie."

Ellipsis/ Ellipse (f.): Omission of a word or phrase that can usually be readily supplied by the reader.

Empfindsamkeit (f.): A culture and type of writing that emerged around 1740. Closely related to the English "Age of Sensibility" (= sensitivity), the movement emphasized the expression of emotions and attention to the finest of stimuli from the natural or social world.

Engaged poetry/ engagierte Dichtung (f.): Poetry that takes up social or political causes.

Enjambment/ Enjambement (n.): A technique in which a syntactical unit runs over from the end of one line of verse into the beginning of another.

Enlightenment/ Aufklärung (f.): The Age of Enlightenment, around 1720–1785, which stressed the priority of reason and science over the emotions. Poetry of the period tends to have a learned or pedagogical aspect.

Epigone/ Epigone (m.): Derived from the Greek, this word means a latecomer or someone born in the wake of a distinguished generation. In Germany, the term was made famous by Karl Immermann's three-volume novel *Die Epigonen* (1836). An epigone is often highly conscious that his work follows a high point of cultural achievement, and in some usages, "epigonal writing" implies that such work is inferior or imitative.

Epiphanic moment/ der "ewige Augenblick": A moment of special insight in which the world is suddenly suffused with meaning and cohesion.

Erlebnislyrik (f.): This concept, which refers to poetry that originates in individual experience, has come into disrepute in recent times, largely because of our understanding that the speaker of a poem is distinct from its author.

Et in Arcadia ego (Latin): "I, too, am in Arcadia." According to most interpretations, the speaker of the phrase should be understood as Death. The phrase is often used ironically, to suggest that even Arcadia is not perfect.

Expressionism/ Expressionismus (m.): An artistic and literary movement beginning around 1910 and continuing into the mid 1920s. Striking colors, often at odds with the natural colors of objects and people, characterize the visual art, poetry, and prose of Expressionism. In response to World War I, the movement became more politically oriented, giving voice to a sense of crisis in the modern world. As a counterweight to depictions of a disintegrating social reality, mystic elements creep into some Expressionist works.

Folk traditions, folk song/ Volksdichtung (f.): Initiated in part by Herder, intense interest arose in *das Volk* and its traditions. German Romantic poets, notably Achim von Arnim and Clemens Brentano, collected old poems of various kinds, polishing them slightly to create what came to be known as *Volkslieder* (see chapters 2 and 6). The *Volksliedstrophe*, derived from a medieval form, consists of four lines, the second and fourth of which rhyme, while the first and third do not (xaxa). Rhyme words in this stanza alternate between feminine (two-syllable) and masculine (one-syllable).

Free verse/ freie Rhythmen: Unrhymed lines of varying length and meter. In German, the term *freie Verse* refers to rhymed lines of varying length and meter.

Genitive metaphor/ Genitivmetapher (f.): In German poetry, metaphors are often created by using a genitive construction in which the term in the genitive is placed before the term it governs; for example, "des Mondes freundlicher Zauberhauch," Goethe). Even when the phrase is not actually metaphorical, this type of genitive (often known as the Saxon genitive or "sächsischer Genitiv") is associated with poetic language; for example, "der Abendwolke Glut," Uhland).

Hexameter (m.): A line of verse modeled on the hexameter of classical antiquity (for details, see appendix on metrics). Do not confuse this line with the six-stressed **alexandrines** used in the **Baroque** period, which should not be termed a hexameter.

Hymn/ Hymne (f.): The German word *Hymne* refers to a free-rhythm poem in the manner of Pindar such as those written by Klopstock and Hölderlin in the eighteenth and nineteenth centuries. A poem sung at church services is called a *Kirchenlied* (n.)in German.

Iamb/ Iambus (m.): An unstressed syllable followed by a stressed syllable.

Imagery/ Bildlichkeit (f.): The metaphors and other figurative language of a poem taken as a whole or discussed in terms of related clusters (e.g., "nature imagery"). The German term for a single image is *Bild* (n.).

Impressionism/ Impressionismus (m.): Like impressionism in painting, impressionism in poetry presents the world as we perceive it through our senses. In addition to visual effects, the speaker of the poem pays close attention to acoustic and olfactory impressions.

Locus amoenus (Latin): This phrase literally means "pleasant place." In poetic tradition, it refers to a trysting place for lovers; it is usually a protected area with a tree or a wooded backdrop, a grassy surface, water, and a gentle breeze.

Madrigal/ Madrigal (n.): Most of us think of a madrigal as a musical piece, usually a part song for two or three voices. The term can also refer, however, to a poetic text that stands alone. In the Romance languages, where the form originated, there are many variations. Lines usually have an irregular number of stresses, and the rhyme scheme, though mainly alternating, may also include multiple lines with the same rhyme or an "orphan" rhyme that has no matching rhyme; the poem may end with a brief set of lines or a single line that is set off from the rest of the poem and departs from its general rhyme scheme.

Märchenton (m.): The syntactic and rhythmic effects cultivated by the Brothers Grimm in their fairy tales. Wilhelm Grimm was mainly responsible for casting the tales in this style.

Masculine and feminine rhyme/ männlicher und weiblicher Reim (m.): In poetry, a one-syllable rhyme is called "masculine" and a two-syllable rhyme (where the stress falls on the second-last syllable) is called "feminine."

Medievalism: The revival of medieval forms and themes undertaken by the Romantic poets. The revival was inspired by the rediscovery of medieval texts in the nineteenth century and the beginnings of philological work on these texts.

Meistersang (m.): In the fourteenth, fifteenth, and sxiteenth centuries, guilds of poet-singers composed unaccompanied songs in the desire of carrying on the tradition of high medieval *Minnesang* (see "courtly love poetry," above). Unlike the *Minnesänger*, the *Meistersänger* were not members of courtly society: most of them belonged to the trades. As singers, they underwent strict training in the highly codified forms of *Meistersang*; their proficiency was tested in singing competitions.

Memento mori (Latin): Reminder of death. Note the spelling, with an "e" in the first syllable.

Metonymy/ Metonymie (f.): In this figure of speech, the intended meaning is replaced by an object related to it in terms of space, time, or cause. An abstraction may be replaced by something concrete, for example. A special form of metonymy is synecdoche (German: *Synekdoche* (f.)), where a whole is represented by a part.

Moderne (f.): One of several German terms for the period of modernity that begins in the late nineteenth century and continues into the early years of the twentieth century. It is not entirely identical with *Modernismus*, which refers more specifically to the experimental modernist movements that flourished in the first several decades of the twentieth century.

Motif/ Motiv (n.): An image that is repeated throughout a text.

New Subjectivity/ Neue Subjektivität (f.): A trend in German poetry during the 1970s characterized by a return (or an apparent return) from political poetry to poetry of everyday life and subjective experience.

Octave/ Oktave (f.): The first eight lines of a sonnet (regardless of whether they are printed as two quatrains or a single unit).

Ode/ Ode (f.): In German, the word *Ode* refers *only* to poems written in ode forms derived from classical antiquity (see appendix on metrics for the most common types). Unlike the English ode, the German *Ode* does not need to be addressed to a person or thing.

Parataxis/ Parataxe (f.): Sentences formed by a sequence of main clauses (in contrast to sentences consisting of a main clause and one or more subordinate clauses).

Pathetic fallacy: A strategy in which the speaker of the poem acts as if nature were joining in or reflecting his or her own feelings.

Persona/ lyrisches Ich (n.): Synonyms for the speaker of the poem. In German, *das lyrische Ich* or simply *das Ich* are the customary terms for the speaking subject.

Petrarchism/Petrarkismus (m.): Key elements of Petrarchism include elaborate syntax, a set of characteristic themes such as love and death, and a catalogue of female features (including the comparison of lips with coral and the bosom with snow). Similarly, Petrarch and his followers connected fire with sexual desire and ice with chastity. Paradox and oxymoron are also common in this type of poetry.

Quatrain/Vierzeiler (m.)/ Quartett (n.): In English, the word "quatrain" refers to a four-line stanza with a regular rhyme scheme. In German, "Vierzeiler" is the general word for a four-line stanza, while the term "Quartett" is used for the two four-line sections in the first half of a sonnet.

Rhyme scheme/ Reimschema (n.): As in English, German poetry uses not only pure rhyme, but also, upon occasion, *unreine Reim* (m.) or half-rhyme. In some periods or dialects, or in the poetry of specific authors, sounds that do not rhyme in modern high German are considered full rhymes. An example is Goethe's frequent rhyming of the sounds *ei* and *eu*. In German, alternating or cross rhyme is *Kreuzreim*, envelope or embracing rhyme is *umarmender Reim*, rhymed couplets are *Reimpaare*, and internal rhyme within a single line is *Binnenreim*. Eye rhyme, where the two words are spelled in the same way but do not sound alike, is *Augenreim*.

Romanticism/ Romantik (f.): The German Romantic period, beginning in the late 1790s and continuing into the 1830s. It is usually divided into two phases: early Romanticism, when the underlying philosophy and poetic theory of the movement was established, and late Romanticism, where its ambiguities and paradoxes became more evident.

Scansion: Analysis of meter using conventional signs to indicate stressed and unstressed syllables (in the case of classical meters, long and short syllables, as well as specific types of pauses within lines). See appendix on metrics.

Schwebende Betonung (f.): A term used to designate a set of two syllables, each of which bears stress and where it is difficult to decide which of the two syllables bears the primary stress and which the secondary.

Self-reflexive/ poetologisch: Used to describe a poem that also reflects on the nature of poetry.

Sestet/ Sestett (n.): The last six lines of a sonnet, whether or not they are divided into separate sections.

Sonnet/ Sonett (n): A poem in fourteen lines. Note the difference in spelling between the English and the German word. The most common form of German sonnets is the Petrarchan form, which concludes with a sestet or two tercets; the Shakespearean form, which ends with a rhymed couplet, is extremely rare in the German tradition. The sonnet was popular in the Baroque period; it was revived by the German Romantics.

Spondee/ Spondeus (m.): In classical antiquity, the spondee was a foot that consists of two long syllables; in German adaptations, it consists of two stressed syllables.

Sprachkrise (f.): Around 1900, writers began to doubt the reliability of language. Hugo von Hofmannsthal's "Ein Brief" is a key text in the literature of the language crisis.

Stanza/ Strophe (f.): A set of lines in a poem that is paralleled by other such sets of lines. If the poem you are discussing does not have regular stanzas, refer to the units of lines as "sections" (*Abschnitte* (m.)). The German term *Stanze* (f.)

refers *only* to the eight-line Italian form *ottava rima*, in which each group of lines is structured by the rhyme scheme ab ab ab cc. *Note:* do not use the English word "verse" to refer to a stanza; in German, the term *Vers* (m.)refers to a single line of poetry.

Stilbruch (m.): A sudden shift in style: a line or passage in everyday language may suddenly appear in a text written in a formal style, or vice versa.

Stollen: This word refers to the two sections in the **Aufgesang** of a medieval poem.

Storm and Stress/ Sturm und Drang: A literary movement that emerged around 1770 and that emphasized strong emotions, idealized the concept of genius, and rebelled against contemporary social order.

Subjectivity/ Subjektivität (f.): This term does not mean "subjective" as opposed to "objective." Rather, it refers to the way the speaker relates to the external world and the way in which this relationship is expressed in the poem.

Symbolism/ Symbolismus (m.): A type of poetry initiated in France in the late nineteenth century and continued in French and other European languages into the early part of the twentieth century. In this movement, "symbols" are not one-on-one equivalents, but rather, evocative images whose power stems from the multiple meanings they suggest.

Synaesthesia/ Synästhesie (f.): A mode of perception in which two or more different senses fuse. One of the most frequent synesthetic effects occurs when sounds are seen as colored, for example.

Tercet/ Terzett (n.): A tercet is any three-line unit in a poem. In a sonnet, the two three-lined sections in the last part of the poem are called *Terzette*. For another kind of tercet, see *Terzinen* below.

Terzinen: A form derived from the Italian (Dante is its best-known practitioner), *Terzinen* are tercets arranged according to the rhyme scheme aba bcb cdc, etc., but ending with the pattern yzy z. This structure gives the final line special emphasis or poignancy.

Topos: A topos is simultaneously a familiar theme and a more or less conventional way of formulating it. An example of such a topos is **locus amoenus**; another example is the notion that "all is transient."

Trochee/ Trochäus (m.): A poetic foot in which a stressed syllable is followed by an unstressed syllable (or, in classical metrics, a long syllable by a short syllable). See appendix on metrics.

Trope/ Tropus (m.), pl. Tropen: This term is used to designate any phrase that cannot be taken literally, but must be interpreted in order to be understood.

Vanitas (Latin)/Eitelkeit (f.): The transience of human life and endeavors. A characteristic theme in the Baroque period.

Volta (Italian): The turn of thought between the octave and the sestet of a sonnet; often, this turn is a reversal.

Waise (m.)[literally, "orphan"]: In rhymed verse, this term refers to a word at the end of a line that has no rhyming counterpart in the poem.

Further reading

Anthologies

Brode, Hanspeter, ed. *Deutsche Lyrik: Eine Anthologie* (Frankfurt a.M.: Suhrkamp Taschenbuch, 1990). An excellent, compact anthology. A welcome feature is that the date of each poem is given below the text; the book's one fault is its misleading line-numbering system.

Detering, Heinrich, ed. *Reclams großes Buch der deutschen Gedichte: Vom Mittelalter bis ins 21. Jahrhundert* (Stuttgart: Reclam, 2007). A scintillating selection of poems that covers a remarkable range. Its size, over 1,000 pages, makes it best for desk reference.

A German guide to the study of poetry

Felsner, Kristin, Holger Helbig, and Therese Manz, eds. *Arbeitsbuch Lyrik* (Berlin: Akademie Verlag, 2009). A complete guide to all aspects of German lyric poetry, with fresh examples and instructive exercises.

Readings of individual German poems (in German)

Gedichte und Interpretationen, vols. I–VI (Stuttgart: Reclam, 1982–1984). A series of interpretations of individual poems from the Renaissance to the present, collected by various editors and with contributions by different hands. Each poem is presented in a reliable text with details of its publishing history; the interpretations pay attention not only to the texts but also to their broader contexts. An additional, unnumbered volume covers medieval poetry: *Gedichte und Interpretationen: Mittelalter*, ed. Helmut Tervooren (Stuttgart: Reclam, 1993).

Kaiser, Gerhard. *Augenblicke deutscher Lyrik: Gedichte von Martin Luther bis Paul Celan* (Frankfurt a.M.: Insel Taschenbuch, 1987). Perceptive readings arranged according to thematic headings: language, representation, experience, self-reflexivity, poetry and reality.

Further reading for individual chapters

Chapter 1

Block, Richard. "Falling to the Stars: Georg Trakl's 'In Venedig' in Light of Venice Poems by Nietzsche and Rilke," *The German Quarterly*, vol. 78, no. 2 (Spring 2005): 207–223

Groddeck, Wolfram. "'Ein anderes Wort für Musik': Zu Friedrich Nietzsches Venedig-Gedicht," in *Gedichte und Interpretationen*, vol. V: *Vom Naturalismus bis zur Jahrhundertmitte*, ed. Harald Hartung (Stuttgart: Reclam, 1983), 20–32

Mornin, Edward. "Ludwig Uhland and the Romantic Mythology," *The German Quarterly*, vol. 62, no. 1 (Winter 1987): 20–27

Thayer, Terence K. "Knowing and Being: Mörike's 'Denk' es, o Seele,'" *The German Quarterly*, vol. 45, no. 3 (May 1972): 484–501

Chapter 2

Barclay, David E. "Medievalism and Nationalism in Nineteenth-Century Germany," *Studies in Medievalism*, 5 (1993): 5–22

Frenzel, Peter. "Minne-Sang: The Conjunction of Singing and Loving in German Courtly Song," *The German Quarterly*, vol. 55, no. 3 (May 1982): 336–348

Gebert, Bent. "'Ach Gott, wir han verschlafen!': Überlegungen zur Tageliedrezeption in Achim von Arnims und Clemens Brentanos *des Knaben Wunderhorn*," *Germanisch-romanische Monatsschrift* 57 (2007): 303–318

Kasten, Ingrid, ed. *Deutsche Lyrik des frühen und hohen Mittelalters* (Frankfurt a.M.: Deutscher Klassiker Verlag, 2005)

Kühnel, Jürgen. "Wolfram von Eschenbach: *Sîne klâwen*," in *Gedichte und Interpretationen: Mittelalter*, ed. Helmut Tervooren (Stuttgart: Reclam, 1993), 144–168

Müller, Jan-Dirk. "Männliche Stimme – weibliche Stimme in Neidharts Sommerliedern," in A. Heitmann *et al.*, *Bi-Textualität: Inszenierungen des Paares* (Berlin: Erich Schmidt, 2001), 334–345

Sievert, Heike. "Das Mädchenlied: Walther von der Vogelweide: *Under der linden*," in *Gedichte und Interpretationen: Mittelalter*, ed. Helmut Tervooren (Stuttgart: Reclam, 1993), 129–143

Wachinger, Burghart, ed. *Deutsche Lyrik des späten Mittelalters* (Frankfurt a.M.: Deutscher Klassiker Verlag, 2006)

Young, Christopher. "Vision and Discourse in the Poems of Heinrich von Morungen," in *Blütezeit: Festschrift für L. Peter Johnson zum 70. Geburtstag*, ed. Mark Chinca, Joachim Heinzle und Christopher Young (Tübingen: Niemeyer, 2000), 29–51

Chapter 3

Felstiner, John. *Paul Celan Poet, Survivor, Jew* (New Haven and London: Yale
    University Press, 1995), especially his section on "Tenebrae," 101–105
Marx, Reiner. "Unberührte Natur, Christliche Hoffnung und menschliche
    Angst – Die Lehre des Hausvaters in Claudius' 'Abendlied,'" in *Gedichte
    und Interpretationen*, vol. II: *Aufklärung und Sturm und Drang*, ed. Karl
    Richter (Stuttgart: Reclam, 1983), 341–355
Reinhart, Max, ed. *Early Modern German Literature 1350–1700* (Columbia, SC:
    Camden House, 2007)
Schmidt, Lothar, "Und wenn die Welt voll Teufel wär: Zu Martin Luthers *Ein feste
    burg ist unser Gott*," in *Gedichte und Interpretationen*, vol. I: *Renaissance
    und Barock*, ed. Volker Meid (Stuttgart: Reclam, 1982), 55–67
Von Mücke, Dorothea E. "1666, February: By order of Friedrich Wilhelm I, King
    of Prussia and Elector of Brandenburg, Paul Gerhardt is removed from
    the office of deacon at Saint Nicolai Church in Berlin," in *A New History
    of German Literature*, ed. David Wellbery *et al.* (Cambridge, MA:
    Harvard University Press, 2004), 309–314

Chapter 4

Burgard, Peter J. "Dead Metaphor Society? From Opitz to Hoffmannswaldau,"
    Neophilologus, 93 (2009): 295–310
Hutchinson, Peter. "Politics and Playfulness in Günter Grass's Sonnet Cycle
    Novemberland," *German Quarterly*, vol. 78, no. 2 (Spring 2005):
    224–239
Kaiser, Gerhard. "'Ihr liebt, und schreibt Sonette! Weh der Grille!'. Das Verhältnis
    von Leben und Dichtung als Thema von Goethes Sonettenzyklus
    1807/1808," in *Augenblicke deutscher Lyrik: Gedichte von Martin Luther
    bis Paul Celan* (Frankfurt a.M.: Insel, 1987), 197–236
Kühlmann, Wilhelm. "Selbstbehauptung und Selbstdisziplin. Zu Paul Flemings
    'An Sich,'" in *Gedichte und Interpretationen*, vol. I: *Renaissance und
    Barock*, ed. Volker Meid (Stuttgart: Reclam, 1982), 159–167
Mauser, Wolfram. "Was ist dies Leben doch? Zum Sonett 'Thränen in schwerer
    Kranckheit' von Andreas Gryphius," in *Gedichte und Interpretationen*,
    vol. I: *Renaissance und Barock*, ed. Volker Meid (Stuttgart: Reclam,
    1982), pp. 222–230
Meid, Volker. "Ein politischer Dichter. Zu Weckherlins 'An das Teutschland,'" in
    Gedichte und Interpretationen, vol. I: *Renaissance und Barock*, ed. Volker
    Meid (Stuttgart: Reclam, 1982), pp. 148–158
Ryder, Frank G. "The Design of Hofmannswaldau's 'Vergänglichkeit der
    Schönheit,'" *Monatshefte*, vol. 51, no. 3 (March 1959): 97–102

Wagenknecht, Christian. "Memento mori und carpe diem. Zu Hofmannswaldaus Sonett 'Vergänglichkeit der Schönheit,'" in *Gedichte und Interpretationen*, vol. I: *Renaissance und Barock*, ed. Volker Meid (Stuttgart: Reclam, 1982), pp. 331–344

Chapter 5

Bell, Matthew. "'Im Herbst. 1775' and 'Warum gabst du uns die tiefen Blicke': Estrangement, Ambiguity, and the Melancholy Voice," *Publications of the English Goethe Society*, 78 (2007): 13–27

Hetzron, Robert. "Goethe's Graffito, or (The) Wanderer's (Second) Nightsong," *The Germanic Review*, vol. 65, no. 1 (1990): 12–19

Hilliard, K. F. "'Nänie': Critical Reflections on the Sentimental in Poetry," *Publications of the English Goethe Society*, 77 (2006): 3–13

Oellers, Norbert. "Das verlorene Schöne in bewahrender Klage. Zu Schillers 'Nänie,'" in *Gedichte und Interpretationen*, vol. III: *Klassik und Romantik*, ed. Wulf Segebrecht (Stuttgart: Reclam, 1984), 181–195

Reed, T. J. "Ein Gleiches," in *Goethe-Handbuch*, vol. I, ed. Regine Otto and Bernd Witte (Stuttgart: J. B. Metzler, 1996), 191–194

Schmidt, Jochen. "'Sobria ebrietas', Hölderlins *Hälfte des Lebens*," in *Gedichte und Interpretationen*, vol. III: *Klassik und Romantik*, ed. Wulf Segebrecht (Stuttgart: Reclam, 1984), 257–267

Segebrecht, Wulf. "Sinnliche Wahrnehmung Roms. Zu Goethes *Römischen Elegien*, unter besonderer Berücksichtigung der *Fünften Elegie*," in *Gedichte und Interpretationen*, vol. III: *Klassik und Romantik*, ed. Wulf Segebrecht (Stuttgart: Reclam, 1984), 48–59

Vaget, Hans Rudolf. "Introduction" to Johann Wolfgang von Goethe, *Erotic Poems*, trans. David Luke (Oxford University Press, The World's Classics, 1988), ix–xliv

Zenke, Thomas. "Der Augenblick der Sensibilität" [on Rolf Dieter Brinkmann's "Einen jener klassischen"], in *Gedichte und Interpretationen*, vol. VI: *Gegenwart*, ed. Walter Hinck (Stuttgart: Reclam, 1982), 386–393

Chapter 6

Bormann, Alexander von. "'Tief Verlangen nach beßrer Lust'. Zu Eichendorffs Gedicht 'Die Heimat. An meinen Bruder'" [on 'Denkst du des Schlosses noch . . . ?'], in *Gedichte und Interpretationen*, vol. III: *Klassik und Romantik*, ed. Wulf Segebrecht (Stuttgart: Reclam, 1984), 451–462

Frühwald, Wolfgang. "Die Erneuerung des Mythos. Zu Eichendorffs Gedicht 'Mondnacht,'" in *Gedichte und Interpretationen*, vol. III: *Klassik und Romantik*, ed. Wulf Segebrecht (Stuttgart: Reclam, 1984), 394–407

Frühwald, Wolfgang, ed. *Gedichte der Romantik* (Stuttgart: Reclam, 1984)

Kaiser, Gerhard. "Mutter Natur als Himmelsbraut. Joseph von Eichendorff: 'Mondnacht,'" in *Augenblicke deutscher Lyrik: Gedichte von Martin Luther bis Paul Celan* (Frankfurt a.M.: Insel, 1987), 178–192

Koopmann, Helmut. "Romantische Lebensfahrt" [on Eichendorff's "Frische Fahrt"], in *Gedichte und Interpretationen,* vol. III: *Klassik und Romantik,* ed. Wulf Segebrecht (Stuttgart: Reclam, 1984), pp. 293–305

Louth, Charlie. "The Romantic Lyric," in *The Cambridge Companion to German Romanticism,* ed. Nicholas Saul (Cambridge University Press, 2009), pp. 67–84

Mahoney, Dennis F., ed. *The Literature of German Romanticism,* Camden House History of German Literature, vol. VIII (Columbia, SC: Camden House, 2003)

Simons, Oliver. "Botschaft oder Störung? Eine Diskursgeschichte des 'Rauschens' in der Literatur um 1800," *Monatshefte für Deutschsprachige Literatur und Kultur,* vol. 100, no. 1 (Spring 2008): 33–47

Chapter 7

Böschenstein, Bernhard. "Inspiration," in *Gedichte von Eduard Mörike,* ed. Matthias Meyer (Stuttgart: Reclam, 1999), 15–25

Häntzschel, Günter, ed. *Gedichte und Interpretationen,* vol. IV: *Vom Biedermeier zum Bürgerlichen Realismus* (Stuttgart: Reclam, 1983)

Meyer, Mathias, ed. *Interpretationen: Gedichte von Eduard Mörike* (Stuttgart: Reclam, 1999)

Müller, Joachim. "An einem Wintermorgen vor Sonnenaufgang. Eine Interpretation," *DVjs,* 25 (1951): 82–93

Ockenden, Ray, ed. *Oxford German Studies,* vol. 36, no. 1 (2007) (special issue on Eduard Mörike; includes articles by several different scholars)

Peucker, Brigitte. "The Poetry of Regeneration: Droste-Hülshoff's Ophelia as Muse," in *Lyric Descent in the German Romantic Tradition* (New Haven: Yale University Press, 1987), 71–118

Rolleston, James. "'Bildung' and the Possibility of History: Eichendorff, Mörike, Droste-Hülshoff," in *Narratives of Ecstasy: Romantic Temporality in Modern German Poetry* (Detroit: Wayne State University Press, 1987), 23–66

Stein, Jack M. "Poem and Music in Hugo Wolf's Mörike Songs," *The Musical Quarterly,* vol. 53, no. 1 (January 1967), 22–38

Chapter 8

Adams, Jeffrey Todd. "'Orplid' as Absolute Poetry," in *Eduard Mörike's "Orplid": Myth and the Poetic Mind* (Hildesheim: Olms, 1984), 117–153

Buck, Theo. "Negative Utopie: Zu Georg Trakls 'Grodek,'" in *Frühling der Seele: Pariser Trakl-Symposion* (Innsbruck: Haymon, 1995): 170–180

Calhoon, Kenneth S. "The Eye of the Panther: Rilke and the Machine of Cinema," *Comparative Literature*, vol. 52, no. 2 (2000): 143–156

Kaiser, Gerhard. "O Lied, mein Land. Eduard Mörike: Gesang Weylas," in *Augenblicke deutscher Lyrik. Gedichte von Martin Luther bis Paul Celan* (Frankfurt: Insel, 1987), 269–282

Kramer, Andreas. "Rilke and Modernism," in *The Cambridge Companion to Rilke*, ed. Karen Leeder and Robert Vilain (Cambridge University Press, 2010), 113–130

Mistry, Freny. "The Concepts of 'Death' and 'Evening' in Hofmannsthal's 'Ballade des äußeren Lebens,'" *Modern Austrian Literature: Journal of the International Arthur Schnitzler Research Association*, vol. 7, nos. 3–4 (1974): 77–86

Schlesier, Renate. "Dionysische Kunst: Gottfried Benn auf Nietzsches Spuren," *Modern Language Notes*, vol. 108, no. 3, German Issue (April 1993): 517–528

Sheppard, Richard. "From the 'Neue Gedichte' to the 'Duineser Elegien': Rilke's Chandos Crisis," *Modern Language Review*, vol. 68, no. 3 (1973): 577–592

Chapter 9

Böschenstein, Bernhard. "Involution" [on Paul Celan's poem "Tübingen, Jänner"], in *Interpretationen: Gedichte von Paul Celan*, ed. Hans-Michael Speier (Stuttgart: Reclam, 2002), 96–103

Celan, Paul. "Der Meridian: Rede anläßlich der Verleihung des Georg-Büchner-Preises," in *Ausgewählte Gedichte*, ed. with afterword by Beda Allemann (Frankfurt a.M.: Suhrkamp, 1981), 133–148

Felstiner, John. "Paul Celan's Todesfuge," *Holocaust and Genocide Studies*, vol. 1, no. 2 (1986), 249–264

Goebel, Rolf J. "Gesamtkunstwerk Dresden: Official Urban Discourse and Durs Grünbein's Poetic Critique," *German Quarterly*, vol. 80, no. 4 (Fall 2007): 492–510

Kaiser, Gerhard. "Paul Celan: 'Sprachgitter,'" in *Augenblicke deutscher Lyrik* (Frankfurt a.M.: Insel, 1987), 373–391

Kiedaisch, Petra, ed. *Lyrik nach Auschwitz: Adorno und die Dichter* (Ditzingen: Reclam 1995)

Minden, Michael. "The Lyric of Negation," in *Modern German Literature* (Cambridge: Polity, 2011), 142–148

Moses, Stéphane. "1952, Autumn. *Mohn und Gedächtnis*, Paul Celan's First Authorized Collection of Poetry, Is Published," in *A New History of German Literature*, ed. David Wellbery *et al.* (Cambridge, MA: Harvard University Press, 2004), 856–861

Chapter 10

Hinderer, Walter. *Geschichte der politischen Lyrik in Deutschland* (Würzburg: Königshausen & Neumann, 2007)

Lamping, Dieter. *Wir leben in einer politischen Welt: Lyrik und Politik seit 1945* (Göttingen: Vandenhoek & Ruprecht, 2008)

Thomson, Philip. "Exegi monumentum: The Fame of Bertolt Brecht," *The German Quarterly,* vol. 53, no. 3 (1980): 337–347

Zenke, Jürgen. "Poetische Ordnung als Ortung des Poeten: Günter Eichs 'Inventur,'" *Gedichte und Interpretationen,* vol. VI: *Gegenwart,* ed. Walter Hinck (Stuttgart: Reclam, 1982), 72–82

Index

Cambridge Introductions to...